202
GREAT WALKS

202
GREAT WALKS
THE BEST DAY WALKS IN NEW ZEALAND

MARK PICKERING

REED

Front cover image: Sea-arch, Haumuri Bluff, Kaikoura.
Back cover image: Godley Head, Christchurch.

Reed Publishing
Te Karuhi tā tāpui o Reed (Aotearoa) (NZ) Ltd

Established in 1907, Reed is New Zealand's largest
book publisher, with over 300 titles in print.

For details on all these books visit our website:
www.reed.co.nz

Published by Reed Books, a division of Reed Publishing (NZ) Ltd,
39 Rawene Rd, Birkenhead, Auckland.
Associated companies, branches and representatives throughout the world.

ISBN 0 7900 0878 5
First published 2003
Reprinted 2004, 2005

© 2003 Mark Pickering
The author asserts his moral rights in the work.

Edited by Sam Hill
Cover designed by Rachel Kirkland
Text designed by Kate Greenaway

Printed in New Zealand

CONTENTS

SOUTH ISLAND

WAITAKI VALLEY, COASTAL OTAGO AND DUNEDIN

CENTRAL OTAGO, CATLINS AND SOUTHLAND

WANAKA AND QUEENSTOWN

FIORDLAND AND STEWART ISLAND

Acknowledgements

Despite having faithfully promised myself there would be no more walking or tramping guidebooks, I have found myself hitting the road once again. A big thank you to the various friends who put me up for the night: Kirsty Woods and Peter Williamson in Wellington, Alan Hooker and Beverley Tatham in New Plymouth, Paula Kibblewhite and Bernie Kelly in Hawke's Bay, Lars Brabyn and Ottilie Stolte in Hamilton, and Jean and Roger Gibson way down in Central Otago. It made my many journeys a lot easier.

Especially deep thanks to my partner, Rachel Barker, and daughter Alex, who put up with my absences but also shared many of my wanderings.

Maps

Map Notes. All the maps in this book are based on the LINZ database (Land Information New Zealand), which has been freed from copyright restrictions by the New Zealand government. However, this database is updated infrequently so some map features may not be correct.

A scale and north pointer has been overlain on all maps, but it is worth remembering that every map is oriented with north at the top, and the squares shown on the maps are always one kilometre in width.

With some of the longer walks (such as Crater Lake or Totara Flats), there was not enough space on the page to show the full map. In these cases a section of the walk is included instead. A full topographical map is essential for these walks.

There is some variation in sharpness of the maps, due to variations in the dpi (dots-per-inch) at which the original maps were scanned.

Map Disclaimer. Because the printed size of these maps is quite small, and some detail has been lost during the publication process, they should not be used as a substitute for a full-scale topographical map.

TopoMap Pro. The maps in *202 Great Walks* were all produced using the TopoMap Pro software (version 2, 250dpi), by Mapworld of Christchurch. My thanks to Mapworld's owner Neville Jones for being able to utilise this excellent map software package. Contact: www.TopoMapPro.com

Author's note

This is a personal selection of walks. I have tried to represent the diversity of landscape in New Zealand fairly, but space limitations have inevitably restricted some choices. For every walk included, there are probably another two or three in most areas that are worth doing. However, some regions are lacking in decent walks: Poverty Bay, Manawatu, Wanganui and Waikato, please note.

I have personally visited all of these walks, and I have utilised information from the many pamphlets and publications put out by various city councils and the Department of Conservation. Every effort has been made to keep the information in the book up to date, but nothing stays the same.

It is the publisher's intention to update the book on a regular basis, and if you do see errors please email the author. Every effort will be made to incorporate the changes in the next edition.

Contact: markpickering@clear.net.nz

PREFACE

Why walk? On the face of it, the answer is obvious: to keep fit, to get some fresh air into your lungs, and to stretch your muscles and your curiosity. Human beings are active bipedal creatures and, although this might surprise some teenagers, we are built to move.

Bodies are not well designed for long periods of sitting, either in front of computers or commuting daily in cars. It makes our breathing less generous, our health more fragile. The whole thrust of our technological improvements takes away our natural state of movement and replaces it with inactivity. The car and the dishwasher are wonderful devices, but so are our legs. We have them for life and we need to use them, or lose them.

There are few things more satisfying than a good walk. It will not kill you, it requires little in the way of equipment or preparation, and there is a profound pleasure in quietly poking around a corner into a landscape different from your own.

Walking also offers a respite from the chronic hurry diseases of modern society and its highly sugared consumerism. It takes us at a slower pace, when society drums on faster. It finds quiet and solitude, when many human spaces are noisy and troubling.

> Above all, do not lose your desire to walk: every day I walk myself into a state of well-being and walk away from every illness; I have walked myself into my best thoughts, and I know of no thought so burdensome that one cannot walk away from it ...
> (Soren Kierkegaard, quoted in *The Songlines*, by Bruce Chatwin.)

But if you have read this far, you are probably one of the converted, or near-converted.

There is a definite change in the air, and according to Hillary Commission statistics walking has become New Zealand's number one recreational activity. In my own backyard of the Port Hills of Christchurch, the number of daily walkers has increased dramatically. On a summer's weekday ten years ago I might have seen nobody else out on these lovely hills, but now all the tracks seem to have persistent little dots moving over them.

Yet I don't feel crowded. There's plenty of space up there, and everywhere and anywhere in New Zealand. Indeed, I hope this book encourages more people to get out walking, though of course I have a vested interest. Walking writers have to make a living too, and to my continuing surprise, manage to do so.

But aside from helping me pay my bills, there is another excellent reason why you should buy this book. It is for a good friend of yours, long taken for granted, who does not grumble much, and has been expected to tick over quietly, efficiently and loyally for decades, with no regular maintenance whatsoever — your body.

INTRODUCTION

WALK NOTES

A GOOD START

For every walk, keep your plans modest if you are unfamiliar with the area, or the exercise. Keep an eye on the weather and tell someone where you are going.

EQUIPMENT

A good parka (or raincoat), energy food or a packed lunch, thermos, map, camera, sturdy and comfortable shoes and a sunhat are good things to start with.

There is now a good range of lightweight tramping boots that are impressively comfortable, and a raincoat is useful for protection against rain and wind, or for sitting on at lunch. For some of the alpine walks warm clothing is essential.

Walking poles are very useful. They are like ski-poles but retractable.

CLEAR INTENTIONS

Before you set off, it is important to leave clear intentions of where you are going with friends, family, flatmates, or a visitor centre if applicable (and don't forget to sign out too). Some walks have logbooks at the start of the track.

TRACKS

No specific gradings are given for these walks, but a general description is supplied, indicating if the track is flat, rolling (up and down) or a hill.

The type of track is also described, such as gravel path, mown grass strip, beach walking, sheep track or four-wheel-drive (4WD) track. The description 'tramping track' indicates a basic track, not necessarily well-marked, and where some experience is useful.

The condition of the track is indicated in the description, especially if there is mud or any rock scrambling.

TIMES AND DISTANCES

It is notoriously difficult to suggest walking times that make sense to everyone. The times suggested here are generous, designed for the plodders. Most averagely fit adults could reduce them.

As a rule of thumb the following scale can be used for flat or well-graded track travel:

2 km — 30 minutes
4 km — 1 hour
8 km — 2 hours.

For hill climbs the actual distance is not as relevant as the amount climbed. On a good track a walker could expect to take the following times:

300 metres — 1 hour
600 metres — 2 hours
1000 metres — 3 hours

SHORTER OPTIONS
Most of the walks in the book have a 1-hour or 2-hour turnaround option. This should suit people with shorter time, shorter legs, or who are short of breath. Usually the return point is at an interesting feature.

WEATHER
New Zealand enjoys a brisk, mild, moist, maritime climate. Long periods of settled weather are unusual, and abrupt changes are the norm. If the weather is not looking favourable, change your plans, for many hill walks are a waste of time if you cannot see the views. It is often windy, so take a wind-jacket, which can also serve as a rain-jacket. The sunlight can be intense so a sunhat is useful as well, and burn time can be short.

WINTER WALKING
The walks in this book are not written for snow conditions, so for example, the walk to Crater Lake, Mount Ruapehu, should only be undertaken in summer or snow-free conditions.

WALK ACCESS
Basic descriptions of how to get to each walk are included, but a good road atlas is essential. There is usually a carpark with signposts at the start of the walk. Other facilities are indicated.

CITY AND TOWN WALKS
Most of the city and town walks have good bus transport to them, but beyond the city or town a private car is virtually essential.

BABY BUGGIES
Baby buggies, mountain buggies or power prams are becoming increasingly popular among families with small children. Despite their advertised virtues they seem to be mainly suitable for flat, sealed paths or flat, well-made gravel tracks. Even a small hill is cause for quite a bit of parental sweat.

Baby buggies can be used on many of the city walks, and this is noted in the text where applicable. However, even the best tracks can have bicycle barriers or awkward corners that require negotiation.

WHEELCHAIR AND DISABLED ACCESS
Only a very few of these tracks are suitable for wheelchairs. Many start in visually interesting landscapes, however, so people with disabilities may not need to venture far to see some spectacular places.

MOUNTAIN BIKING
Mountain biking has become an enormously popular sport, and a few of these walks are shared with mountain bikes or cross over mountain-bike trails. Unless otherwise stated, or the track is designated multi-use, walkers have priority.

WALK INFORMATION

INFORMATION CENTRES

Throughout New Zealand there are wonderful information centres in all large and small towns, usually clearly indicated by the big 'i ' sign. These centres are usually open seven days a week and are an invaluable starting point in areas you are unfamiliar with.

DEPARTMENT OF CONSERVATION

The Department of Conservation (universally known by the acronym DoC) is the government department responsible for the protection and management of wilderness areas in New Zealand. It manages all national parks as well as marine reserves, and many other types of land from high country tussock landscapes to urban swamplands. Something like 25 percent of New Zealand's land area is in wilderness regions of one type or another.

Many of the walks in this book come under DoC's aegis, and nearly all the national parks and forests have visitor centres. These are excellent places to start from, providing track advice, pamphlets and maps, weather updates, and information on track closures and upgrades.

DoC has placed its pamphlets in most information centres, and in some towns has actually combined with the centre to provide a joint information base. A great idea!

PAMPHLETS

On most of the walks described here a further source of information is indicated, such as a pamphlet or map. However, there is no guarantee that these pamphlets are available, and some may even be out of print. The Department of Conservation should be your first stop, but local libraries can often help with out-of-print pamphlets and booklets.

MAPS

For the more serious walks always take a topographical map. The maps printed with most walks are extracts from the 1:50,000 topographical database and were accurate at the time of publication. However, many of these maps are not being updated or corrected in any meaningful way, and this needs to be taken into account when using them.

WALK COURTESY

KEEP TO TRACKS

Please keep to the marked tracks and avoid shortcuts. This is particularly important in fragile wetland areas and farm parks.

FENCES AND GATES

The farm rule is generally to leave a gate as you find it, whether open or shut. Most fences will have stiles, but if not, climb over the fence by the main strainer posts or where the gate is hinged.

SHEEP AND CATTLE

Sheep are rather nervous beasts and easy to panic, whereas cattle display the opposite trait of excessive curiosity. Walk quietly around stock, and if they are moving away give them time to do so.

LAMBING AND TRACK CLOSURES

A number of tracks pass through rural areas and may be closed from August to October for lambing. Other reasons for closure include fire risk and wildlife management. Please respect these closures.

DOGS

Most dog owners are responsible and careful, and keep their dogs under firm control. This is particularly important in rural areas where stock is present, and in wildlife areas. For ground-nesting birds the continual presence of dogs can jeopardise breeding, making it difficult for the birds to re-establish.

Dog fouling is an unpleasant nuisance on walking tracks, and it is the owner's responsibility to remove it. Carry that plastic bag, or at least clear it off the track with a stick, or cover it with earth.

FIRES

Many areas have restrictions or a total ban on fires; please observe these. If you see a fire contact the emergency services.

WALK NUISANCES

LITTER

Litter is not a major problem on tracks, and mostly occurs in carparks. Having a plastic bag and a pair of gardening gloves in the car or backpack is a positive way of ensuring our beaches and tracks stay litter free.

INSECTS

The two main problems are sandflies and wasps. Any good insect repellent should keep away the small sandfly, a type of black fly that is at its worst on the West Coast of the South Island. Mosquitoes appear only at night, so if you are camping a good insect-proof tent is useful.

Wasps are particularly prevalent in the beech forests where there is honeydew, and are at their peak in March–April. They are generally manageable but if you do get stung move quickly, for it usually means you have disturbed the nest and the first sting will be quickly followed by others. If you are allergic, take precautions.

There are no poisonous insects except the katipo spider, which few New Zealanders have ever seen; no leeches, snakes, horse-flies, bears, scorpions, man-eating spiders and so on.

VANDALISM AND GRAFFITI

All walks suffer periodically from vandals and graffiti. If you see evidence of this behaviour please contact the track managing authority immediately. If you actually see vandalism, or suspicious behaviour, and can identify a vehicle, take down its number and report it to the police.

CAR BREAK-INS

It is unlikely your vehicle would be broken into while you are on a daywalk, but to avoid becoming a victim don't leave valuables in cars.

WATER QUALITY

A water-borne parasite protozoan called giardia exists in some freshwater streams and can cause diarrhoea and vomiting. Fortunately it is easily cured and for most people is a nuisance rather than a threat. Carry your own water if you are doubtful of the local stuff, and generally treat any water running through farmland with caution.

It is a pity to have to automatically distrust all freshwater creeks in wilderness areas, and I have no intention of doing so. Recent scientific articles suggest that in order to absorb the ten giardia cysts necessary to start an infection you need to drink something like 100 litres of water from a stream. Cheers, mate!

WALK APPRECIATION

APPRECIATE WITHOUT POSSESSING

Many of these walks are in fragile areas where if everyone grabbed a chunk of interesting material the consequences of degradation would be obvious very quickly. People may think 'their small bit' doesn't make a difference, but it does. Interesting stones, driftwood, flowers and so on should be left for others to appreciate. Historic sites should be treated the same way; taking souvenirs of curious bits would soon mean there was nothing left to see.

FOOD GATHERING

The wildlife is usually more dependent on the food sources than you are. Shellfish beds can get depleted very quickly by humans, and people invariably take more than they really need. Collect for yourself and your family, not for all your mates.

WILDLIFE

If you see a wild creature keep a reasonable distance and be patient. Most birds and animals give warning signals or movements if they feel uncomfortable, so respect their space, and withdraw. Do not come between animals and their escape routes (for example, between seals and the sea). If chicks or young animals are present, be especially discreet.

The Department of Conservation advocates a policy of not feeding wild animals, especially 'friendly' ones like the weka and kea. It is usually the wrong sort of food and lures them away from their natural environment. Get expert help for the 'rescue' of injured wildlife.

GUIDEBOOKS TO PLANTS AND BIRDS

New Zealand is rich in unique plant and bird species, and there are many excellent books on New Zealand plants and birds.

For plants, Andrew Crowe has produced a series of attractive books — *Which Native Tree*, *Which Native Fern*, and so on — which are full of information on how to identify plants and their uses by Maori.

For birds, *The Hand Guide to the Birds of New Zealand* (Penguin) by Hugh Robertson and Barrier Heather is excellent, and lightweight.

Two useful series of books are the *Reed Field Guides* and *Reed Nature Series*, which cover a wide range of topics.

CONSERVATION

'Take only photos, leave only footprints' is the best motto. Wilderness is not a replenishable resource, and we cannot buy any more of it if we run out. Nor can we preserve its peaceful and uncluttered environment if we take our noisy, busy culture into it.

North Island

CAPE REINGA
A spirited headland track

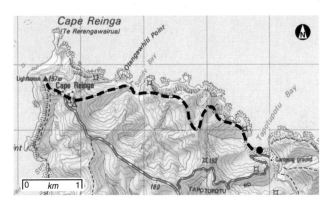

TRACK
A rolling coastal headland path, mostly grass, well signposted.

WALK TIME AND DISTANCE
1.5–2 hours one way Tapotupotu Bay to Cape Reinga; 3–4 hours (7 km) return.

ONE-HOUR WALK
Up onto Tapotupotu headland return.

ACCESS AND FACILITIES
From Kaitaia drive north almost 100 km on State Highway 1F. Just before Cape Reinga there is a signposted turn-off to Tapotupotu Bay, 2 km, where there is an excellent camping area beside a fine sandy bay. This campground gets packed in summer.

INFORMATION
Te Paki, Department of Conservation booklet.

It would be a dreadful letdown to come all the way to the top of New Zealand and be disappointed with the view. Cape Reinga is 450 km from Auckland, and the last 100 km is dusty and dull, but when you arrive at Tapotupotu Bay it is worth it. For this rare and remote place has a very fine landscape indeed — swathes of golden sand, windswept heathlands and big cleaving headlands. The walk from Tapotupotu Bay has brilliant views, and overlooks the constant jostling of the seas that meet at Cape Reinga.

From Tapotupotu Bay the track zigzags steeply up onto the grassy headland, marked by red posts. Manuka is the common coastal tree, with an aromatic scent. The track climbs to the top of the headland, where it turns inland along an old vehicle track, then cuts across the top of a gully onto another headland.

You can see the Cape Reinga lighthouse now, as the track descends into the sheltered and unimaginatively named Sandy Bay, which the Maori called Ngatangawhiti Bay. This cove is pretty and secluded, with shady pohutukawa and rock platforms to explore. It is a good place for lunch, and about halfway to Cape Reinga for those who want a 2-hour return walk.

It is a steep climb up the open spur to the carpark, and at the lighthouse there are good views of the Three Kings Islands. Reinga has been translated as 'place of

leaping', or 'underworld'; Maori legend says that all souls travel to the pohutukawa tree on the headland of Cape Reinga and descend into the underworld by sliding down a root to fall into the sea. The souls climb out again up onto Ohaua, the highest point of the Three Kings Islands, where they bid their last farewell before leaving finally for the world of their ancestors.

Cape Reinga is enormously popular with tourists, and 'sold' as the most northerly point of New Zealand. In actual fact the most northern point is North Cape, 30 km away to the east, but let us not quibble, for it is no hardship to swing back along this soaring headland track.

OTHER WALKS

This coastal path is part of a longer coastal walkway that starts at Spirits Bay and skirts around Cape Reinga to the top end of Ninety Mile Beach.

The headland track at Cape Reinga, looking back to Tapotupotu Bay.

Fishing from South Head (see page 22).

SOUTH HEAD
Seascape and signal station

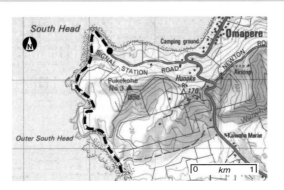

TRACK
Grassy paths and low-tide beach walking, some climbing.

WALK TIME AND DISTANCE
1 hour on headland and beach, 2–3 hours (6 km) return to Waiwhatewhata Stream Bay and point. A low or mid tide is definitely best.

ACCESS AND FACILITIES
From Omapere on Highway 12, drive south for 1 km then follow Signal Hill Road 2 km to the well-situated carpark.

INFORMATION
Arai-te-Uru, Hokianga Historical Society pamphlet.

South Head commands the entrance to Hokianga Harbour. In 1838 John Martin erected a signalling mast to help boats cross the dangerous bar, and he acted as pilot once vessels had entered the harbour. Martin also built a small cottage and boatshed at the waterside. Following the decline of the timber trade, the signal station's long period of service was brought to a close in 1951.

There is a good view from the carpark, but it is even better from the short walking track to the old signal site, with the huge, barren sand dunes on the North Head of Hokianga Harbour gleaming white in the sun. There's a short historic trail around the headland (10 minutes), and plenty of opportunity to explore the coast at low tide, when the cleared path for the historic pilot's boat ramp can still be seen.

A graded track goes down to the main beach, but to continue south you need to climb up onto the next headland and follow the track around a recessed rock cove. The track follows the fenceline around farmland before dropping through sand dunes into Waiwhatewhata Stream Bay.

There are extensive tidal platforms here, and the track continues around to the point at the south end of the bay. If you wish, you can continue along this wild and remote shoreline for several days. It is tempting.

OTHER WALKS
South Head is at the top end of the Waipoua Coastal Track, a three-day tramping trip that travels past the Waipoua Kauri Forest then over Maunganui Bluff to the Kai Iwi Lakes. There is also a low-tide route from South Head to Omapere settlement.

WAIPOUA FOREST
King kauri

TRACK
Flat and easy walking on good forest paths. Okay for baby buggies.

WALK TIME AND DISTANCE
Tane Mahuta is 10 minutes return, Four Sisters 5 minutes return, Te Matua Ngahere 30 minutes return.

ACCESS AND FACILITIES
Waipoua Forest is on Highway 12, about 30 km south of Opononi and 60 km north of Dargaville. There's an information centre and motor camp at the forest headquarters, about 8 km past Tane Mahuta. The forest lookout is worth a side trip.

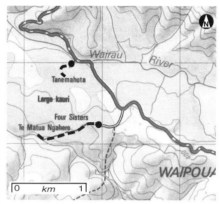

These walks are short but unique, for the Waipoua Forest is the last and only place in New Zealand where you can see big kauri in their proper context of an unaltered forest. These huge trees never fail to impress, and when you consider that they were part of the era of the great moa and the giant eagle, then in the pre-human history of New Zealand a biblical quotation seems apt — 'there were giants on the earth in those days'.

Everything about kauri is larger than life. They can live up to a thousand years, and a tree like Tane Mahuta could be milled to make ten houses. Kauri is a conifer, and starts life as a normal looking tree in a nursery forest like manuka, grows through a teenage or 'ricker' stage, then thickens into middle age and swells into a vast cylinder while the crown gets thin. The bark flakes off in pieces the size of dinner plates, which prevents epiphytes establishing a hold. Waipoua is the kauri's last sanctuary, 2600 hectares of mature kauri that was preserved only as late as 1952.

The Tane Mahuta walk goes to the largest kauri in existence, awesome, with a 13-metre girth and 17 metres to the first branch. The Four Sisters walk follows an elegant boardwalk around four 'sisterly' kauri.

The Matua Ngahere ('father of the forest') walk is the most impressive of the three, mainly

Tane Mahuta.

because you have time to become absorbed by the forest as you go deeper into it. The silence is deafening, and big trees slide by in a splendid parade until you reach the second biggest kauri in existence.

TUTUKAKA HEAD
Interesting islets and curious coves

TRACK
Grass footpath and stairs, some beach walking and a short bush track. You need a mid or low tide.

WALK TIME AND DISTANCE
1 hour (2 km) return.

ACCESS AND FACILITIES
From Tutukaka, take the northern road then the Tutukaka Reserve Road on the left, 400 metres past the Tutukaka Hotel. Not well signposted, but this narrow lane leads to quite a decent carpark with sea views.

Tutukaka Head is a succession of islets with tiny jewel-like bays on either side, where the sea sweeps right through when it wants to. Surf scours the tide platforms, and Kukutauwhao Island anchors the whole fragile assemblage of islands together.

The main track leads over the grassy headland, then sharply down a staircase to the beach. The little sandy bays are perfect, and so are the rock platforms that skirt both sides of the peninsula. Kids will love to play hide and seek among the rock stacks and sea-sculptured rocks.

If they get bored, the final part of the walk clambers up a bush track onto Kukutauwhao Island. At the high point a lighthouse watches over the Poor Knights Islands, with views everywhere.

There is an alternative track from the carpark, which goes down to an unnamed bay where there is nothing more than sand, grass and solitude.

The steps down to the beach, Tutukaka Head.

A.H. REED MEMORIAL KAURI PARK
& WAIMAHANGA WALKWAY

Urban kauri forest and coastal causeway

TRACK

A.H. Reed Memorial Kauri Park: excellent boardwalk from the middle carpark, suitable for wheelchairs and baby buggies. Other bush tracks are more basic.

Waimahanga Walkway: good flat gravelled track, suitable for baby buggies on causeway. Bush track to Waverley Street.

WALK TIME AND DISTANCE

A.H. Reed Memorial Kauri Park: middle boardwalk 10-minute circuit; full walkway 30 minutes (1 km) one way. Waimahanga Walkway: 1 hour (3 km) one way; 2 hours (6 km) return; circuit 1 hour 10 minutes (Cockburn Street, causeway, Waverley Street, Raurimu Avenue).

ACCESS AND FACILITIES

A.H. Reed Memorial Kauri Park: from the city take Mill Road and Whareora Road to either of three carparks: top waterfall, middle boardwalk, or lower.

Waimahanga Walkway: Onerahi Road leads to: (1) Old Onerahi Road and Waimahanga Road; (2) Waverley Street (this has the best carparking); (3) Raurimu Avenue to Cockburn Street.

INFORMATION

Whangarei Walks, Whangarei District Council pamphlet.

A.H. REED MEMORIAL KAURI PARK

This splendid walk can be fitted into most people's schedules. There is a spectacular short boardwalk around several thick-waisted kauri and a waterfall higher up.

To do the best walk in this park, get dropped off at the top carpark and walk down to the lower carpark. First you descend past the sudden 24-metre waterfall (although there seems to be no decent lookout onto it), then the track wanders through lush forest to the middle boardwalk.

At times the walking platforms are a giddy 10 metres above the valley floor, and the gentle stream underneath is softened by deep-green, moss-encrusted boulders. The track winds down easily to the bottom footbridge at the lower carpark.

WAIMAHANGA WALKWAY

Good exercise for flat walkers or power prammers, as the causeway follows an old port railway line built in 1911. The views are a bit scant, blocked by the fine mangrove forest, but there are two bridges where you can watch the estuary gurgle in and out through the mud.

From the Cockburn Street carpark follow the causeway to the first wooden truss bridge, then it is another 10 minutes to the George Point footbridge. There are some views of the port here, and the main track continues on to Waimahanga Road carpark, but it is a good idea to take the side-track.

This leads past a footbridge (and another side-track to George Point Road) and into a fine remnant of coastal forest with totara trees and lush ferns. This track exits onto Waverley Street opposite the sewage treatment works and kindy (good town planning!) and it's not a bad circuit to go up onto Onerahi Road and down Raurimu Avenue to the Cockburn Street carpark.

A boardwalk section of the A.H. Reed Memorial Kauri Park walk.

An old bridge on the Waimahanga causeway.

MOUNT MANAIA
Volcanic rock plugs and spectacular views

TRACK
A steep hill walk on a tramping track, sometimes muddy.

WALK TIME AND DISTANCE
2–3 hours (3 km) return.

ONE-HOUR WALK
Bluff lookout return.

ACCESS AND FACILITIES
From Whangarei follow the airport road then the coast road to Whangarei Heads and Urquharts Bay, then take the Ocean Beach Road 1 km to a carpark and information sign. At McLeods Bay (1 km before Mount Manaia) there are toilets, picnic tables and a children's play area.

INFORMATION
Mount Manaia Ridge Scenic Reserve and *Bream Head Scenic Reserve*, Department of Conservation pamphlets.

This striking mountain can be seen from many points around Whangarei Harbour and Bream Bay. Fingers of volcanic rock stretch up from a coastal forest, and DoC has built a viewing platform that is spectacular and nerve-racking. The andesite rock is the remains of a volcano that erupted 20 million years ago, and the peak is of important cultural and spiritual significance to Ngati Manaia and Ngati Wai.

From the large carpark follow the signs past the Early Settlers Memorial and through the carved Maori gateway. At first shingled, the track quickly becomes more basic as it sidles through thick bush of kauri, nikau palms, rewarewa and puriri. There are some large specimen trees as the muddy track lurches upwards around the base of Mount Manaia to the bluff lookout, where there are good views of Bream Head and the Hen and Chicken Islands.

The track steepens, then reaches the main ridge, wriggling past increasingly forbidding rock pinnacles. After passing the alternative track down, the main track stops beside a viewing platform right beside a rock pinnacle. From the top you can see the isolated trigged summit of Mount Manaia. According to Maori lore, the local tribes used to bury their dead warriors and chiefs on these peaks, though I cannot imagine how they did it.

Don't go beyond the platform if you suffer from vertigo, and in any case there is really nowhere to go. Oddly, there is a picnic table underneath the platform.

On the return, fit walkers can take the steep alternative track. The worst part is at the top, with a scramble down rocks and roots, but there is a wire to help you down a gully. After that it becomes easier. This used to be the main track to the peak before the easier route was established.

OTHER WALKS IN THE AREA
Bream Head, Smugglers Cove.

TAWHARANUI REGIONAL PARK
Peninsula of promise

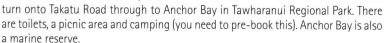

TRACK
An easy rolling walk on farmland, with bush groves and some mud.

WALK TIME AND DISTANCE
1–1.5 hours (4 km) return (if including Tokatu Point add another hour).

ACCESS AND FACILITIES
From Highway 1 at Warkworth, follow the road to Omaha Flats, then turn onto Takatu Road through to Anchor Bay in Tawharanui Regional Park. There are toilets, a picnic area and camping (you need to pre-book this). Anchor Bay is also a marine reserve.

INFORMATION
Tawharanui Visitors' Guide, Auckland Regional Council pamphlet.

Northland seems to have a baffling surplus of coastal scenery, and each twist and turn of the road to Tawharanui reveals another magical indentation. Matronly peninsulas shepherd close-knit groups of islands, and each bay is a golden slice of summer all year round. This coast offers a perpetual promise of escape.

Anchor Bay is an open, sandy beach broken with tidal platforms, offshore reefs and headlands with sea caves. Large pohutukawa trees rustle on the beach edge. It is hard to walk away from all this, but if you choose to do so, there is a fine walking circuit around the peninsula.

From Anchor Bay follow the farm road up onto the broad tops of the peninsula, crossing the Ecology Trail. There are good views along the farmland past grazing Hereford cattle and Romney sheep. After about 2 km you reach a track junction that is about 90 metres above sea level, where you have the option of following the peninsula out to Tokatu Point (spelt Takatu Point on some maps). You can see cloud-capped Little Barrier Island in the distance, and Kawau Island nearby to the south.

Follow the track along the south coast and turn onto the side-track that drops through a shady stream with stands of manuka and puriri, then follows alongside a dam, meeting the Ecology Trail again on the way. Shortly you exit out to Anchor Bay again and that stunning stretch of sand.

OTHER WALKS
South Coast Track, Ecology Trail and sand dune circuit.

KAWAU ISLAND
Time out on a timeless island

TRACK
Well-graded bush track, or rock-hopping at low tide to get to the old copper mine engine-house.

WALK TIME AND DISTANCE
1 hour return (4 km) to copper mine.

ACCESS AND FACILITIES
Daily ferry service from Sandspit, a wharf about 10 km from Warkworth. The worst part about Kawau Island is the expense of

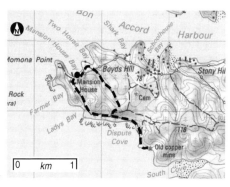

getting there. The adult fare on the ferry from Sandspit to Kawau Island was $24 return; the ferry takes about 30 minutes one way, with commentary. Rather overpriced I thought, so perhaps take your own boat?

DoC charges $4 per adult to go inside the Mansion House. There are toilets and tearooms, and plenty of places to picnic.

INFORMATION
Kawau Island Historic Reserve, Department of Conservation pamphlet.

As Te Kawau-tu-Maro, 'island of the motionless shag', Kawau Island was a prime fishing ground for Maori, but when Samuel Marsden landed in 1820 it was deserted. Manganese was discovered here in New Zealand's second underground mine, then copper in 1844. Cornish miners were brought in, with some 300 miners and their families at the height of the industry; the 'Mansion House' began life as the mine manager's house, built in 1847.

In 1862 Governor George Grey bought the island. He owned it for 25 years, during which time he enlarged the house and established a cultured paradise of exotic birds, plants and conversation. From 1888 onwards a succession of owners ran Mansion House as a guest house, holiday camp and watering hole for boaties. Restoration started in 1976 and the renovated Mansion House was officially opened in 1979.

From the wharf, walk past the Mansion House, persistent peacocks and exotic plants, onto the Coach Road that leads to Lady's Bay, a small, discreet cove. The track continues on to a lookout on a grassy clearing, and from here you take the Miners' Track down to Dispute Cove — nice snoozing spot.

Either take the inland track to the copper mine, or if it is a mid- to low tide wander on the tidal platform to the massive ruin of the engine house. The rich colours of copper stain the rocks and the stillness is broken only by scavenging gulls.

On the return you can explore the broad tidal platforms around to Lady's Bay, or follow the Redwood Track down to Two House Bay and around the point to the Mansion House. Of course, you have to allow some time to explore the grand Mansion House, and by then you will be scampering to catch the return ferry.

You quickly run out of time in Kawau.

SHAKESPEAR PARK
A happy alchemy

TRACK
Rolling farmland and short bush tracks. Some mud and small hill climbs.

WALK TIME AND DISTANCE
2- to 3-hour circuit, 6 km return.

ONE-HOUR WALK
Headland return.

ACCESS AND FACILITIES
Turn off Highway 1 onto Whangaparaoa Road, which leads to a carpark. There are picnic facilities, pukeko, peacocks, toilets and a camping area at the far end of Te Haruhi Bay.

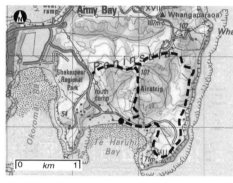

INFORMATION
Northern Parks and *Heritage Trail*, Auckland Regional Council pamphlets.

At the end of the Whangaparaoa Peninsula is Shakespear Park, named not after the bard but after one W.H. Shakespear, who purchased the land in 1883. A shrewd buy, most people would think, for it included a glorious beach at Te Haruhi Bay, wide swathes of tidal platforms, some pockets of bush reserves and excellent views along the sea-eaten coastline. In 1967 another shrewd buyer came along, and the Auckland Regional Authority purchased the land for a park.

And the public have not been slow to enjoy this gorgeous park, which is alive with choices for the lazy or the walker. The best circuit walk starts from Te Haruhi Bay and follows the Tiri Tiri track up onto the headland, then swings along the easy farmland tops, displacing the well-fed sheep and passing a short side-track down to Pink Beach.

Platoons of perambulating pukeko peck in the paddocks, but the main track climbs up to a farm road and wanders around to the lookout platform, with the Hauraki Gulf spread out before you. The main poled track continues down a spur to Te Haruhi Bay, completing a circuit that should take about 2–3 hours. And the peacocks are still prowling on the foreshore.

OTHER WALKS
The Heritage Trail features forest, wetland and Maori sites; 1–2 hours return.

People and peacocks on the Shakespear Park foreshore.

OKURA BUSH
Seashore and sea forest

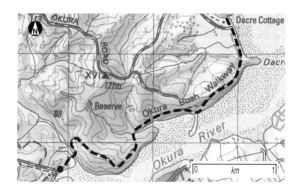

TRACK
A good graded gravel track most of the way, some solid climbs, and a beach stretch.

WALK TIME AND DISTANCE
3–4 hours one way; 3–5 hours return to Dacre Cottage. It is a good solid walk to Dacre Cottage so take lunch. 8 km return to Dacre Cottage.

TWO-HOUR WALK
Mangrove beach and point return.

ACCESS AND FACILITIES
South: off East Coast Road (Highway 25) onto Haigh Access Road to a miserable carpark. North: off East Coast Road (Highway 25) onto Spur Road and Duck Creek Road to Stillwater Park.

INFORMATION
Auckland Walkways, Department of Conservation pamphlet.

A long walk along a forest shoreline that is surprisingly untouched considering it is only 20 km north of Auckland city. Dense bush, mangroves, and a wide beach at Karepiro Bay, where the tiny and historic Dacre Cottage stands. The carpark at Haigh Access Road is limited to say the least, but this part of the walk to Dacre Cottage is the most scenic.

From the carpark the track turns a corner and strides across a long bridge and boardwalk over a mangrove forest and stream. This is a good place to view birds, and white-faced herons can often be seen poking about the mudflats. After this the track starts a steady climb to 100 metres above sea level and a forest thick with nikau palms and young kauri.

The track then descends slowly to the shore and winds along to a beach where there are mangroves and a small finger of land that juts out into the broad estuary of the Okura River. A good return point.

Otherwise continue up through bush and pine trees to Dacre Point and a sharp descent to Karepiro Beach. About 1 km along here is the locked Dacre Cottage, built in about the 1850s and now restored. There are toilets here.

The track continues from Karepiro Bay by crossing a stream and climbing a low ridge, then following alongside the Weiti River estuary to Stillwater Park.

MURIWAI GANNET COLONY
Soaring by sea cliffs

TRACK
Easy, well-made walking tracks.

WALK TIME AND DISTANCE
30 minutes return gannet colony; 1 hour return via Flat Rock. Add 30 minutes for visiting Maori Bay.

ACCESS AND FACILITIES
From Auckland follow Highway 16 towards Helensville for 25 km, then turn off at Waimauku, some 12 km from Muriwai. The last stretch of road down to Muriwai is steep and narrow; watch out for pedestrians. The closest access to the gannet colony is at the Maori Bay carpark, where there are toilets and superb information panels. There is also extensive car parking and a general store by the main beach.

INFORMATION
Muriwai Regional Park, Auckland Regional Council pamphlet.

A short walk to an amazing sight: a squabbling, jostling, cackling, thriving gannet colony. There are a thousand nesting pairs of gannets at Muriwai. The viewing platforms are only metres away, and give a marvellous birds'-eye view of what it is like to be a gannet. When they are not fighting for their space on the cliff edge they are whooshing overhead, bringing back food for their young or effortlessly soaring over the Pacific.

The headland updraughts make it easy for the gannets to get to and from the nesting sites, and the abundance of food has enabled the colony to expand. It started on the offshore Oaia Island, then moved onto Motutara ('island of the sea birds') and when this rock stack became overpopulated the gannets started a mainland colony.

You can also walk past the viewing platform and down to Flat Rock, which is a popular fishing spot despite being both slippery and dangerous with a surf breaking. From the beach it is a short walk past the main carpark and up Maori Bay track to the carpark there.

There's pillow lava at the far end of Maori Bay carpark, and you can follow a locked access road to the dark volcanic bay, which is dotted with the corpses of gannets that didn't make the grade.

The Muriwai gannet colony.

AUCKLAND CITY WALK – TUFF CRATER
& ONEPOTO BASIN
Hidden city craters

TRACK
Gravel paths, boardwalks and grass swales, some short climbs.

WALK TIME AND DISTANCE
1 hour circuit (including Tuff Crater and Onepoto Basin), 5 km return. 40 minutes (4 km) return Tuff Crater.

ACCESS AND FACILITIES
Small carpark at Heath Reserve, at the end of Exmouth Road. The Tuff Crater track starts here, and there is also a footbridge over the motorway to the grandly named City of Cork Beach — more name than beach really.

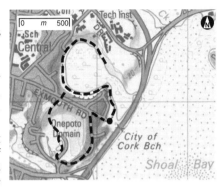

Motorists making the daily numbing drive to work from the North Shore to the city will barely have noticed these two discreet volcanic basins. Both are delightful, and provide an ideal urban walking environment, with many places to explore throughout Northcote suburb.

There are track links from Onepoto Basin to Onepoto Stream, which can also be directly connected to the Kauri Glen Scenic Reserve, and then just across Onewa Road to Le Roys Bush and further on to . . . well, you get the idea. Splendid backyard discovery stuff.

From the Heath Reserve an excellent track wanders into Tuff Crater and follows a boardwalk past the thick mangrove forest. There are junctions to Exmouth Road, Arahia Street and a lookout platform at St Peters Street, then the track loops right round to the romantically named 'The Warehouse Way'.

On the return you can wander up to Exmouth Road, then cross and descend a broad grass swale down into Onepoto Basin and its popular lakes. A good return here could be up Sylvan Avenue and Heath Avenue to the reserve and carpark.

The lookout platform beside Tuff Crater.

AUCKLAND CITY WALK – HARBOURVIEW
Great space, great place

TRACK
Flat, easy paths on gravel and boardwalks. Baby buggies can be taken just about all the way.

WALK TIME AND DISTANCE
1 hour (4 km) return.

ACCESS AND FACILITIES
Off Te Atatu Road, then Harbour View Road to a carpark.

INFORMATION
Harbourview, Waitakere City Council pamphlet.

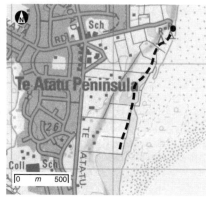

The Waitakere City Council has been doing some good things on its side of the city. Walks at Opanuku Walkway, Paremuka Lakeside, Henderson Creek and Waipareira are stunning examples of what can be done to provide urban walkways in the heart of the city. Harbourview just about tops them all, with its view across the glittering Waitemata Harbour to the tall, metallic skyscrapers downtown. The walkway starts by a carpark and a totally useless but utterly stylish picnic platform.

A short boardwalk circles the pond, but the main track wanders south along the shoreline, where shore birds dabble among the ponds and creeks. There is one historic building along the track and several exit points to Te Atatu suburban roads. The walk ends too soon, but it is a lovely return.

Picnic platform and pampas, Harbourview.

AUCKLAND CITY WALK – PANMURE BASIN
Joggers' and strollers' retreat

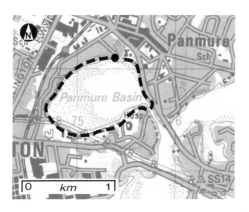

TRACK
Flat, easy walking on good paths. Suitable for baby buggies.

WALK TIME AND DISTANCE
1 hour (3 km) return.

ACCESS AND FACILITIES
Access from Panmure roundabout onto Ireland Road, then Cleary Road to plenty of carparking. There are other access points off Ireland Road and Waipuna Road. Children's play area and toilets.

INFORMATION
An Auckland road map would be useful.

Auckland has many nooks and crannies to explore, and if you can overcome the horrible traffic (getting up *really* early seems to work), the Panmure Basin offers a unique urban recreation circuit. Ideal for easy walkers, power prammers and very popular with joggers.

Dawn is a fine time. Old pohutukawa trees edge the basin, and the first rush-hour traffic roars all around as the first light comes through the winking streetlights. It is an easy, undemanding stroll, your head nodding in acknowledgement to all the regular loopers, and each lap represents 3 km.

It is better than I have made it sound.

RANGITOTO ISLAND
Easy access to a volcanic icon

TRACK
Good gravel tracks and paths up a steady 259-metre hill.

WALK TIME AND DISTANCE
2–3 hours (6 km) to summit and return; 4–5 hours (12 km) summit and McKenzie Bay return. Take water. Remember to check the ferry pick-up time before you leave the wharf. I have noticed that the ferry return times do not suit walkers who want to do a full circuit, unless you can turn the power on.

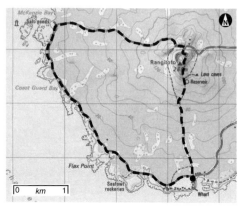

ONE-HOUR WALK
Pohutukawa Stop return and Fern Walk.

ACCESS AND FACILITIES
Tour boats leave from the main Auckland city wharf daily. There are toilets, a barbecue area, an occasional shop, a saltwater swimming pool and an information shelter at the wharf.

INFORMATION
Rangitoto, Department of Conservation pamphlet.

Rangitoto's shallow volcanic cone is an icon for Auckland and a great escape for the city. It has New Zealand's largest pohutukawa forest, extensive lava fields, mangrove swamps, and a fine walking network. There are no cars, and the only hustle and bustle is the rush of walkers off the ferry. A good day out in any weather, rain or fine.

From the wharf take the popular and broad summit trail, with its many excellent information panels on the way to slow you down. The black scoria rock and rustling pohutukawa create a strange landscape. You pass two track junctions, to Wilson Park Walk and the Lava Caves walk, then the track steepens slightly to the final summit and a splendid panorama.

From the summit take the track down to the cross-island road and follow this down to pretty McKenzie Bay – this can be a hot walk. Follow the coastal road past the side-track to a lookout over the black-backed gull colonies at Flax Point. The main track continues over a mangrove inlet back to the wharf and that tempting ice-cream shop.

KITEKITE FALLS & USSHER CROSS
Waterfall wander in the Waitakeres

TRACK

A good gravel track on the south-side walk to Kitekite Falls, rougher on the north side. Cowan Track to Ussher Cross to Kitekite Falls are well-marked bush trails.

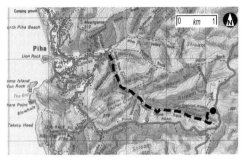

There are many track junctions and choices, which can be confusing even with all the good signposting. Take a map.

WALK TIME AND DISTANCE

Kitekite Falls: 1 hour (2 km) return.

Kauri Grove — Ussher Cross — Kitekite Falls: 2 hours (5 km) one way.

ACCESS AND FACILITIES

Kitekite Falls: drive to Piha and along Glen Esk Road to the carpark.

Ussher Cross–Kitekite Falls: on the road to Piha look out for the carpark at the Cowan Track.

INFORMATION

Waitakere Ranges: Recreation and Track Guide, Auckland Regional Council map. An extremely useful publication that details the mayhem of all the different tracks and track options. Don't walk in the Waitakeres without it.

This walk gives you a smorgasbord of what the Waitakeres have to offer. Superb forest on the higher slopes, a clear cascading stream, then the sudden leap into nothingness as a waterfall appears under your feet. Finally a rich coastal belt of nikau palms, waving and opening up to the definitive beach.

The best walk option is to get dropped off at the Cowan Track carpark on the Piha road, and walk down to Kitekite Falls and Piha. The Cowan is a short track that drops steeply and links to the Kauri Grove Track. This sidles easily alongside the Glen Esk Stream to the four-way junction of Ussher Cross.

Keep going on the Kauri Grove Track a short way further to the top of Kitekite Falls, then follow the Connect Track down steeply to meet the main Kitekite Track. For the falls themselves, walk back uphill a short way — it is worth it, a graceful gusher. You can keep going on this track, climbing a little then sidling easily around the valley and down to the forest floor. Then it is a broad track past several junctions and attractive bridges to the carpark and a justly famous beach.

OTHER WALKS

Kitekite Falls (from Piha carpark), 1 hour return. This starts as an easy stroll through dense groves of nikau palms and past various side-tracks and bridges. The path then steepens and climbs around the valley slopes to come right round and under the falls themselves. The track down the other side is not quite as smooth, but just as interesting.

WHATIPU COAST
Wildness of wind and shore

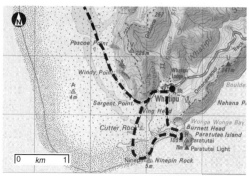

Detail: Whatipu beach area

TRACK
All flat beach and coastal walking. The headland walk to Karekare beach involves a scramble and you need a low tide.

WALK TIME AND DISTANCE
2–3 hours (12 km) return to Tunnel Point; 4–5 hours (16 km) return to Karekare beach.

ONE-HOUR WALK
A circuit can be made from the carpark to include Paratutae Island, Ninepin Rocks and Cutters Rock.

ACCESS AND FACILITIES
From downtown Auckland drive to Titirangi and follow the coastal road past Huia to the north head of Manukau Harbour at Whatipu carpark, about 25 km. There are toilets and an information board.

Sticking out on the north edge of the Manukau Harbour, Whatipu is one of the truly great beaches — wild and stinging on windy days, haunting on calm mornings. There is an abundance of coastal scenery here, with a huge beach plain, headlands, islets, tidal platforms, ephemeral dune ponds and swathes of jointed rush waving in the equally abundant wind.

Historic features include the old wharf on Paratutae Island, the wreck of HMS *Orpheus* (New Zealand's biggest shipwreck, in 1863, with the loss of 167 lives), the caves used by Maori for shelter, and the tunnel and timber tramway that can be traced all the way to Karekare beach.

For the best walk you need pre-arranged transport and a low tide to go right through to Karekare. If that is awkward you should still be able to get right through to Karekare and back, as long as you time the tides right and don't dilly-dally on the way.

From the carpark follow the track to the sea caves, which the Maori used as shelter; the largest is called 'Te Ana Ru'. A 4WD road leads past dune lakes, and once around the corner it is not far to the distinctive prominence of Pararaha Point; about 4 km from the Whatipu carpark.

Stay close to the cliffs and you will reach the old tramline and the historic tunnel. The railway was built in the 1870s to carry kauri timber from Karekare to a wharf at Whatipu. Once through the tunnel it is easy walking to Cowan Point and the bluff at Kaka Point. It is barely a kilometre to Karekare but you definitely need a low tide to cross the tidal platforms, then follow the scrambly track. You pass remnants of the old tramway then round the corner and reach Karekare. But remember, if you are returning, not to enjoy this beach too long.

Manukau Heads, Whatipu coast.

Kitekite waterfall (see page 37).

OTUATAUA STONEFIELDS
An ancient place

TRACK
No formed tracks, but marked trails over the pastureland and stone mounds.

WALK TIME AND DISTANCE
1–2 hours (2–4 km) return.

ACCESS AND FACILITIES
Very near Auckland airport but not as well signposted as you would expect. From Highway 20A (just before the first airport roundabout) turn onto Ihumatao Road for 3 km, then go down Oruarangi Road and into Ihumatao Quarry Road. There are signboards and a carpark at the end of the road.

INFORMATION
The Otuataua Stonefields: official opening commemorative brochure, Manukau City Council booklet.

Some eight hundred or a thousand years ago Polynesians landed in New Zealand, bringing with them the seeds and tubers of their island homes. Essentially tropical crops like kumara need careful maintenance, and they struggled to grow in this unfamiliar land. The gardeners learnt that by manipulating stone mounds to create microclimates they could warm the earth, protect the crops from winds, reduce moisture loss and make their kumara flourish.

Every stone in these coastal fields has been shifted, first by the Maori, then by Europeans, who crisscrossed the land with dry-stone walls. The result is an ancient matrix of agriculture that was later discarded and left to the sweeping winds off the Manukau estuary.

The three self-guiding trails — historical, botanical and geological — all become muddled up with each other, and people just seem to wander off on their own personal explorations and discover all sorts of things — a Moreton Bay fig tree, 800-year-old storage pits, a barberry hedge, a saucer-shaped volcanic cone, a karaka grove. Or they sit by the shimmering coastal edge, gazing out to the Manukau Heads and wondering what it must have been like to come to an empty land where your crops wouldn't grow.

Old stone fences and a Moreton Bay fig in the Otuataua Stonefields.

CLEVEDON SCENIC RESERVE
Puriri forest and hill lookout

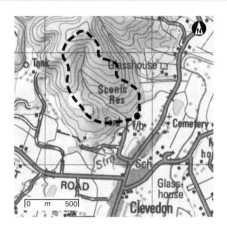

TRACK
Gravel paths at first, then worn forest trails up a steady hill. The downhill fenceline track is a bit rough.

WALK TIME AND DISTANCE
1–2 hours (2 km) return. Some of the signposting is unclear.

ACCESS AND FACILITIES
From Clevedon take North Road and Thorps Quarry Road to the carpark and picnic area.

This is an eerie, sensuous forest, where the huge puriri trees turn the light silvery and calm under the canopy. Nikau palms are also dominant, as well as tawa, broadleaf and ferns. This little bush reserve is just a remnant, sticking out oddly from the well-manicured and green, rolling farms of Clevedon. It is a walk that combines well with a Clevedon cafe.

From the carpark, walk past Camp Sladdin across the vehicle ford and past the quarry picnic area to the signposted walk intersection. There are two short loop tracks that are almost too short to be useful. Take the right-hand gravel track to the summit, as it wends up through the gorgeous puriri forest. A steady climb leads to the scrubline and the summit lookout platform at 210 metres.

The easiest and best-graded return is back down the gravel track, otherwise take the alternative track as it drops back through the scrub into the forest. It then follows a rather uninteresting and steepish fenceline down and then up, before passing a track junction and dropping easily through kauri forest to the carpark.

OTHER WALKS
Omana Regional Park (1 hour coastal and rural circuit) and Tawhitokino Beach, near Kawakawa Bay (1 hour coastal walk).

MIRANDA WETLANDS
The margin of the land

TRACK
Old farm track, stopbank, shellbanks and mudflats.

WALK TIME AND DISTANCE
1 hour (2 km) return.

ACCESS AND FACILITIES
Miranda is at the lower end of the Firth of Thames, along the coastal road from Clevedon to Waitakaruru. Alternatively you can access Miranda off Highway 25 some 10 km from Waitakaruru.

There are several access points to the Miranda foreshore, including rest areas along the highway. The best access is about 800 m south past the Miranda Trust building, where there is a stile and signpost, and a bird-hide a short distance from the road.

Early mornings at Miranda spill washes of gentle colour over the flat horizon. The sea turns from black to silver and then blue, and the shellbanks reflect the first glitter of the morning sun. This is one of the best sites for wading birds in the country, birds with exotic and faraway names that reek of Asia Minor — red-necked stint, terek sandpiper, lesser knot, whimbrel, eastern curlew, turnstone, bar-tailed godwit and Pacific golden plover.

Miranda does not involve much walking, and the best times to visit are at dawn and dusk. High tides bring the birds closer, while low tides reveal the slither of the tidal streams as they trickle through the exposed mudflats. From the stile a vehicle track wanders through the Robert Findlay Wildlife Reserve to the bird-hide.

Keen birdies will need a good pair of binoculars, but anyone can enjoy the open, pure expanses of Miranda, and the occasional buzzing car on the coastal highway does not disturb the peacefulness. It is 100 km from Auckland — a world away.

WAIRERE FALLS
Graceful waterfall and historic Maori trail

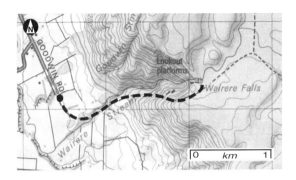

TRACK
An easy walking track that turns into a steep tramping track. Some boulder-hopping and river crossing, and the track is not suitable after rain.

WALK TIME AND DISTANCE
2 hours (3 km) return to waterfall lookout; 3–4 hours (4 km) return to top of waterfall.

ONE-HOUR WALK
To third bridge return.

ACCESS AND FACILITIES
From Te Aroha drive south beside the bushy escarpment of the Kaimai Range along the straight Te Aroha–Gordon Road–Okauia Road, some 25 km to a right-angle corner. The Wairere Falls carpark is signposted 1 km down the unsealed Goodwin Road.

A showpiece waterfall that, if you are game enough, you can admire from both the graceful foot and the stomach-heaving top. There are stream crossings, attractive footbridges, and a scary route up to the Kaimai escarpment.

The track starts by wandering up the Wairere Stream in a regenerating forest of kawakawa, then crosses a bridge and drops back beside the stream. The stream is attractive, with rich mosses on the big boulders, and there are two more bridges to cross. There is one awkward river corner that might be tricky to get past after heavy rain.

The track climbs away from the stream to the foot of a steep staircase, with a number of landings to pause on. Shortly afterwards there's a side trail to a lookout platform where you can admire the waterfall framed by bush as it tumbles down in two leaps of 73 and 80 metres. It is about two hours return to here.

The bush track continues to zigzag steeply up through to the top of the escarpment. Because Wairere Falls is a natural break in the mountain defences, the Maori used the route for hundreds of years. At the top, the old Maori trail is followed for 15 minutes to a side-track that takes you to the dizzy lookout platform at the top of the waterfall. The views of the Waikato are amazing, and on a clear day you can see the distant peaks of the Tongariro plateau.

HAMILTON CITY WALK – JUBILEE PARK
& RIVERSIDE WALKS

Rare kahikatea forest and river walks

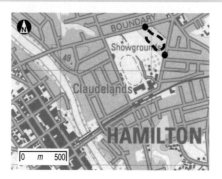

TRACK
Flat boardwalk. Suitable for baby buggies and wheelchairs.

WALK TIME AND DISTANCE
15 minutes return.

ACCESS AND FACILITIES
For Jubilee Park drive from Hamilton city across the Whitiora Bridge then onto Boundary Road. There is also access off Brooklyn Road, but neither road is particularly good for carparking.

There is quite a lot wrong with this short walk – lousy carparking, no interpretation panels, and the picnic tables beside the busy car-fuming roads must be some sort of council joke. On the other hand, local rumour has it that the Hamilton City Council is planning to re-orientate access in the future, and to provide better carparking. There is also talk of better information, and this kahikatea forest deserves it – it is superb.

The deep shade of the forest provides a welcome short sojourn away from the busy roads that surround it, and 'short' is right. The walk is brief, on broad boardwalks that sweep around the kahikatea, tawa, mahoe and pukatea. But if you do the boardwalk twice, it actually seems better the second time. This is a remnant of the lowland swamp forest that once covered the Waikato Plain; today only 4 percent still stands.

OTHER WALKS ALONG THE RIVERSIDE
It is well worth combining Jubilee Park with a riverside walk, though you will need a good road map. There are generally good paths and trails on both sides of the river. Here are two suggestions:

1. Victoria Bridge down to Cobham Bridge and on to Hamilton Gardens, then back to Cobham Bridge and onto the other bank of the river to Victoria Bridge.

2. Fairfield Bridge (or Milne Park) along the riverbank to Whitiora Bridge, Claudelands Bridge to Victoria Bridge. Then walk across and through Memorial Park to Claudelands Bridge and return on the same side of the river that you came down on.

HAMILTON CITY WALK – HAMMOND PARK
Some silence in the city

TRACK
Boardwalk and quiet road footpaths. Accessible to baby buggies, and wheelchairs part of the way.

WALK TIME AND DISTANCE
1 hour (3 km) return.

ACCESS AND FACILITIES
Rather complex access, so take a road map. From Cobham Drive turn down Howell Avenue, then Louise Place and right into Malcolm Street, and right again when Malcolm Street forks down a road to a pretty riverside picnic and car-turning area.

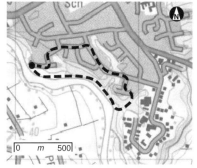

This is an unexpected gem that even many Hamiltonians do not seem to know about. It is an easy, friendly little circuit that you could safely take your grandmother on.

From the clipped and tidy river park, turn upstream and you will reach an architect-designed boardwalk. This zigzags amiably along with good views of the river (as well as people's backyards) until it reaches Hammond Park. With all the native bush and birds, this stretch of boardwalk really seems a long way away from busy city life.

Across the grassland of Hammond Park there is a steep access path (you may have to push granny at this point) up onto Balfour Crescent. To complete the circuit continue up to Hudson Street, then left along to Malcolm Street. Short, but very sweet.

A boardwalk along the Waikato River, Hammond Park.

MOUNT KARIOI
Weird and wonderful

TRACK
A steep tramping track, some rock scrambles and mud.

WALK TIME AND DISTANCE
3–4 hours (4 km) return to rock lookout; 4–5 hours (7 km) return to summit. Total climb to lookout 420 metres.

ONE-HOUR WALK
Fenceline return; good views.

ACCESS AND FACILITIES
From Raglan take the Whaanga Road, which becomes increasingly narrow, dusty and dramatic, until you reach the carpark overlooking the sea.

INFORMATION
Raglan R14 map.

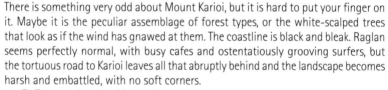

There is something very odd about Mount Karioi, but it is hard to put your finger on it. Maybe it is the peculiar assemblage of forest types, or the white-scalped trees that look as if the wind has gnawed at them. The coastline is black and bleak. Raglan seems perfectly normal, with busy cafes and ostentatiously grooving surfers, but the tortuous road to Karioi leaves all that abruptly behind and the landscape becomes harsh and embattled, with no soft corners.

Te Toto track to the Mount Karioi summit starts climbing through kanuka and lancewood forest, then gets out into open grasslands that must have been burnt over. Twisted, whitened trees are a testament to the constant wind, and out to sea you can see significantly sized islands that do not show up on many maps.

Along the track there are a couple of rocky outcrops to negotiate, with wires bolted on and a ladder to help on a tricky bit. You get some good views here, though if it is windy (it is always windy) you will be concentrating on holding on.

The track dips down to a thick forested saddle and climbs up to the foot of a rock bluff, then sidles sharply left. There is a very steep scramble up through a dirty gully with big tree roots and a wire to help, then you reach a flattish point where the side-track goes on to a rock lookout with a brilliant view.

Is the true summit worth it? Probably optional – the views are a bit better, but there is still an hour to go, including several rock outcrops with wires and ladders, before the transmitter is reached.

Back at the carpark, if you follow the fenceline down a short way over the farmland you can look into the deep, verdant basin underneath the black escarpments. Apparently you can get down there, but I have not yet tried it. It looks alluringly strange.

WAIKATO RIVER
Stopbank walk by a broad river

TRACK
Grass stopbanks and rural paths.

WALK TIME AND DISTANCE
3-4 hours (18 km) return (to Te Kauwhata pumphouse). The entire walkway is 18 km long, but the stretch from Dragway Road to the pumphouse is the most interesting. The second section from the pumphouse to Rangiriri entirely follows Churchill East Road and is (in two words) dead boring.

ONE-HOUR WALK
Along the stopbank.

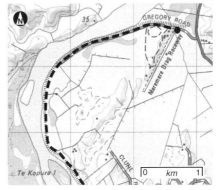

Detail: Waikato River walk

ACCESS AND FACILITIES
Dragway Road is signposted just south of Meremere, and there is a small carpark and a boulder with a plaque on it.

This new walkway is part of the proposed Te Araroa Walkway, a long-distance path that its advocates hope will run the length of the country. It is hoped that other segments of Te Araroa will be more exciting than this one, which, despite being opened by Sir Edmund Hillary and the Topp Twins, is dull. Still, there are few public walking tracks along the Waikato River, and this peaceful section of the track follows stopbanks around a rural corner of this broad and absorbing waterway.

From Dragway Road you follow the stopbank straight across the cow paddocks and alongside a curious 'plantation' of kahikatea trees. Closer to the river now, the stopbank follows through several patches of bush past Te Kopura Island to Hayton Downs Road. Shags can often be seen, as can kingfishers and white-faced herons. The track wanders through a mix of farmland, bush and wetland areas.

It is hard to determine a clear turnaround point, but near Karihoa Island might be a good place. If you have pre-arranged transport then it is worth going on to the pumphouse exit.

The Waikato River from the stopbank walk.

RUAKURI CAVERN &
MANGAPOHUE ARCH
A labyrinth of limestone

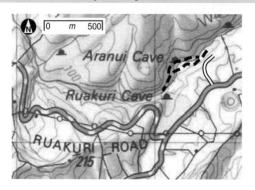

TRACK
A well-made gravel track with directional arrows (Ruakuri Cavern), and a farm track with some mud (for Mangapohue Arch).

WALK TIME AND DISTANCE
1 hour (2 km) return Ruakuri Cavern; 30 minutes (1 km) return Mangapohue Arch.

ACCESS AND FACILITIES
From Highway 3 drive 8 km to Waitomo resort, 1 km to Tumutumu Road, and 2 km along this to a signposted side-road down to a large carpark beside the Waitomo Stream. There are shelter, toilets and information boards here.

For Mangapohue Arch continue from Waitomo along the Marokopa road some 20 km to the signposted carpark; toilet, information boards.

INFORMATION
West to Marokopa, Department of Conservation pamphlet.

Water on limestone creates peculiar landscapes, and some of the oddest lie in a band of rock from Waitomo to the Marokopa coast. Here you can find caves, tunnels, archways, tomo (the Maori word for sinkholes), 'disappearances' where water runs underground, and the attractive 'karren', water-sculpted rocks. Both these walks are short, but splendid.

RUAKURI CAVERN
This walk swings from the carpark into a moist gorge and around a gantry over the Waitomo gorge above the downstream entrance of the natural tunnel. The track dives through a 'squeeze' then over the top of a natural 'bridge' and down to several spectacular lookout points.

It is somewhat baffling. One spectacular viewpoint is from a platform right inside the natural tunnel itself. Back in the daylight there is a lookout at the upstream end of the tunnel, then the track returns to the carpark by a devilish route. It crosses the natural bridge again, drops down steps and platforms, and twists underneath these in a spiral through another limestone 'squeeze'. At last the track settles down to a calm run back over the footbridge onto the main track.

MANGAPOHUE ARCH

From the dusty, scrubby carpark you get little warning of what's ahead. The archway is 17 metres high, and a grandiose remnant of an old underground waterway. There are clusters of stalactites on the roof and a smaller archway inside the main one. Cross the bridge and walk easily into the archway, where there is a lookout platform on top of the inner arch.

The track continues through the tunnel to the farmland, then climbs up past strangely shaped rocks (one with giant oysters fossilised in it) and eventually descends back to the carpark.

OTHER WALKS — OPAPAKA PA

Next to the Weaving Centre (a few kilometres before Waitomo) there is an inconspicuous Maori archway. An unassuming bush trail leads past interesting signs on Maori medicinal use of plants, and at the farm fence the trail goes on to the high point of Opapaka Pa, with a surprising and soothing vista. 1 hour return.

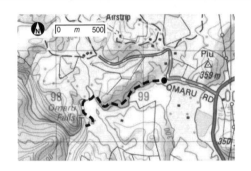

OMARU FALLS
Remote waterfall in the King Country

TRACK
A reasonably easy bush and farm track, but it can get muddy through the cow paddocks.

WALK TIME AND DISTANCE
1 hour (2 km) return.

ACCESS AND FACILITIES
From Highway 4, on a major bend, take the Omaru Road; 1 km to signpost.

The King Country has always been different. It is hard to define its boundaries, and often harder to define what makes it special, though the geology helps. Peculiar papa (mudstone and sandstone) sediments make the rivers flow dark and thick through steep brown walls, and every now and then bands of old basalt intrude and force the river to leap.

At Omaru Falls the stream leaps magnificently into a rock bowl of sandstone, and it is a fine example of the many waterfalls throughout the King Country and Waikato.

The walk starts across farmland, then follows through bush along the Mapiu Stream. At one point the stream cascades across broad plates of rock in the riverbed. There is no real warning of the waterfall, and you need to walk around another piece of farmland to the lookout.

Here you can ponder the strange, undeniable, inscrutable urge that humans have to visit falling water.

The Omaru waterfall.

MOUNT PUREORA
Mountain at the heart of the North Island

TRACK
A tramping track on a steady climb, with boardwalks in places. Sometimes muddy. You need a fine day to make the climb worthwhile.

WALK TIME AND DISTANCE
2–3 hours (4 km) return.

ONE-HOUR WALK
Forest tower return.

ACCESS AND FACILITIES
A good road map is important. From Highway 32 it is about 15 km along Link Road through the Pureora Forest Park to the saddle summit and the start of the Link Track to Mount Pureora. The road is

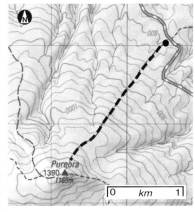

winding, narrow and gravelled, and most unsuited to people in a hurry, though there are always a few forestry workers who are. There is a picnic and camping area at Kakaho, 5 km from the highway.

Link Road continues right through the forest park to Barryville Road; left is the park headquarters, right is to Barryville on Highway 30. There is an information shelter, a carpark and toilets opposite the park headquarters.

For the forest tower follow the signs from Barryville Road to Pikiariki Road, then past the Buried Forest turn-off to a signposted junction after 4 km. It is then 500 metres down a side-road to the carpark.

INFORMATION
Pureora Forest Park: hut and track information, Department of Conservation pamphlet.

Mount Pureora is not quite the dead heart of the North Island, which lies some 5 km to the northeast, but it feels like it. From the soft summit you can look out over the vast sweep of the central highlands, as far as the snowy peaks of Mount Egmont/ Taranaki and Mount Ruapehu.

From the carpark saddle the track climbs steadily through beautiful bush, with occasional streams tinkling. There are several boardwalked sections, but no views at all until almost the very top.

As you scramble up the last eroded sections of track you enter a tiny fragment of alpine herbfield. Mount Pureora, at 1165 metres, is just high enough to allow this alpine ecosystem, and of course it provides the superb views.

FOREST LOOKOUT TOWER
A short walk through the forest leads to the lookout tower, where ladders zigzag past platforms up four storeys to high up in the bush canopy. Kaka, parakeets and bellbirds are all commonly heard, and there is an early morning chance of hearing the rare kokako.

Coromandel

TRACK

A well-graded gravel track, with most of the climbing on the return.

WALK TIME AND DISTANCE

1.5 hours (3 km) return.

ACCESS AND FACILITIES

From Tairua take Highway 25 and drive 15 km to Whenuakite Junction, then follow the signs a further 10 km to the settlement of Hahei. The Cathedral Cove road climbs above Hahei and on to a fine lookout at the carpark. Toilets, information boards.

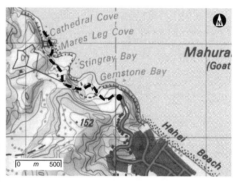

INFORMATION

Te Whanganui A Hei, Department of Conservation pamphlet.

Captain Cook observed the transit of Mercury here in 1769, and Joseph Banks enthusiastically noted a 'truly romantick' archway. Maori lived along this coast for centuries and there was once a fortified pa site right above the archway itself. It is a short, eye-catching walk, massively popular in summer, so get in early.

From the carpark the track wanders in and out of scrubby gullies and past a side-track through a puriri grove, which is well worth taking. These puriri are immense trees, famous for the hardness of their wood. A bit further along there is another short side-track down to Gemstone Bay, and still further on another side-track to Stingray Bay. Both these secluded bays are good for snorkelling, with crystal-sharp water.

The main track winds over farmland with good views of Mercury Bay, then zigzags down a flight of steps to Mare's Leg Cove. This delightful bay was named for an unusual offshore rock formation shaped like a horse's hind leg, but this has since collapsed.

The archway is on your left. Twenty metres high and 10 metres wide, it leads through to Cathedral Cove itself, which is dominated by Te Hoho or Sail Rock. On a hot day the lapping water, sculptured rocks and sparkling views over Mercury Bay are so overwhelming you just have to lie down and take a nap.

Walkers on the Cathedral Cove track.

KAUAERANGA KAURI TRAIL
An historic circuit through the Coromandel highlands

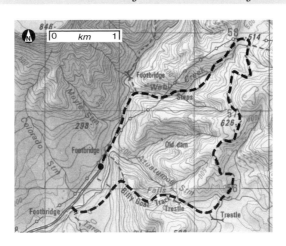

TRACK
Well-marked tracks that vary from gravel to rock to red mudstone, which can get unnervingly slippery when wet. A steep climb at first, then up and down travel past the trestles, with a final sharp descent.

WALK TIME AND DISTANCE
4–5 hours (7 km) return.

TWO-HOUR WALK
Hydro Camp return.

ACCESS AND FACILITIES
From Thames drive south 2 km to Kauaeranga Valley Road, and follow this attractive valley 13 km to the visitor centre and carpark. Note the gate closing times. It is another 9 km on a winding, unsealed road (with some beaut potholes) to the road-end. There are toilets, information boards and many sheltered campsites along the road.

INFORMATION
Kauaeranga Kauri Trail, Department of Conservation pamphlet.

The Kauaeranga Kauri Trail seems a perverse name for a track circuit that has barely any kauri on it. However, there are plenty of sites of the mechanisms that helped rid the world of kauri, including old dams, trestles, skidded roads, tramlines and steam haulers. There are also waterfalls, historic pack-tracks and fine outlooks. A very good all-round day walk in fact – pity about the kauri.

From the carpark take the footbridge over the Kauaeranga River. The track follows along the river at an easy grade, through groves of nikau palms. At the track junction, take the Webb Creek and Pinnacles track as it climbs steeply up this narrow stream.

There are pretty waterfalls in this valley, as well as three swing bridges, and the original hand-cut stone staircases that were built to assist packhorses up this steep grade. The track flattens out at an open manuka terrace, the site of the 1940s Hydro Camp, where workers camped when taking powerlines to the east coast.

The Billygoat Basin track starts on the right and follows an old bulldozer line on top of an historic pack-track up to a saddle with good views over the Kauaeranga Valley. The track winds through thick manuka (and the occasional juvenile kauri) down to Atuatumoe Stream, and shortly afterwards there is a side-track to the remains of the long trestle — originally 160 metres long, and 11 metres above ground at the highest point.

The main track passes a junction with the Tarawaere Dam track and you get good views of the Billygoat waterfall as the Atuatumoe Stream plunges down a series of cascades. After some tramway cuttings (and the remains of the short trestle) the lovely graded track becomes steep as it follows the historic incline. Steam-haulers were used on this steep tramway to lower the kauri logs down to the valley.

Eventually the track eases and sidles away from the incline, and winds down to the Kauaeranga River by the old swing bridge. Usually you can boulder-hop directly across the river, and the bridge is only for emergency use. It is about 500 metres back along the road to the main carpark. A thoroughly good circuit.

Billygoat waterfall on the Kauaeranga Kauri Trail.

COLLINS DRIVE
Wandering water races and tenacious tunnellers

TRACK
Steep, narrow, well-worn tracks, with quite a bit of hill work. You will need a torch for the big tunnel, and should expect to get wet feet.

WALK TIME AND DISTANCE
2–3 hours (3 km) return for the Collins Drive circuit. Not all the tracks are shown on the mapboards at the road-end, which can be confusing.

ONE-HOUR WALK
Water race return.

ACCESS AND FACILITIES

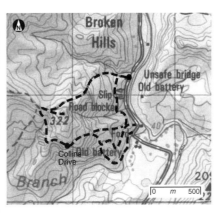

The area is known as Broken Hills, or sometimes Golden Hills, and the main access is off Highway 25A at Hikuai, then some 6 km up the Puketuie Valley Road to a carpark and an extensive (and exceedingly attractive) camping area. The Tairua River pauses here in several gorgeous pools, so take the tent and the kids, and make a weekend of it. The old through-road on to Puketui Road and Highway 25A is absolutely closed, even for 4WDs.

INFORMATION
Broken Hills Recreation Area, Department of Conservation pamphlet.

Adits, drives and tunnels are all the same thing — artifically created holes in the ground. The Collins Drive is a spectacular 500-metre-long tunnel, and part of a track circuit that also includes three craftily chiselled water-race tunnels and a complicated network of mining ruins. If gold-mining history is your thing you will love this place. Even if it is not, you will still be impressed.

From the carpark follow the old road over the footbridge and turn uphill on the signposted track. It is a steep, hard climb through bush past the Water Race Track junction and up to a saddle. Here a side-track climbs steeply to a sort of lookout, with some good views towards the pinnacles of the Coromandel Range.

Down from the saddle the track reaches the entrance of Collins Drive, and you squelch in. A third of the way along the drive has a short side-tunnel with glow-worms, halfway through there is a kink in the tunnel's length, and just before the end there are two boarded-up side passages with very good glow-worms.

Phew, you're out. Take the steep steps down from the 'aerial hopper' sign to the Water Race Track, then turn right (upstream) and go through three elegant tunnels, which were driven to take the water at an even gradient. Beyond the last tunnel there is another track junction; take all the downhill options back to the old road, and follow this back downriver to the carpark.

OTHER WALKS
There are many short walks in this area, including Gem of the Boom, Golden Hills Battery and Broken Hills Battery.

KARANGAHAKE GORGE
Railway and relics of the gold era

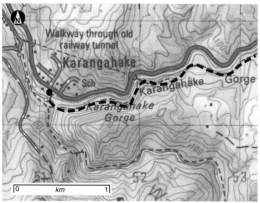

Detail: start of gorge walkway

TRACK
Flat, easy walking on well-gravelled tracks. The tunnel has a light on a time switch.

WALK TIME AND DISTANCE
2 hours (7 km) one way.

ONE-HOUR WALK
Circuit at Karangahake via the tunnel, or wander about the Victoria Battery site.

ACCESS AND FACILITIES
The two main access points are at Karangahake, where there is a carpark, information shelter (and a cafe across the road), and at Waikino carpark at the other end, with a visitor centre in the historic station. Toilets and picnic tables at both ends. An excellent track for baby buggies.

INFORMATION
Karangahake Gorge Historic Walkway, Department of Conservation pamphlet.

It is hard to grasp the size and scale of the gold batteries at the Karangahake Gorge until you walk among the ruins. The Victoria Battery was the largest in New Zealand, with 200 stampers, and by 1909 the output from the Karangahake quartz mines was 60 percent of the total gold produced in the country. In the early twentieth century the Karangahake Gorge was one of the most intensely concentrated industrial sites in the country, the equal today of the Aramoana aluminium smelter or the Marsden Point oil refinery.

There is plenty to see here, with old battery sites, railway formations, tunnels and bridges, as well as a pretty gorge and waterfalls, and superb interpretation panels along the way. Ideally the walk should be done one way, with pre-arranged transport at the other end.

From Karangahake cross the new footbridge and turn left over another footbridge across the deep-coloured and steep-walled Waitawheta River (see the Waitawheta Gorge walk). Almost totally lost in the bush at this corner is the Woodstock Battery and Talisman Batteries. You will be amazed at what is here (I was) and there is much intriguing and hazardous exploration potential.

The railway line swings around to the end of the tunnel, which has a light on a time switch, and provides a good quick return to Karangahake. Otherwise stroll past the remains of an old timber dam and on to the quarry and pretty waterfall site with its sheltered rest area.

The railway track continues around to the Owharo Falls and Waitawheta Road carpark, then veers around to the massive Victoria Battery site. There is an information circuit here, before the main track crosses the historic railway bridge to the visitor centre.

The historic tunnel and railway bridge in the Karangahake Gorge.

WAITAWHETA GORGE
Magnificent gorge walkway

TRACK
Well-graded, mostly flat track with modest climbs following an old tramway. Baby buggies can be taken some of the way.

WALK TIME AND DISTANCE
2–3 hours (6–8 km) return (to Dickies Flat Road).

ONE-HOUR WALK
First footbridge return.

ACCESS AND FACILITIES
Off Highway 2 at the impressive

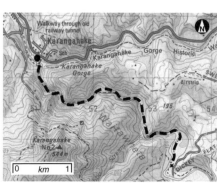

Karangahake carpark, where there are toilets, information panels, and a cafe across the road.

This is a superb new walkway that cuts up a sheer-sided gorge, its walls stained with the peculiar red and yellow oxides of minerals. Tunnels, tramways and other old mining relics give a tremendous sense of the past, a time when this slim poetic chasm rang out with hard, unromantic industry.

The first footbridge over the Karangahake is an old-fashioned beauty, then at the immediate junction the Waitawheta track slips into the gorge. It follows the line of an old tramway and later water supply pipeline, and edges around steep cliff faces to the second footbridge. There is a tunnel here, and a side-track that leads up to an old mine shaft.

From the bridge the track wanders around the corner where the river is slick and calm, and across gantries and platforms, heading further up the Waitawheta River to an old underground pumphouse beside a deep pool of the river. There was a DoC sign here stating that the track beyond was 'closed', but judging from the boot prints the track gets plenty of use. In my role as a responsible guide-book writer I headed up the forbidden track and found a well-made benched trail (with a bit of mud) that wanders up the Waitawheta River and eventually reaches Dickies Flat Road after another 2.5 km. However, you have left the best part of the gorge by then, and will want to turn around long before.

On the way back, just past the first footbridge down, look up and across to the bluff walls on the other side. You should see black holes that the locals call 'windows', which is just what they are. Behind them are hidden mine adits and passageways, just a hint of the extraordinary scale and complexity of mining that took place here.

Note: after a few phone calls I found out that the 'track closed' sign is on the DoC boundary between the Waikato and the Bay of Plenty, and I am assuming this little incoherence will be sorted out soon.

OROKAWA BAY
A lonely, lovely bay

TRACK
A well-graded and rolling coastal path along an old bridleway.
WALK TIME AND DISTANCE
2 hours (4 km) return.
ONE-HOUR WALK
Second headland return.
ACCESS AND FACILITIES
From Waihi Beach settlement make your way to the far north end of the beach by the large carpark. The very first part of the walk may get blocked at high tide (or you need to wade), though an hour either side should be fine.

A straightforward and pleasing walk that starts from the popular Waihi Beach, scene of some teenage New Year revelries in the past. The track turns the first headland corner into a much quieter world; Orokawa Bay has no roads leading to it, and is the ideal place for reveries.

In essence the track ambles along about 200 metres above the sea, slipping through attractive bush gullies and wandering around headlands with good views back over the coast. You can see Mayor Island and White Island, occasionally gushing white smoke.

The first view of Orokawa Bay is seen through waving toetoe and there is a seat from where you can appreciate it. Then it is a quick descent to an untrammelled piece of coast with a white and glorious beach, backed by rustling pohutukawa.

There is plenty to explore here, including the fishing rocks, and there is a roughish track up Orokawa Stream. This crisscrosses the stream to the William Wright Falls, dropping over a band of rock. The coastal forest is lush, tropical and silent.

Orokawa Bay from the headland track.

PIOS HEADLAND
Short walks to headland views and sheltered beaches

TRACK
Grass and gravel paths, sometimes muddy.

WALK TIME AND DISTANCE
1 hour return to headland summit; 1 hour return to Shelly Bay; 1 hour Anzac/summit circuit. All 3 km return.

ACCESS AND FACILITIES
From Highway 2 take the Athenree Road, then Steele Road and Emerton Road to the main beach on Seaforth Road. Alternatively drive from Waihi Beach to Seaforth Road and follow this all the way to Anzac Bay where there is a carpark, toilets and an extensive picnic area. There are popular campgrounds at both Athenree (with hot pools) and Bowentown, and the entire area, with its sandy beaches, pohutukawa coast, estuaries and general facilities, is perfect for a family weekend.

The Tauranga Harbour is a huge inland lagoon, stretching from Mount Maunganui in the south to Pios Beach in the north. The Pios headland is a relaxed and miniature version of the more famous Mount Maunganui hump, with short, easy walks to a terraced pa site, fishing beaches and a marvellous outlook over the Bay of Plenty. None of the walks take more than an hour, but if you include the summit, the pa and a beach swim the time just flies away.

From Anzac Bay (which is part of Bowentown Domain) walk up onto the rocky headland and pa site. There are fine views of the entrance, and the pa Te Kura a Maia is magnificent, with lines of terraces sloping down to the sea. The track goes on up to the top carpark and wanders past a side-track to Cave Bay, a popular fishing spot.

There are good views from the summit and a good track that circles underneath and goes down the other side to sidle above the motor camp back down to the access road and Anzac Bay.

The track to Shelly Bay leaves from Anzac Bay and follows a well-benched (if muddy) path up through pohutukawa forest and over a grass clearing down to Shelly Bay. There seem to be trails all over the place, either up onto the summit or down to prime coastal fishing spots. Yet despite its popularity, it seems to be quite easy to find a cosy corner of your own on Pios headland.

WAIKAREAO WALKWAY

Urban track around an estuary

TRACK
Flat gravel paths and boardwalks. Suitable for baby buggies.

WALK TIME AND DISTANCE
2–3 hours (9 km) one way for the whole Waikareao circuit.

ONE–HOUR WALK
Maxwell Road to Coach Road carpark return.

ACCESS AND FACILITIES
The Waikareao estuary is in the heart of Tauranga. A good starting point is Maxwell Road, off Chapel Street, but there are many other access points.

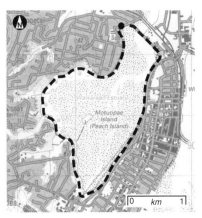

This is an intimate and interesting estuary walk alongside urban reserves and mangrove inlets. There are no roads to cross and plenty of unhurried places along the way, with linking tracks into other parts of the city.

At the attractive carpark and picnic area by Maxwell Road, take the well-signposted track along the Daisy Hardwick section of track around to the Goods Road carpark. The track travels between the sparkling estuary and a profusion of urban plants spilling over from people's backyards.

At Goods Road there is a patch of coastal forest, then the botany changes character as the track winds along a mangrove inlet. Just near the Coach Road carpark there is a boardwalk out into the estuary, with an information panel and a lookout platform with seats.

The main track follows a beautiful boardwalk, cutting across the mangroves, then goes around the point and passes the low-tide road to Motuopae Island. This is a good return point if you want to stay on the quieter sections of track.

Although the next part of the walkway wriggles along coastal mangroves, it quickly reaches the busy Waihi Road, then turns along the even busier Waikareao expressway. This is still a good track though, popular with runners, with footbridges linking to Graham Park and Tauranga Domain. The last section of track follows Chapel Street back to Maxwell Road.

The mangrove estuary and boardwalk to the lookout on the Waikareao Walkway.

MOUNT MAUNGANUI

An easy walk round (and up) a landscape icon

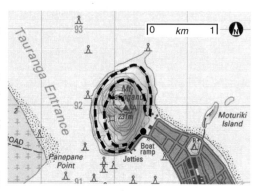

TRACK
Well-graded tracks through coastal forest.

WALK TIME AND DISTANCE
2- to 3-hour (9 km) circuit return from Pilot Bay (description below).

ONE-HOUR WALK
1 hour return round the coast; 1 hour return to the summit.

ACCESS AND FACILITIES
From Tauranga cross the bridge, drive 2 km to Mount Maunganui beach and then to Pilot Bay. Toilets and carparking.

'The Mount' is the emotional and cultural icon of the Bay of Plenty, and it sticks up far more than its mere 230-metre height would suggest. The Maori knew the mount as 'Mauao', and used the hill as habitation, lookout and pa refuge. It provides good easy walking and plenty of views, and the cafes and bars of the town are not far away.

From Pilot Bay the coastal track stays 50 metres above the coast, but further along a short side-trail goes down to a pretty, sandy beach where you get good views of the harbour entrance and the Tangaroa statue. This stretch of coast and reef is also an important scientific reserve.

The coast track rounds Stoney Point, with views of the dead-flat Rabbit Island, and the pohutukawa provide shade. North West Rock is a popular surf-fishers' hang-out, and at low tide you can scramble about the reef platform. Round the corner there are several attractive sandy coves at low tide.

The track climbs slightly to a track junction; follow up the historic 1860 stone steps and join the Oruahine Track as it continues up onto a plateau and turns steeply uphill to the Waikorere Track junction.

Follow the Waikorere Track as it climbs steadily through regrowth forest, past a side-track to a lookout, then up onto the beacon on the summit of the Mount. There are excellent views, of course, particularly of the beach, township and Mayor Island. It is then easy walking down the old vehicle track as it winds down through scrub and farm country, passing a large reservoir, before reaching Pilot Bay.

Mount Maunganui.

TUAHU TRACK
Ancient Maori trail into the Kaimai mountains

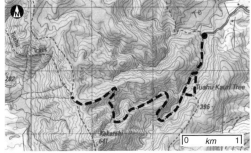

TRACK

A good benched track that climbs steadily through forest to the ridgeline.

WALK TIME AND DISTANCE

4–5 hours (12 km) return. 40-minute walk Kauri tree loop track return.

ACCESS AND FACILITIES

Turn off Highway 2 onto the Hot Springs Road and follow this 5 km past the Sapphire Springs motor camp to the road-end carpark and toilets. The motor camp has a large swimming pool, coldwater pools and a food store.

The Tuahu Track is a long, easy climb to the crest of the Kaimai Range. Originally it was a Maori trail, but it was widened to a bridle path in the late 1890s. Although the total climb is 400 metres, it is so gentle and genial that it does not seem like it, and the eventual view is worth the effort.

About 10 minutes after leaving the carpark you reach a side-track that goes up to a large kauri – well worth the deviation. This side-track then continues and regains the main Tuahu Track. Note also the side-track to Sentinel Rock.

The main Tuahu trail wanders in and out of stream gullies, climbing very steadily, and with little in the way of views until you are nearly at the top. Eventually the track reaches the crest of the ridge at a four-way track junction. Follow the Tuahu Track for another 5 minutes to get broad views of the Waikato, or turn up the track towards Te Rereatukahia Hut to find an immediate flax and tussock clearing with a panorama of the Bay of Plenty and Mayor Island.

A great munch spot, safe in the knowledge that the downhill return on the Tuahu Track is a romp.

The view from the Waikato side of the saddle, Tuahu Track.

TARAWERA FALLS
Magical meeting of escarpments, disappearances and waterfalls

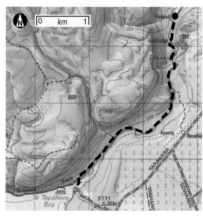

TRACK
Bush track, with a short hill and some clambering.

WALK TIME AND DISTANCE
2–3 hours (8 km) return from lake. You could arrange a transport pick-up from the Lake Tarawera picnic area.

ONE–HOUR WALK
Waterfall return.

ACCESS AND FACILITIES
From Kawarau take River Road then Waterhouse Street across the bridge and past the forestry headquarters to a T-junction. Tarawera Falls is signposted, and it is 15 km to the carpark. The road to Tarawera Falls is a public access easement but the gates by the forest headquarters are closed every night. Note any fire restrictions, and restrictions imposed by logging operations.

In the midst of the bland uniformity of pine forest around Kawarau are the energetic and quirky Tarawera Falls — bluffs, tomo, waterfalls, swimming holes, a wonderland of surprises and variety, tinged with a touch of Tolkien in the thick forest interior.

The track from the carpark goes through kanuka forest to an elegant footbridge, then through tawa and rewarewa forest with silver fern underneath. The Tarawera Falls thunder out from a natural fissure halfway up a rock face. Many people do not go beyond here, but they miss half the fun.

The track climbs cleverly and steeply up through the bluff walls, and once on top it divides. The left-hand track goes in a spectacular loop directly above the Tarawera Falls, winding past bridges and streams to the tomo where the Tarawera River disappears into a narrow rock cavern. The loop track joins the main track again, and continues upriver through a deep, dense bush of moss and unlikely boulders.

It soon reaches another waterfall, then a cascade and, in the reflective river reaches, a deep swimming hole with a platform. From here on the track is more sedate, as it goes through second-growth forest towards the swampy margins of Lake Tarawera. Finally, there is a swing bridge across the Tarawera River to the carpark and picnic area on the other side.

If you are unable to arrange a car to pick you up it is no particular hardship to retrace your steps down the river for another dose of wonder.

Previous page: Copper mine ruins, Kawau Island.

Above: Anchorage Bay, Tawharanui Regional Park.

Below: Twisted tree stumps on the hill track up Mount Karioi.

Opposite: Early morning in the Miranda wetlands.

Opposite left: Mt Taranaki from near
Fanthams Peak.

Above: Sunrise Hut and the tops
beyond.

Right: Looking towards the reef,
Castlepoint.

Left: Wellington's 'Eiffel Tower', atop Mount Kaukau.

Below: Tumbledown Bay.

Opposite: Palisades, Otara pa.

Next page: Whariariki Beach — it doesn't get any better than this!

NGAHOPUA – CRATER LAKES
Mysterious lakes and virgin forest

TRACK
Forest trail in hilly bush country.
WALK TIME AND DISTANCE
1 hour (3 km) return.
ACCESS AND FACILITIES
From Highway 30 turn down the Lake Okataina Road. The Ngahopua/Crater Lakes track starts just opposite the short road to the Outdoor Centre, where there is good carparking.

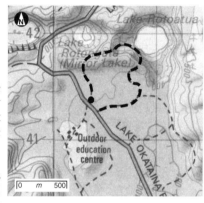

The Maori word 'Ngahopua' means 'depressions' or 'bowls', and these old volcanic craters have filled to form lakes – Rotongata and Rotoatua. Because the track does not go down to the lakeside, but peers at them at a distance from the thick bush rim, they seem remote and mysterious – like sacred places you are not allowed to reach.

The track is straightforward and climbs from the road through beautiful bush, with big tawa and rimu dominating the canopy. Epiphytes, or tree-hanging plants, fill every niche in the lush forest. At some point you become aware that you are on the rim of a large crater, with all the land falling away, and shortly you see Lake Rotongata, silent and girdled with reeds.

Lake Rotoatua.

The track then continues along the well-defined rim, with several lookouts on the way, and at the last lookout there is a fine view into Lake Rotoatua. The lake is deep, with sheer walls. It was formed 3500 years ago but seems somehow timeless. After this point you descend quite quickly to a junction with the Anaha Track, and then onto the road, where the spell is broken.

OTHER WALKS
At the end of Lake Okataina Road there is the Eastern Lake Okataina Walkway, a good walk, 3 hours one way.

ROTORUA CITY WALK – # LAKE FRONT
& SULPHUR FLAT
A hot walk!

TRACK
Footpaths, forest trails and boardwalks. Well signposted, but do not venture off the boardwalks onto the sulphur plain itself. The whole track is suitable for baby buggies.

WALK TIME AND DISTANCE
1–2 hours (8 km) return.

ACCESS AND FACILITIES
On the Rotorua lakefront. There is good carparking off Memorial Drive by the Village Green park, also toilets, picnic tables and children's play equipment.

The city of Rotorua sits precariously on top of a thermal field, and you sometimes wonder if by banging your foot down too hard you might start another geyser. The place reeks (literally) of thermal action, and the city walkway across Sulphur Flat is an immediate and exciting way to enjoy it.

   This attractive urban walkway can be started from the busy jetty area on the waterfront, and circles the peninsula and golf course at Motutara Point. There are good views over the lake, plenty of birdlife including scaup, shags and swans, and many interesting lakeside corners to explore. It is a walk that does not get dull.

The track then meanders through fringes of manuka and passes close by the historic Tudor Bath House, then around to the thermal area by Sulphur Flat. Hot steam seeps out of holes and weird colours stain the grey plain. The boardwalk crosses the thermal area crisply, as if in a hurry to get across, but there are information panels on the way to slow the visitor.

   Eventually the track reaches Puarenga Stream and goes on to the busy Te Ngae Road, so Sulphur Flat is a good turnaround point. After rain the place can really steam.

Sulphur Flat, Rotorua.

ROTORUA CITY WALK – WHAKAREWAREWA REDWOODS

Easy strolls under tall giants

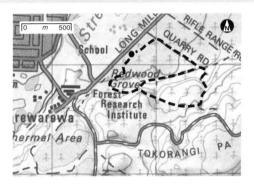

TRACK
The Redwood Trail is a wide and flat forest path, suitable for baby buggies. The Quarry Lookout Track is a narrower bush track, with a steady climb and descent.

WALK TIME AND DISTANCE
1–2 hours (4 km) return.

ONE-HOUR WALK
Redwood circuit.

ACCESS AND FACILITIES
From Highway 30A (to Rotorua airport) turn onto Tarawera Road, then take Long Mile Road to the carpark by the Forestry Information Centre; toilets and information here.

INFORMATION
There is a large range of walks at Whakarewarewa, and it is also popular with mountain bikers. It is useful to have a map with the various walks marked on it. The information centre also has detailed leaflets on walking, mountain biking, and tree species.

Redwood tree plantations were established throughout New Zealand in the early part of the twentieth century, but few survived. These huge trees are fussy, and need deep, fertile soils, even rainfall and no frosts. Probably the best surviving example of redwood forest is this 6-hectare lot in Whakarewarewa Forest. Some trees have reached 65 metres – pretty impressive, although in their native California they can reach 110 metres!

From the information centre follow the easy (and colour coded) trail into the redwood forest as it winds around the giant trees. The trail takes an easy course around the forest, and there are boardwalks in places.

The Quarry Lookout Track is signposted in another colour. This track climbs slowly, branching off from the Tokorangi Pa Track, then up and around to a reasonable lookout over the forest. The track descends quickly back to the flat, and you are faced with a muddle of track choices back to the carpark. You can shortcut directly back, or continue left along the Quarry Lookout Track as it takes a longer loop back to the carpark.

HOROMANGA RIVER
Back-country river splashing

TRACK
Worn path and lots of river crossings. Do not attempt after rain or if the river is high.

WALK TIME AND DISTANCE
2–3 hours (8 km) return.

ACCESS AND FACILITIES
From Highway 38, just south of Murupara, turn onto Troutbeck Road; it is some 15 km to a sign, and a 1-km side-road to a large, dusty carpark.

INFORMATION
Urewera National Park 273-08 map; good for showing the access roads. *Short Walks in the Urewera-Galatea (Kuhawaea)*, Department of Conservation pamphlet.

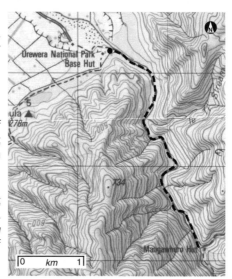

You need a warm, muggy day to enjoy the Horomanga River — a day when it does not matter how much you splash, or how far you go. There are 34 crossings in all to get to Mangawhero Hut (17 there, 17 back) and you crisscross up a lazy river, with waving toetoe beckoning.

Do not be surprised if you find horse floats or horses hitched up at the carpark, for the Horomanga River is a popular horse-trekking area, and people regularly cross over the Ikawhenua Range into the Whakatane River catchment. It is a different world in the Urewera, and the sight of horses and riders splashing across the stream is exciting and nostalgic.

The first few crossings have some deep pools that often tempt people to linger, looking for trout, otherwise the river travel is straightforward. The bush valley is confined but the entry and exit paths are well marked with the standard orange triangles.

Mangawhero or Red Hut ('whero' means red) sits on a terrace across the river. The hut has six bunks and an open fireplace, but there are better places for a brew on any number of the riverflats. From the hut, other tracks disappear off into the Urewera hinterland, but it is a sure-fire 17 river crossings to get back to your car.

Mangawhero or Red Hut, on the Horomanga River.

WHIRINAKI RIVER
Simply the best

TRACK
Well-benched and mostly flat bush pathway.

WALK TIME AND DISTANCE
2–3 hours (9 km) waterfall circuit.

40-MINUTE WALK
Moerangi junction return.

ACCESS AND FACILITIES
From Highway 38 turn right towards the Minginui turn-off, then turn right over the Whirinaki River bridge to meet River Road. There is a DoC camping area at this road junction. Follow River Road upvalley for about 7 km to the carpark and signboard. It is useful to have the Urewera National Park map.

INFORMATION
To Save a Forest: Whirinaki, by John Morton, book.

Until I receive word to the contrary, I am prepared to state that this is the best forest in New Zealand. Statuesque and dense, it is a forest of exceptional quality and calibre. Trees like rimu, kahikatea, matai and miro grow to extraordinary heights at Whirinaki and have a profound effect on the visitor.

The Whirinaki track starts by passing through the Oriuwaka Ecological Area, a scientific reserve where there are outstanding podocarp trees, then crosses the Whirinaki River at Te Whaiti-nui-a-toi canyon. This is a deep, attractive slot in the rockbed. After the canyon the track settles into an easy, well-benched grade along the river terrace, passing the side-track to Moerangi.

The birdlife can be thick, with robins, shining and long-tailed cuckoos, parakeets, kaka, songthrush, blackbirds, tui and bellbirds. There is a footbridge over the Mangamate Stream and not long afterwards a side-track goes down to the Whirinaki waterfall. This is a thundering leap, with a viewing platform from where you can take it all in.

A bridge crosses the top of the waterfall to other vantage points, and this track can be followed back to the carpark. It travels along an old logging road on the other side of the Whirinaki River, and makes the visual point that this magnificent forest came within a few hundred metres of being eradicated.

The Whirinaki River.

ARAHAKI LAGOON
Lagoon in the heart of the forest

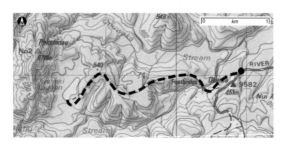

TRACK
A bush walking track, benched at first, with some small climbs. After rain the lagoon can be quite large, but much of the time it is a grassy swamp with a worn trail around it.

WALK TIME AND DISTANCE
2–3 hours (4 km) return.

ACCESS AND FACILITIES
From Highway 38 turn right towards Minginui, then just before Minginui itself turn right over the Whirinaki River bridge to meet River Road. There is a DoC camping area 2 km downvalley of this road junction, but follow River Road upvalley to the Whirinaki Track carpark, then continue on a much rougher road some 2 km to the mangy carpark.

INFORMATION
To Save a Forest: Whirinaki, by John Morton, book.

This is an ancient place that smothers your thoughts with the silence of centuries — a lonely lagoon in the midst of a circling rim of kahikatea trees. The thick silence is broken only by the calls of kaka, robins and bellbirds.

The track starts unexceptionally, wandering through an old logging area with manuka and lancewoods, then it descends to a footbridge to cross the Waiatiu Stream. A short, steepish climb brings you into dense tawa forest with the occasional massive rimu, and the track softens onto a ridge, passing through groves of perfect tree ferns. There is little windfall, and the forest seems undisturbed by the outside world. The descent is hardly anything at all and quite suddenly you arrive at the lagoon.

I was there after a wet summer and the lagoon was full, almost touching the stately kahikatea. The frogs sounded like an orchestra of didgeridoos, and large black shags and kaka flapped melodiously across the empty marsh. Little else disturbed this pond of tranquillity.

It truly is an other-worldly place.

LAKE WAIKAREITI &
LAKE RUAPANI CIRCUIT
Lakes, ponds and swamps.

TRACK
A garden path to Lake Waikareiti, then a standard and rolling bush track.

WALK TIME AND DISTANCE
5–6 hours (16 km) Lake Waikareiti–Lake Ruapani circuit.

ONE- TO TWO-HOUR WALK
Lake Waikareiti return.

ACCESS AND FACILITIES
Highway 38 is an unsealed, tortuous and narrow road that passes through Urewera National Park to the visitor centre and carpark for Lake Waikareiti. There are toilets here. Rumour has it that this road is going to be sealed, but do not hold your breath.

INFORMATION
Waikaremoana Walks, Department of Conservation pamphlet.

Enjoy a fulsome forest daywalk, visiting in a slow circuit Lake Waikareiti, isolated ponds and strange silted-up lakes, with their own 'tundra' of wetland plants and subalpine species. You feel psychologically displaced in this remote landscape, and the views across the dry ponds seem positively Jurassic — you fully expect to see a moa strolling across the meadow.

The track to Lake Waikareiti is as smooth as a garden path and climbs effortlessly past a fern forest with red beech dominating the canopy. The path climbs steadily and reaches a low saddle where there is a toilet and shortly afterwards a lakeside shelter. This is a useful place for a breather, out of sandfly habitat.

A more ordinary bush track approximately follows the shores of Lake Waikareiti for 2 km to the junction with the Lake Ruapani track. Soon there is the eerie tranquillity of Puna Hokoi, a clearing and wetland, followed by two small ponds, Hine Rere and Ngutu Manu. The track follows a stream that disappears, then climbs a small saddle to Whane o Ruapani, a larger pond.

It is 1 km over a bigger hill to Lake Ruapani itself. Orchids are often found on the wetland margins of the lake and, surprisingly, black-backed gulls and spur-winged plovers can also be seen. After this the track goes over another short hill and down a streamside to the Waipai Swamp and a respite from the engulfing bush, then it is 2 km back to the carpark and out of the woods.

GISBORNE CITY WALK – GRAY'S BUSH
A precious remnant of kahikatea forest

TRACK
Flat bush trails, not always obvious or well-marked.

WALK TIME AND DISTANCE
1 hour (1–2 km) return.

ACCESS AND FACILITIES
From Gisborne take the Back Ormond Road 9.5 km from the city to the carpark.

INFORMATION
Gray's Bush Scenic Reserve, Department of Conservation pamphlet.

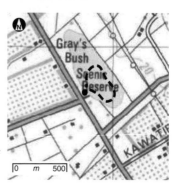

Not much lowland kahikatea forest remains on the Gisborne plains, and this is the best example. Many of the trees are between 400 and 500 years old and some reach higher than 40 metres. It is a pocket handkerchief reserve really, barely large enough to be self-sustaining, but still not to be sneezed at.

The bush is semi-coastal in character, with puriri, kohekohe, mahoe and kawakawa underneath the kahikatea. Nearly 12,000 people visit Gray's Bush every year, which puts enormous pressure on the reserve, so DoC limits access to the southern half to allow the rest of the forest to grow undisturbed.

The track is roughly in a figure of eight, and it does not take long to cover the ground. You have to force yourself to go slowly, linger, and admire. The air always seems more heavy and silent under this sort of canopy, with a hundred different sorts of greens blending and smoothing the smoky light.

If you can, arrive early, very early, just as sunlight is catching the top canopy and there is no traffic on the roads; then you capture just a brief sensory moment of what it must once have been like over much of the Poverty Bay plains.

GISBORNE CITY WALK – TE KURI FARM WALK
Farm circuit and lookout over Gisborne

TRACK
Rolling country with farm tracks, forest trails and grass paths. Well signposted, with some mud. Closed for lambing between August and mid-October.

WALK TIME AND DISTANCE
2–3 hours (6 km) return.

ACCESS AND FACILITIES
From Gisborne's Ormond Street turn onto Ballance Street, then Barkers Hill, then follow Shelley Road to the carpark.

INFORMATION
Te Kuri Farm Walkway, Department of Conservation pamphlet.

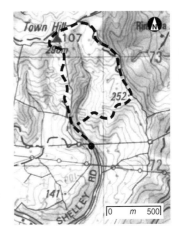

I find it difficult to get excited about farm walkways. The compromises needed to sustain both a commercial farm and an attractive walking route seem intractable, and too many fences, shelter belts and buildings get in the way.

That this walk is worth doing at all is a credit to its handiness to Gisborne city and the good panorama it provides over it. But there is also a desperate shortage of good walking opportunities near Gisborne.

From the carpark the walkway passes the other end of the circuit, crosses fences and starts a steady climb up through a remnant of coastal forest. It is over a 200-metre climb up to the panoramic lookout, where there are views as far as the Mahia Peninsula. The track goes through a pine plantation, then descends open slopes down a long hill through paddocks back to the carpark. A good leg stretcher – that's about it really.

WHEROWHERO LAGOON
Rich in space and light

TRACK
Flat beach walking to the spit.
WALK TIME AND DISTANCE
2 hours (6 km) return to end of spit.
ACCESS AND FACILITIES
From Highway 2 take Browns Beach Road, which peters out in a confusing welter of 4WD tracks and sand dunes. Be careful if you are in only a car.

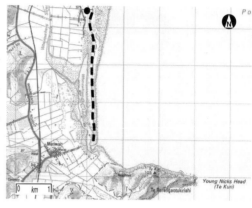

Wherowhero Lagoon is a transitory place for migrating birds, and for lonely anglers watching the ebb and flow of the tides. It is a wide open space, with all of Poverty Bay laid out before you; Gisborne to the north, and to the south, the long, white-knuckled finger of Young Nicks Head.

There's not much to do but wander through the sand dunes, with their twisted limbs of driftwood and busy banded dotterels running briskly over the sand. Oystercatchers roam along the wet sea edge, and on the spit you will see the elegant white-faced heron and perhaps hear its ugly 'kraaak' call.

Black swans will be patrolling the lagoon and with a good pair of binoculars you might see migratory birds with strange names, such as Asiatic whimbrels, red-necked stints, turnstones and knots. At the far end of the spit Young Nicks Head looks stunning, especially in the morning light, but of course you have to get up as early as the birds to see that.

Driftwood and Young Nicks Head from the Wherowhero Lagoon walk.

MAHIA RESERVE
Hilltop views and gutsy forest

TRACK
A bush track down and up a steep reserve.
WALK TIME AND DISTANCE
1.5–2 hours (4 km) return.
15-MINUTE WALK
Lookout return.
ACCESS AND FACILITIES
From Highway 2 drive to Mahia Beach, then take Kinikini Road as it scrambles up steep hills (which can get greasy after rain) and surmounts the ridgeline in a scenic switchback for some 7 km before reaching the Mahia Reserve carpark.
INFORMATION
Mahia Peninsula Scenic Reserve, Department of Conservation pamphlet.

You have got to have a good stomach for this road, but what a view — full horizons of clouds and glittering seas on either side. You feel right on top of Mahia Peninsula and there is a remoteness about the land that is refreshing; the reserve is also a cool escape from a classic hot Mahia day.

Walk up the road from the carpark to the start of the track and past the junction, where the track starts to drop steeply through dense tawa, rewarewa and rimu forest, with lancewood, ngaio and karaka. The track follows a stream down to an open clearing with a picnic table.

Then comes the hard part, a robust climb up beside a stream then up a spur back to the ridgeline. Just above the road there is a lookout, which is okay, but hardly any better than the views you get from the carpark, perched high above the glistening waters of the Pacific.

The lookout from the road opposite Mahia Reserve.

TAUPO TOWN WALK —
CRATERS OF THE MOON
Simply steaming

TRACK
Flat boardwalks and gravel paths, suitable for baby buggies. The warnings to keep to the track are serious.

WALK TIME AND DISTANCE
1 hour (3 km) return.

ACCESS AND FACILITIES
Craters of the Moon is off Highway 1, signposted about 4 km north of Taupo, and down a short 1-km side-road to a carpark, toilets and information shop. Free entry.

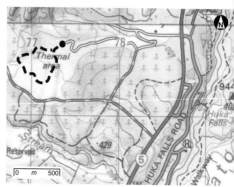

The beauty of visiting this thermal steamfield is that it is one of the best, it is growing, and it is free! Many geothermal sites in the Rotorua/Taupo area are commercially operated, and the Craters of the Moon is one of the rare exceptions. Since the forced closure of many of Taupo's private geothermal bores the thermal activity in the region has recovered noticeably, and the Craters of the Moon has become more active.

From the carpark the easy track goes into the thermal area where large craters give vent to clouds of white steam, which after rain are sometimes so thick it is like walking through a hot fog. Everywhere the surface is alive with little vents between the big craters and wafts of sulphur, creating an alien outpost. Plants struggle in this area, and those that succeed can be suddenly blighted when a steam vent opens unexpectedly underneath them.

The track does a circuit through the steamfield, with lookouts and information panels at appropriate places, demonstrating the finer points of steam vents, fumaroles, mud craters and the like. Changes in the activity of steam vents can occur daily. An alive place.

OTHER WALKS
Huka Falls, 15 minutes return.

Steamfields and umbrellas, Craters of the Moon.

MOUNT TAUHARA
A grunty bush climb to a high peak

TRACK
A tramping track up a steepish hill, with mud and a trench and some clambering in places.

WALK TIME AND DISTANCE
3–4 hours (5 km) return.

ONE-HOUR WALK
Water tank return.

ACCESS AND FACILITIES
From Highway 5 take Mountain Road to the carpark and signpost. Permission to cross the land and use the track is allowed by the Maori trustees.

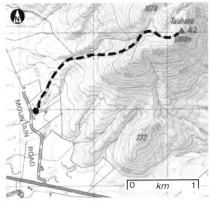

This is a strenuous track leading to a volcanic peak overlooking Lake Taupo, and it is surprisingly popular considering the going is quite rough in places. On any weekend day there might be 20–30 people winding up through the dense bush to the rock lookouts. Take a lunch, for the view is superb.

From the carpark the track crosses a farm paddock then follows up an easy grass spur and along a fenceline to a water tank on the bush edge. There are fine views here. The track twists through the thick bush of kamahi and manuka, climbing erratically as it passes a seat. Higher up it passes quite close to a good-sized stream (I found it drinkable), and gets easier as it wanders onto a 'saddle'.

There are some short stretches of track along deep earth trenches, then the bush becomes more alpine as you walk up the final slopes to the beacon, where there is an excellent panorama. A side-trail turns along a ridge to more rock outcrops, and (if you find it) a worn trail cuts down to the main track again.

Climbing towards Mount Tauhara.

OPEPE GRAVES
Walks that take you back

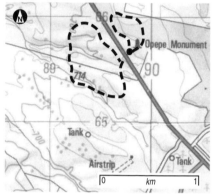

TRACK
Rolling forest tracks, okay surface, but some mud.
WALK TIME AND DISTANCE
1–2 hours Southern Loop, 4 km return.
ONE-HOUR WALK
Northern Loop.
ACCESS AND FACILITIES
Off Highway 5 about 20 km from Taupo. Carparking off the highway.

Like all signposted walks beside busy highways, once you are sizzling along at high speed it is less than tempting to slow down and investigate what the signs mean. But Opepe is well worth stopping for. On one side of the road there are massive rimu and matai trees, and a graveyard for soldiers who died during a surprise attack by Te Kooti. On the other side a track visits the old constabulary redoubt and a totara water trough, and for a while you have exchanged the hustle of the modern highway for the slow horse pace of the 1860s.

The Northern Loop goes through bush to the rather well-kept cemetery where headstones still stand, readable and telling. Continue on the bush loop track, which is interrupted by some massive trees — rimu, matai and totara.

The Southern Loop passes the track junction and goes to the cleared grassy site of Opepe township, which once had up to 600 people living in a mostly sawmilling community. The track then descends and joins the old Napier–Taupo road, with occasional telegraph poles. The regrowth forest is thick and silent. A side-track leads to a large old totara water trough, where it is not hard to sense the bullock teams pausing.

Now the track climbs, eventually reaching a junction to a pitsaw site where giant totara were imaginatively turned into telegraph poles. You can hear the traffic now, and soon after you close the loop and are back in your own time.

An historic gravestone, Opepe.

TE IRINGA FOREST
Beech forest climb to an old hut site

TRACK
A steady hill climb on a bush pack-track.

WALK TIME AND DISTANCE
2–3 hours (6 km) return.

ONE-HOUR WALK
To first stream return.

ACCESS AND FACILITIES
Turn off Highway 5 onto Takarua Road and travel 10 km to Clements Road, a narrow road that after some 5 km leads to a carpark; picnic tables and toilets in a sheltered, secluded wee glade.

The charm of this trek is that you are a long way from anywhere, in a forgotten far north section of the Kaimanawa Forest Park. It is likely that all you will have for company are the birds and the mountain streams, and the track swings through the thick, rich forest of red and silver beech like a lullaby.

From the carpark it is all red beech to the first stream, and some of these trees are massive. Then the track climbs more and eases into silver beech, with umbrella-like tree ferns plugging any gaps in the canopy. Once over a smaller stream the walk finally reaches a sort of saddle, and as the benched track wanders along the ridge you can get peeping views of the Kaimanawas and the Tongariro plateau.

The path slips down a mite and around to an old hut site, which has a signpost and an air of absence. Even the dunny has gone. This grass clearing is about the only place you will find any sun, but it seems lifeless compared to the forest. I read somewhere that forests always feel better because there is more oxygen inside them. I rather like that.

The old hut site, Te Iringa Forest.

PORERE REDOUBT
The last battleground

TRACK
Gravel track.

WALK TIME AND DISTANCE
1 hour (2 km) return. There are
several quite well-made and
unmarked tracks that lead from the
top redoubt, and it is suspected
they lead to the Outdoor Pursuits
Centre. However, I have not tested
that theory.

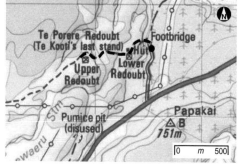

ACCESS AND FACILITIES
From the township of National
Park, drive north on Highway 47, past the turn-off to Whakapapa, some 18 kilometres.
Porere is indicated on the left by rather a small sign that you could miss. Carpark.

INFORMATION
Te Porere: battle site of the Maori Wars. A rather old brochure, obtainable from the
Tongariro National Park visitor centre at Whakapapa.

Not much of a walk, but a powerful return to the past, and the site of the last
pitched battle in the New Zealand Wars. In 1869 Te Kooti Rikirangi Te Turuki led
about 300 men and women here, and built a redoubt that was attacked by a mixed
government force of Armed Constabulary and Maori warriors from the Wanganui,
Taupo and Hawke's Bay areas, perhaps about 500 men in all. This place was
immortalised as Te Kooti's last stand.

The track crosses a bridge over the small Whanganui River, and climbs up to the
lower redoubt. A platform gives you a view of the layout of the trenches, but this
redoubt was quickly overrun. The attackers would have continued along the line of
the track now, up to the high redoubt, with its network of slit trenches, rifle loopholes
and fiercesome 4-metre-high walls that stood out boldly on the brow of the ridge.

Te Kooti's men had seen the government forces crossing the open tussock
grasslands, but they had the bush at their back to escape into. The final attack was
swift, and Te Kooti's defenders killed only four of the attackers before becoming
overwhelmed, losing 37 in the bloody engagement. Many of Te Kooti's men fired on
the attackers from outside the redoubt, and then melted into the bush.

The battle was won, and lost.

Te Kooti was defeated, but gave the government forces the slip. However, he
was never again the same threat. He later founded the Ringatu church, and was
eventually pardoned in 1883 and died in 1893. Porere Redoubt is now a peaceful
scene, calmed by the silence, but by no means forgotten. At the end of one of the slit
trenches there is a small plaque in remembrance of 'Te Kooti's men'.

TONGARIRO CROSSING
Venture into the interior

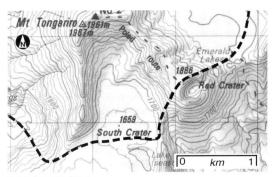

Detail: Tongariro Crossing

TRACK
A well-marked track with some steep climbs and loose scoria. Do not attempt this in poor weather since you will not see a thing, and will have a miserable time. Take plenty of water, food and warm clothing. Even in summer the temperature can drop quickly.

WALK TIME AND DISTANCE
One-way crossing 6–8 hours, 20 km.

ONE-HOUR WALK
Mangatepopo Hut return (or if starting from Ketetahi 1.5 hours return to bush edge).

ACCESS AND FACILITIES
From National Park take Highway 47 and turn onto the unsealed Mangatepopo Road, travelling some 6 km to the carpark. The Ketetahi Springs side-road is off Highway 47A, and leads to information boards, a shelter and toilets. The springs are on Maori land and access is not necessarily permanent or permitted, so check with DoC first. In summer, several companies arrange transport pick-ups for either end of the track. See DoC at Whakapapa.

INFORMATION
The Tongariro Crossing, Department of Conservation pamphlet; *Tongariro T19* map.

This is dubbed the finest one-day walk in New Zealand, and perhaps it is. A volcanic heartland of steaming hot springs, lakes daubed with unearthly colours, barren volcanic craters and the grey, brooding cinder cone of Ngauruhoe. It is popular, and busloads of people are dropped off at Mangatepopo and sent scurrying into this god-forsaken wilderness with scant idea of what they are in for. They mostly survive, but if you want to beat the crowds start early.

From the bleak Mangatepopo carpark the track hurries past the junction to Whakapapa and a side-track to Mangatepopo Hut and up the gradually confining valley. You can smell the soda springs (but they are not hot), and then start up the first serious climb (The Giant's Staircase) to the South Crater.

It is breathtaking on top, with good fast travel across the plateau as you blithely slip by Tongariro on the left and Ngauruhoe on the right. The sharpest climb is now

200 metres up the ridge onto Red Crater itself, at 1886 metres the highest point in the crossing.

So many places to explore but little enough time, so bounce past the two Emerald Lakes, looking like green serpents' eyes, and wander over the vast plain past Blue Lake to the far lip of Central Crater. At this saddle the track leads down a zigzag trail to Ketetahi Hut, then on to the hot springs, distinguished by the permanent puff of cloud that hangs over the flank of the mountain.

An easy trail goes over tussocks and sweet-smelling turpentine scrub to the bush edge. Enjoy the final views of Lake Rotoaira and Mount Pihanga, and follow the track through the totara forest over the undrinkable stream and on to the carpark.

Lunch by the Emerald Lakes, Tongariro Crossing.

The Taranaki Falls (see facing page).

TARANAKI FALLS
Volcanic plateau walk to a 20-metre waterfall

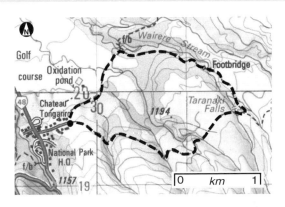

TRACK
Generally well gravelled or boardwalked, but can get muddy.

WALK TIME AND DISTANCE
2 hours (7 km) return.

ONE–HOUR WALK
30 minutes along the track and return.

ACCESS AND FACILITIES
From Highway 48, at the Chateau turn down Ngauruhoe Place to the carpark.

This is a justly popular walk on the pumice plateau, with unrivalled views of the twin volcanoes of Ruapehu and Ngauruhoe, plus a streamside beech forest and a fine waterfall. The air is keen and sharp, and the starting altitude of this walk is 1140 metres. Take warm clothes, some scroggin, and a camera.

From the carpark you weave along a well-made trail through fields of tussock and scoria. There are numerous small gullies to cross, with bridges and mountain streams, and at one point you climb up onto the edge of an old andesite lava flow, formed about 15,000 years ago.

You quickly reach the edge of the Taranaki Falls, which roar over the lava rock. There are lookout points near the waterfall, though the track soon meets a junction, and turning left there is a quick, sharp drop through mountain totara down to the base of the waterfall.

There are plenty of lunch or picnic rocks here and on a hot Tongariro summer's day it is a great place for an afternoon siesta. The track now closely follows the Wairere Stream, first over tussock, then into cool mountain beech forest.

After the footbridge the stream runs down many cascades, and there is a short side-track to one of them. Turn left at the track junction and you quickly break out of the bush and onto the tussock plain again. A few more gullies to cross and you are back at the carpark.

CRATER LAKE
Hard yakka, but what a view!

TRACK

An ambitious day tramp to the volcanic crater lake of Mount Ruapehu. The chairlift runs through the summer holiday season, but beyond the chairlift there is no real track, just a steady climb over rocks following boot trails and a confusing array of cairns. In the future, DoC may provide a marked route during summer.

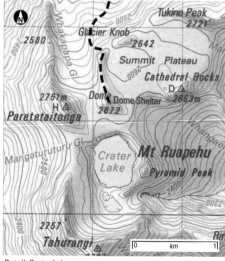

Detail: Crater Lake

Note: This is a walk (more a day tramp) for the experienced and well-equipped; take a map and compass. You need good clear weather: in the mist the potential to get lost is considerable. This description assumes there is no snow on the route, usually implying a January to March walk.

WALK TIME AND DISTANCE

5–7 hours (9 km) return, 1000 metres total climb (utilising chairlift). If walking from the Top o' the Bruce carpark add 2 hours.

30-MINUTE WALK

From the top chairlift a summer nature trail is laid out.

ACCESS AND FACILITIES

From the end of Highway 48 beside the Chateau, follow the road up to the Top o' the Bruce and Iwikau village, where there is a carpark, toilets and many ski huts. The chairlift operates during the summer period and saves 300 metres in height. It operates between 8.30 a.m. and 4 p.m., charge $15.

INFORMATION

Tongariro National Park 273-04 map. This map is especially good as it has a highly detailed 1:12,500 map of the whole crater lake walk.

Mount Ruapehu sits like a massive, grumpy grandaddy in the middle of the North Island, sometimes fuming to itself, occasionally erupting, but usually placid. At 2797 metres Ruapehu is not as inaccessible as it looks, courtesy of a skifield road to 1600 metres and a chairlift beyond that. This is a formidable walk, but immensely satisfying, looking down upon the grey-green crater lake and standing almost on the top of the North Island.

From the Top o' the Bruce the unmarked route basically weaves up through the skifield huts, keeping the main chairlifts on your left. It takes one hour to plod up to the New Zealand Alpine Club Hut, the highest private hut on the mountain, with a fine view of the Pinnacles Ridge.

Descend to the nature trail at what is marked on the maps as Delta Corner. You are now on the standard route, as if you caught the chairlift. Follow up the worn boot trails under The Cirque bluffs onto Restful Ridge, a somewhat ironic name, I feel. To avoid a non-negotiable bluff, the worn trail slips off the ridge into a feature called The Trough, then sidles back onto Restful Ridge again.

The last of the chairlift pylons has petered out, and the large, smooth rocks of Restful Ridge are coloured orange, with occasional old snow patches. There are plenty of cairns to guide you. This is good walking, and you are out on an open mountain with your destination well in sight. Near the crater rim the boot trail becomes very distinct and zigzags sharply up onto the crater wall.

The summit plateau looks magnificent, and in summer this large, flat plain is mostly free of snow. The rugged Te Heu Heu peak is to the left and Cathedral Rocks are straight ahead — but where is the lake?

The trail continues along the crater wall onto the significant bump of Dome at 2672 metres, and the ungainly Dome Shelter. Note the entry via the 'chimney'. The crater lake lies sullenly, and silkily, below you. The Taharangi high peak is on the other side, with multi-coloured and writhing strata bluffs surrounding the lake. The North Island is like a mirage. Pretty good, eh?

The Crater Lake, Mount Ruapehu, and the top of the North Island.

Cliff and seaweed on the Whitecliffs Walkway (see page 86).

WHITECLIFFS WALKWAY
Dramatic cliffs on an historic coastal walk

Detail: Whitecliffs Walkway

TRACK
Beach walking, then steep steps, a bush trail and rolling farm tracks. A low tide is essential as the cliffs are steep, with no escape routes. The inland track is closed for lambing between July and September.

WALK TIME AND DISTANCE
3–4 hours (8 km) Waipingau Stream and 'pipe' track circuit. Add 2 hours to include the historic stock tunnel. The Whitecliffs Walkway continues on to the Tongaporutu River.

ONE-HOUR WALK
Along the beach to the natural archway and return.

ACCESS AND FACILITIES
From New Plymouth it is 36 km to the turn-off into Pukearuhe Road and 11 km to the end of this road. Carparking at the actual road-end is non-existent, so park in the historic reserve (signposted) and walk the last 500 metres down to the beach.

INFORMATION
Walks in North Taranaki, Department of Conservation booklet.

Here on this magnificent coast is a walk of great drama. Pukearuhe was one of the finest defensive and fighting pa in the country, and it overlooks a rollercoaster beach and formidable sea cliffs. There is unique history here, with the pa site, a European redoubt, and a military tunnel that was built in 1880 to assist the garrison, but later employed as a humble stock tunnel.

First walk down the road ramp to the coast, where at low tide you wander past a graceful sea arch and tidal platforms onto the Waipingau Stream. After rain, waterfalls slip-slide over the sea cliffs. From Waipingau Stream it is a good side trip, again with a low tide, along the shoreline to look at the historic tunnel.

The main track picks its way up Waipingau Stream along an old vehicle track, and the valley is full of nikau palms, tawa and rewarewa. At the junction you are faced with the prospect of 670 steps up the spur to the Mount Davidson saddle.

This track follows a public easement along the top of the 200-mm Kapuni gas pipeline, and after the sweat uphill the views are excellent from the 250-metre-high Mount Davidson saddle. All the hard work is over now, and it is easy walking on a poled route down through the sheep paddocks and along the vehicle track back to the carpark. You can see Mount Egmont/Taranaki on a clear day.

NEW PLYMOUTH CITY WALK – TE HENUI
A subtle city walkway – sea, cemetery and stream

TRACK
A mixture of gravel paths, bush trails, footpaths and grass paths, with a steady climb up a stream, then a descent. Generally well-marked, though a town map or the information pamphlet is useful.

WALK TIME AND DISTANCE
1.5–2 hours (6 km) return.

ACCESS AND FACILITIES
In New Plymouth start from East End Reserve, off Buller Street. There is a carpark, picnic place, toilets and a children's play area. There are many other access points to Te Henui Walkway.

INFORMATION
Te Henui Walkway, New Plymouth District Council pamphlet.

New Plymouth has an outstanding network of urban walkways, utilising both the beach frontage and the bush gullies that trickle through the town. Te Henui Walkway has something of everything: sea coast, an intimate bush stream, an historic pa site and a cemetery – what more could you possibly want?

From the Buller Street carpark cross the outlet of Te Henui Stream beside the sea, and negotiate the signposts around the first bend and across another footbridge. The track settles into a streamside bush walk, passing obliviously under the busy Devon Street East bridge and wandering up a quiet dell.

Under Northgate Road the track passes plantings of camellias and magnolias, and Te Henui cemetery. It then crosses another footbridge and, keeping close to the stream, winds past small reserves and residential backyards up to Cumberland Street.

Turn down the other side of Te Henui Stream here, and follow the signposts down past small bush and grass reserves then up to Timandra Street. The walk is quite high above the stream now, and goes through the open parkland of Avery Reserve and Puketara Pa then on to Te Henui cemetery.

The signposts somewhat desert you here, and you have to pick your own way through the dead to find one of several tracks that lead down to Te Henui Stream again, and back to the living shoreline.

OTHER WALKS IN NEW PLYMOUTH
Coastal Walkway (11 km one way), Barrett Domain (1 hour return) and Huatoki Walkway (3 hours return).

LAKE MANGAMAHOE
Picturesque lake circumference

TRACK
Forest trail through bush and pine plantations, and finally roadway, mostly flat. Suitable for baby buggies quite a lot of the way.

WALK TIME AND DISTANCE
1 hour (3 km) return.

ACCESS AND FACILITIES
Off Highway 3, 8 km from New Plymouth. Pleasant picnic facilities and toilets.

INFORMATION
Guide to Walkways New Plymouth District, New Plymouth District Council pamphlet.

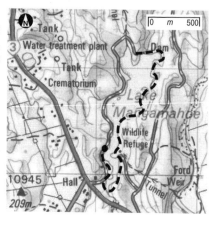

A peaceful and undemanding walk around Lake Mangamahoe, which was created as part of the Mangorei hydroelectric scheme. Placid waters with a good range of waterfowl, and many picnic spots and restful areas along the lakeside. A good walk for small children, with enough features to keep them interested, but not too long.

The track is reasonably well marked. It goes through bush around the western end, then follows through cutover forest and pine plantations to the dam and spillway at the eastern end. There is a nice picnic area here, then a kilometre of road to return to the starting point.

Lake Mangamahoe.

KORU PA
Sacred and silent pa site

TRACK
Farm vehicle track down to the pa site, then bush trails.

WALK TIME AND DISTANCE
1 hour (2 km) return.

ACCESS AND FACILITIES
From Highway 45 at Oakura turn down Wairau Road and Surrey Hill Road to parking by the roadside near the sign. Well signposted.

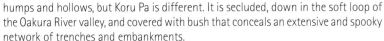

Many Maori pa sites are little more than grassy paddocks with a few nondescript humps and hollows, but Koru Pa is different. It is secluded, down in the soft loop of the Oakura River valley, and covered with bush that conceals an extensive and spooky network of trenches and embankments.

From the road follow the poles down the farm track, then across a paddock to the edge of the reserve. The pa is covered with regrowth forest, so at a distance it looks like a bushy hump. It is only when you are walking on the bush paths that you realise the hill is actually substantial earthworks, terraced in several levels with defensive walls. Some of these walls are supported by the original stonework.

As you wander about you discover old kumara storage pits (rua) and a complex network of paths, some of which lead down to the river with its smooth grey boulders like dinosaur eggs. The silence is intense, and you cannot help but feel the presence of the early Maori who lived and loved in this once great pa.

The distinctive boulders by the Oakura River, Koru Pa.

THE PLATEAU
Traversing the high slopes of Mount Egmont/Taranaki

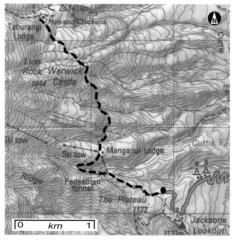

TRACK
Good gravelled track above the bushline, climbing slowly to Tahurangi.

WALK TIME AND DISTANCE
To Tahurangi Lodge 3–4 hours (6 km) return. An alpine walk, suitable as a summer walk only; you need to be well equipped and pick your day.

ONE–HOUR WALK
Skifield return.

ACCESS AND FACILITIES
From Stratford and Highway 3 take the Stratford Mountain House road up the zigzag to a huge skifield carpark simply called The Plateau. There is a lookout platform and toilets here.

INFORMATION
Taranaki National Park 273-09, Egmont P20 maps.

On a fine summer's day this walk cannot be beaten. It starts at 1100 metres, and traverses steadily up and around the side of Mount Egmont/Taranaki. It trawls under impressive rock formations and through a tussock landscape with shy alpine flowers, and offers extensive views across the tidy plains to Ruapehu and Ngauruhoe on the horizon.

From the carpark the track is easy and well-graded as it passes through a shrub belt of leatherwood and koromiko. After you pass the flying fox the track angles into a narrow gorge. You often get old avalanche snow lingering in the valley but there will usually be footsteps to follow. A short climb out of the gorge and you are at the desolate skifield, where there is a large public shelter with toilets.

The track sidles out of the skifield and across various mountain streams and alpine gullies filled with buttercups and daisies in spring. The views are marvellous, the gradient gentle, and the track well poled as it sidles under the volcanic outcrop of Warwick Castle in expansive slopes of tussocks.

It is not long before the television pylon and Tahurangi Lodge come round into view. There is a small, unlocked emergency shelter underneath the lodge. The return to the Plateau carpark is an easy and pleasant downhill task.

YORK HISTORIC CIRCUIT
Railway ruins in the bush

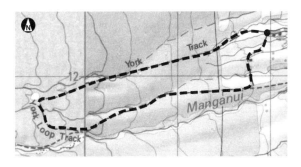

TRACK
Generally flat and easy paths following old tramways, railway lines and access roads. Sometimes a bit overgrown, with a smidgin of rock-hopping along a stream.

WALK TIME AND DISTANCE
2–2.5 hours (6 km) return.

ONE-HOUR WALK
Sand trap return.

ACCESS AND FACILITIES
From Highway 3 turn down York Road and go right to the road-end; there is a small carpark and turning area 50 metres before the very end. Good interpretation sign.

The York track is one of those obscure places that is immensely interesting once you have discovered it, making you wonder why you did not go before. The track follows old railway lines into a huge crusher site, now buried in the bush, and the walk does a circuit, with remnants of industrial history all the way round. There is enough to keep the kids interested and a good place for a food stop halfway round.

Through the gate the track is immediately in thick, luxuriant regrowth forest and quickly reaches a track junction. Turn left to the crusher site, where large concrete structures look appropriately Byzantine in the thick bush. Rock was crushed on this site in the 1940s and railed out to help build the Wellington–New Plymouth railway line.

Fifteen minutes or so further along the track (and water pipe) is the strange concrete sand trap, near the Manganui River. The track continues on an old tramline and along a pretty stream to a footbridge, which makes a pleasing picnic or halfway resting area. A tad further is the small clearing known as the 'foot station', then it is a dead straight line back to the carpark — a fine downward romp on the old service road.

DAWSON FALLS
Through goblin forest to a waterfall

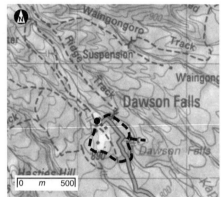

TRACK
Good bush tracks with some up and down.

WALK TIME AND DISTANCE
1–2 hours (1.5 km) Dawson Falls circuit on the Kapuni Loop Track.

ACCESS AND FACILITIES
From Stratford and Highway 3 take the Opunake Road some 12 km, then follow Manaia Road 8 km to the top carpark; visitor centre, public shelter, lookout platform, information boards, toilets.

INFORMATION
Visitor centre and information boards at top carpark. Study the map boards at the carpark or visitor centre carefully, for there are numerous track options in this area and although the colour coding sounds clever, it is not. There is plenty of opportunity for confusion.

Dawson Falls is a popular scenic walk to a dashing waterfall and can be made into a circuit from the carpark. The forest is thickly crusted with lichens and mosses, giving the trees a fairytale look, hence the local name 'goblin forest'. In rain or mist this forest can look even more spectacular.

Find the right colour coding then walk back down the road a short distance and pick up the start of the track. It passes one footbridge, with a view of Kapuni Stream, then the track drops down on a river terrace above Kapuni Stream.

There is another footbridge right above the falls themselves, and just around from here an excellent lookout for people who do not want to drop down to the base of the falls themselves. However, the signposted side-track is worth taking; the 18-metre-high falls look better from below, and on a hot day you might fancy a bracing shower.

The Kapuni Track circuit now continues uphill, crosses the road and climbs slowly back up to the public shelter and carpark.

OTHER WALKS
Wilkies Pools Loop Track (1 hour), Konini Dell Loop Track (1 hour) and Ridge Loop Track (1–1.5 hours).

FANTHAMS PEAK
Soaring views on the way to a high peak

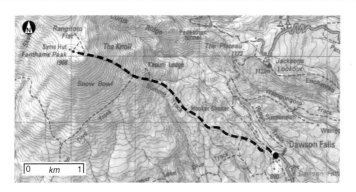

TRACK
A well-marked bush track up steps to boardwalk through tussocks, then soft, pluggy scoria following poles to Fanthams Peak, climbing all the way.

Despite the ease of access, this can be tough country in bad weather, and Mount Egmont/Taranaki has a notoriously fickle climate. This walk is suited to the experienced and well equipped, and there is no point in going unless you can see the views, so wait until you get a good forecast. It will be worth the wait.

WALK TIME AND DISTANCE
5–6 hours (7 km) return.
1.5-hour walk
Hillary Seat return.

ACCESS AND FACILITIES
From Stratford and Highway 3 take the Opunake Road some 12 km, then follow Manaia Road 8 km to the top carpark; visitor centre, public shelter, lookout platform, information boards, toilets.

INFORMATION
Egmont National Park 273-09, Egmont P20 maps.

Mount Egmont/Taranaki is not perfectly symmetrical: there is an odd subsidiary pimple on one side and this is called Fanthams Peak. The walk to it is steep, starting from the goblin forest (see Dawson falls) and up to a volcanic plain, with views right over the heart of the North Island to the volcanoes of Ruapehu and Ngauruhoe. Fanthams Peak is at 1966 metres.

The summit track is well marked as it crosses a footbridge and climbs steadily through a heavy and mossy forest. After passing a couple of junctions the track reaches the Hillary Seat, and the first good view of Mount Egmon/Taranaki.

The track now eases somewhat and pulls up more gradually to the Hooker Shelter, which roughly marks the edge of the bush and start of the subalpine belt. Good views now, and a steady, stepped walk up towards the junction to Kapuni Hut. These steps can be a bit of a curse, but they are a feature of tramping on Taranaki.

The Kapuni Hut verandah is the last sheltered spot, then the track cuts through the last of the alpine scrub and reaches the upper rock slopes – pluggy going in the porridge-like scoria. The route is well poled, but there are trails everywhere, which in misty weather can cause some confusion. At last you reach the edge of Rangitoto Flat, a volcanic plain with crusty scoria and bright-stained rocks. Stick to the poled route as it climbs a little above Rangitoto Flat and sidles directly to the glinting iron sides of Syme Hut.

Plenty to see and do up here, and the hut sits in a commanding position. The return should be straightforward, but make sure you stay on the poled route if the weather closes in.

Rangiwahia Hut (see facing page).

RANGIWAHIA TOPS
Mountain cedar forest and tussock tops

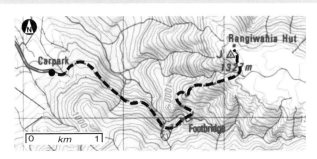

TRACK
A pack-track that climbs steadily.

WALK TIME AND DISTANCE
3–4 hours (8 km) return to hut. Allow another 1–2 hours to get to the main ridge and back.

ONE-HOUR WALK
To footbridge return.

ACCESS AND FACILITIES
From Highway 1 at Mangaweka township turn off to Rangiwahia. It is about 15 km to the turn-off onto Te Para Para Road and a further 4 km to Renfrew Road, then 4 km to the carpark.

This well-graded track was put in by early runholders to take sheep up onto the tussock tops, and the first Rangiwahia Hut was a shepherd's hut. Later Rangiwahia became the second skifield in New Zealand, but today it is a stunning escape from the urban rat-race where you can see the triptych of North Island volcanoes – Mount Egmont/ Taranaki, Mount Ruapehu and Mount Ngauruhoe.

From the carpark the track wanders up through some attractive rimu forest with pepper tree (horopito), rangiora and wineberry (makomako) underneath. Then there is a grove of red beech and an elegant footbridge over a gorge.

You enter mountain cedar (kaikawaka) forest, a distinctive pyramid-like tree with a rich red straight trunk. The track keeps its easy grade, and zigzags up through the subalpine leatherwood (tupare) forest to the tussock grasslands.

The 12-bunk hut has a verandah on which to eat lunch and take in the views, and beside it on the small hilltop there is an even better lookout. There is a worn tussock track a short way above the hut, but it is more than 3 km to Mangahuia, the 1580-metre-high summit. If you have the time, go there.

WANGANUI CITY WALKS – WESTMERE LAKE
& OTHER DIVERSIONS
Placid and peaceful pond

TRACK
Flat bush paths, sometimes muddy.
WALK TIME AND DISTANCE
1 hour (3 km) return.
ACCESS AND FACILITIES
Off Highway 3 down Rapanui Road to
a carpark.

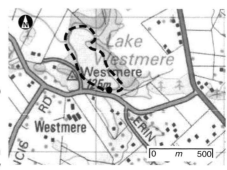

WESTMERE LAKE
This is a rather scruffy little lake, in
need of some TLC, which is a pity
because it is an attractive diversion that is suitable for people wanting a 1-hour
forest escape. Good birdlife and plentiful ducks, as the path does a gentle
circumference around the lake.

OTHER WANGANUI WALKS
There are a number of short, 1- to 2-hour walks around Wanganui city. The Riverside
Walk (1–2 hours return) follows the Whanganui River from downtown along Somme
Parade to Aramoho (Philippa Baker Walkway). The Virginia Lake circuit takes 1 hour.
The Durie Elevator is an unusual public lift that goes from the riverside up to the
suburb of Durie Hill. You walk down a long tunnel to the bottom of the lift where
the attendant takes your money and the lift climbs up to the suburb right beside the
Durie Tower. However, for walkers there
are alternative steps, and the path zigzags
up the hillside with good views, coming
out beside the top of the elevator. The walk
up to and including the Durie Tower is a
vigorous 1 hour return.

Durie Tower.

TOTARA RESERVE
Several walks in a fine forest reserve

TRACK
Bush tracks with some mud.

WALK TIME AND DISTANCE
2–3 hours (5 km) Fern Walk circuit.

ONE-HOUR WALK
Lower Fern Walk loop.

ACCESS AND FACILITIES
Off Highway 3 take the Pohangina West Valley Road through Ashhurst to a bridge, campground and picnic area by the river. Toilets and shelter here.

INFORMATION
Totara Reserve, Manawatu District Council brochure. Take a topographical map as the brochure maps are just about impossible to read.

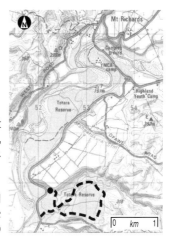

The Totara Reserve is about 300 hectares of straggling bush reserves along the Pohangina Valley Road. It somehow lacks a clear identity, as if the Manawatu District Council has not yet worked out what to do with it. The tracks are disconnected from each other, the signposting is half-hearted, the walks a little ragged, and some are overgrown or unclear.

This is all a great pity, for the reserve has the potential to be a very fine recreational area, with some wonderful stands of podocarp forest and a highly scenic picnicking and camping area beside the Pohangina River. It is a good place for a weekend family camp, with plenty of interest in the river and several short walks.

The Fern Walk starts about 3 km down the Pohangina Valley East Road. There is a short, flat walk of 30 minutes through tall totara, kahikatea and rimu forest. It exits a bit further along the road, which can be followed back to the car.

The main Fern Walk is much longer, taking a 2- to 3-hour loop across the Mangatuatou Stream and up onto a higher bush plateau. It is occasionally rough in places. There is a viewpoint of the Ruahine Range about halfway through the circuit.

Note: a letter written to the Manawatu District Council in 2001 elicited the assurance that more work was being planned to upgrade the Totara Reserve.

OTHER WALKS
Old Coach Road (1 hour).

PALMERSTON NORTH CITY WALK —
RIVERSIDE WALKWAY
Stopbank saunters

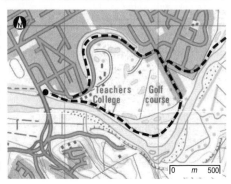

TRACK
Gravel paths or grass trails on flat stopbanks or riverside banks. Suitable for baby buggies.

WALK TIME AND DISTANCE
2-3 hours (12 km) Victoria Esplanade to Ruamahanga Wilderness Area return.

ACCESS AND FACILITIES
Victoria Esplanade Gardens are off Park Road and have toilets, picnic areas, and children's play areas.

INFORMATION
Palmerston North City Walkways and Kiwi Walks, Palmerston North City Council brochure.

Palmerston North (like New Plymouth) has got its act together on urban walks, and has made the best of its geographical features. The Riverside Walkway follows stopbanks along the Manawatu River, and can be made long or short depending on your keenness. It is very accessible to the city and very popular, with many possible variations of route.

From Victoria Esplanade Gardens the river path heads east under the Fitzherbert Avenue bridge and around the broad loop of the river alongside the Manawatu Golf Course. The track does a wriggle at Albert Street then returns to the river, running behind Waterloo Park to Fitzroy Bend Reserve.

There are several trails past the Palmerston North Golf Course and into a scruffy woodland area known rather grandly as the Ruamahanga Wilderness Area. Although the paths go a little further to Riverside Drive, this is a good turnaround point.

On the return it could be a pleasant diversion to go up Albert Street to Centennial Drive, and follow past an old oxbow lake of the Manawatu River, now called Centennial Lagoon, back to the Fitzherbert bridge.

A footbridge near the university section of the Turitea Walkway (see facing page).

PALMERSTON NORTH CITY WALK –
TURITEA WALKWAY
Varied and interesting urban walkway

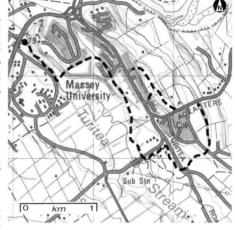

TRACK
All sorts, including footpaths, bush tracks, gravel paths and grass trails. Rolling country but very well signposted. This description is for the full walk circuit but there are numerous other variations.

WALK TIME AND DISTANCE
2–3 hours (7 km) return.

ONE-HOUR WALK
Bledisloe Park to Atawhai Park is about an hour return.

ACCESS AND FACILITIES
Turn off Tennent Drive, just before Massey University, into the carpark, which is easy to miss. Watch for signposts, otherwise there are various other access points off the campus, or Springdale Grove, Old West Road, and so on.

INFORMATION
Palmerston North City Walkways and Kiwi Walks, Palmerston North City Council brochure.

A real hidden gem of a walkway, craftily designed to follow the tinkling Turitea Stream around the university and through the new southern suburbs. The track negotiates parks and gardens, urban streets, streamsides, pockets of bush, farmland and ponds. A little bit of everything, although at the time of writing (2002) some stages were still being completed.

From the carpark turn into Bledisloe Park, an attractive area of native trees, flowering shrubs and footbridges beside the Turitea Stream. The track is sheltered and private here as it crosses the stream a couple of times then turns uphill to Atawhai Park and a narrow gully to Springdale Grove.

Across the road the track nips through a pleasant pocket of bush known as Barbers Bush, then climbs through pine trees and farm paddocks to the Old West Road. There is a short stretch along this road and Turitea Road, then across more farmland to Pacific Drive; excellent views here.

The walkway crosses the road to a lovely stretch of track beside a lake and around to Aokautere Drive. It is intended that the walkway will continue down another stream to Pork Chop Hill viewpoint, but this section is not finished. Walk down Aokautere Drive to the Poutoa Walkway, which follows through pleasant reserves to come out on Summerhill Drive, almost opposite Springdale Grove. Return to Bledisloe Park.

MANGAONE WALKWAY
Foothills bush tramway

TRACK
A well-graded bush track with some stream crossings. Wet feet a certainty within 2 minutes if you start from the southern end.

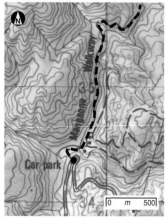

WALK TIME AND DISTANCE
2 hours (7 km) one way, 4 hours (14 km) return. If you have not organised transport at the end, you could return from the saddle.

ONE-HOUR WALK
30 minutes up tramway and return.

ACCESS AND FACILITIES
For the southern access from Waikanae turn off Highway 1 onto Reikorangi Road, then follow Mangaone South Road to the old sawmill site, boiler and carpark. The northern access is off Highway 1 at Te Horo, then along Te Horo/

Detail: Southern end of Mangaone Walkway

Hautere Cross Road and up the winding Mangaone North Road to the carpark and sign.

INFORMATION
Mangaone Walking Track, Department of Conservation pamphlet.

A laid-back sort of track that ambles along an old bush tramway that in many sections has been improved to a well-made logging road. The absence of cars is a real treat, and there is plenty of silence to engulf the walker.

I prefer the northern entrance. The Mangaone North Road is a bush backblocks little lane, and you do not have the pother of wet feet after 50 metres, as you do when you start at the southern end. The track on this northern side wanders up an easy gradient to a saddle, past pine plantations and regrowth bush, with some fine

specimens of rimu, rewarewa and tree ferns. It continues down to a clearing then back into the bush on the tramway.

And the views? On the two occasions I have walked the track the hills were romantically wreathed in mist, while romantic rivulets of rain ran down my neck — so you will have to do your own research on the views.

An old boiler at the southern end of the Mangaone Walkway.

WAIKANAE TOWN WALK –
WAIKANAE RIVER WALKWAY
River path meandering and dune lagoons

Detail: Waikanae River track

TRACK
Flat riverbank paths and stopbanks, urban footpaths, and beach walking.

WALK TIME AND DISTANCE
2–3 hours (8 km) return (from Otaihanga to Highway 1).

ONE-HOUR WALK
To rivermouth return (2.5 km return).

ACCESS AND FACILITIES
From Highway 1 turn onto Otaihanga Road then follow Makora Road to the large Otaihanga Domain, which has toilets, picnic tables and a huge footbridge across the river. There are many other entrances and exits onto the river walkway.

This is a pretty little pathway through willows and native sedges beside the Waikanae River, as it makes its unhurried progress to the sea. Quite private, and Waikanae residents have had the pleasure of this footpath all to themselves for too long.

The Otaihanga Domain is a good starting point, and once you cross the footbridge you can choose from two alternatives. The short walk down the Waikanae River to the rivermouth passes dune lakes and gaggles of black-backed gulls roosting noisily on the shoalbanks. The longer walk is upriver, on a quiet riverside path on the north bank. It links various reserves along the riverbank, including the Karu Reserve, Edgewater Park, Jim Cooke and Memorial Park, and you can wander in peace and quiet all the way until you reach the fairly frantic Highway 1.

A fine footbridge over the Waikanae River.

STINGRAY BAY
Casual surfers' track to a popular bay

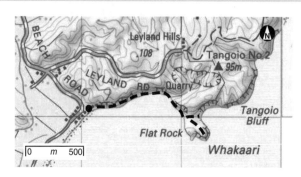

TRACK
A roughish coastal path, slippery when wet, with some beach walking.

WALK TIME AND DISTANCE
1–2 hours (3 km) return.

ONE-HOUR WALK
Old hut bay.

ACCESS AND FACILITIES
Off Highway 2 down Tangoio Beach Road. Carparking on the grass, next to the surfers' cars.

A rough and ready coast with battered baches, old huts, sea cliffs and stony coves — two grass hillocks make ideal coastal lookouts, and there are dark swathes of tidal platforms to explore. Surfers have made this trail their personal highway, pattering on bare feet as they cart their boards towards the singing surf of Stingray Bay.

From the Tangoio Beach baches pick up the well-worn coastal path, which wanders north along pebbled coves under big cliffs. There are some interesting rocks here, and an old hut halfway, before the track goes on to the flat grass sward of a small peninsula.

On the far side is the pretty Stingray Bay, and there are trails up through the thick grass onto both little hills. Alternatively, at low tide you can follow the tidal platforms and rough trails right around the peninsula itself and watch the surfers swinging on the wave breaks.

A great wee place.

Coastline on the way to Stingray Bay.

MOUNT KAWEKA
Many walks on a high saddle

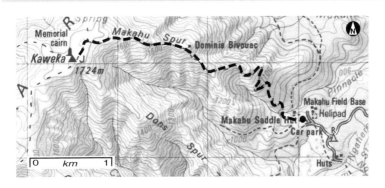

TRACK
Bush track initially, then a steady climb through tussocks and scree to the alpine ridge. Suits well-equipped and experienced walkers.

WALK TIME AND DISTANCE
4–5 hours (5 km) return. Total climb of 700 metres.

ONE-HOUR WALK
Ngahere Loop track, Dons Spur track.

ACCESS AND FACILITIES
It is 70 km from Napier to Makahu Saddle. Take the Rissington–Puketitiri Road, then Whittle Road and Kaweka Road to Makahu Saddle carpark and toilets.

INFORMATION
Makahu Saddle, Department of Conservation pamphlet.

Do not be put off by the 'mountain'. The long, lonely gravel road climbs to over 1000 metres, but you are still in the beech forest at Makahu Saddle. And then there is a surprise, for this sheltered area has a good choice of long and short tracks, including this one to the summit and soaring views of the Kaweka Range.

A benched track travels quickly past scattered mountain beech and Makahu Saddle Hut (4 bunks), and climbs up through scrubland and pine trees onto Makahu Spur. The main track passes the Trials Spur Track (an alternative descent) then gets its teeth into the hill climb.

Shrublands give way to tussocks and steep shingle faces, and the poled track climbs steeply past the other end of the Trials Track to reach the battered Dominie bivouac. There are splendid views from here, and the track onward is not quite as steep. The track is well cairned for another 400 metres to the easy rolling tops of the Kaweka Range.

Turn south past the memorial cairn and onto the broad high point of Kaweka J and its storm-worn beacon. In spring there might be shy gentians and daisies in the foreground, and in the background, views as far as the three Tongariro giants.

OTHER WALKS
Littles Clearing (20 minutes return) and Trials Spur (2 hours return).

103

NAPIER CITY WALK – AHURIRI ESTUARY
Irresistibly easy estuary stroll

TRACK
Flat gravel paths and boardwalks. Suitable for baby buggies all the way.

WALK TIME AND DISTANCE
1 hour (4 km) return.

ACCESS AND FACILITIES
From Napier city it is 1 km to either the Humber Street carpark or alongside Meeanee Quay.

INFORMATION
Wild Walks: sixty short North Island walks, by Mark Pickering, book.

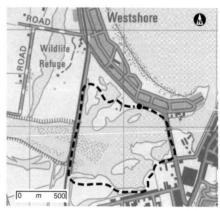

A short and sweet estuary walk, watching the wading birds, and the tides sifting in and out. The estuary is visually best in the early morning and at sunset, when the light turns the waters gold. Over 55 bird species have been recorded at Ahuriri, so take some binoculars if you are keen on this sort of thing. Otherwise enjoy the peacefulness and excellent interpretation signboards.

From the Humber Street carpark the track crosses a footbridge and skirts a line of factories past plantings of ngaio and eucalypts. After 15 minutes the track reaches the embankment bridge, which is closed to cars and forms a perfect viewing platform.

Just here there is an unmarked side trail that crosses a water control gate and follows a stopbank alongside the upper Ahuriri lagoon. This is a good place to look out for roosting spoonbills and the shyer waders. Migrant birds from as far away as Siberia, Alaska and Australia stop over at the Ahuriri estuary, including birds like godwits, turnstones and knots.

The main track crosses the road bridge and winds over boardwalks through attractive saltmarsh ponds and glasswort back around to Meeanee Quay, and the busy Pandora bridge.

Boardwalk over the Ahuriri estuary.

NAPIER CITY WALK – OTARA PA
Authentic pa and palisades

TRACK
Farm tracks and grass paths, with some up and down.

WALK TIME AND DISTANCE
1 hour (3 km) return.

ACCESS AND FACILITIES
From Napier and Taradale take Gloucester Street to the Springfield Road carpark. Toilets and information boards.

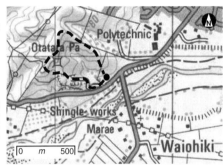

INFORMATION
Otara Pa, Department of Conservation pamphlet.

A splendid double pa site spread over 33 hectares, comprising both Otara Pa and Hikurangi Pa. Defensive earthworks, site terracing and food pits are all evident, but what is particularly striking is the reconstruction of palisades and pou pou (memorial poles). These give a haunting authenticity to the site, and reveal the personality and power of this pa.

It is not difficult walking. From the carpark an old vehicle track leads up under and around the extensive palisades, and you get a sharp idea of how invading tribes would have encountered the defensive fortifications. It also makes you realise how necessary those defences were.

Higher up, the track weaves past kumara pits and terracing to the top of the reserve, where the outlook is marvellous. The pa were situated here for the good defensive boundaries and for access to the rich natural lagoons that surrounded Taradale 800 years ago. An easy grass spur leads back down into the valley and carpark.

TE MATA PEAK
Walk circuit in a limestone landscape

TRACK
Generally well-signposted grass and forest trails, plenty of up and down.

WALK TIME AND DISTANCE
3–4 hours (4 km) return. Any number of track junctions and false trails, so having the pamphlet map is useful.

ONE-HOUR WALK
Chambers Walk, returning via the Nature Trail.

ACCESS AND FACILITIES
From Havelock North take Simla Avenue to Te Mata Peak Road and the Kiwani carpark (the lower carpark).

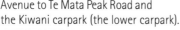

Not all tracks shown

INFORMATION
Te Mata Trust Park, pamphlet. The information board at the Kiwani carpark has all the tracks marked on it. Study it carefully.

For years I was under the quaint delusion that this was called 'Tomato' Peak, for which I blame the Kiwi accent. Te Mata o Rongokako is 'the sleeping giant' or the face of Rongokako, and Te Mata Peak and Trust Park are extremely popular. You can drive to the top lookout, paraglide off the escarpment, mountain bike through the pine forests and walk along the limestone valleys. There is something for just about everyone, and this walk circuit takes in most of the best scenery, including the summit, the limestone faces and the redwood grove.

From the Kiwani carpark take the easy Chambers Walk as it sidles down to a track junction, then turn uphill past another junction onto the Nature Trail and into a dry limestone valley. The well-graded track reaches another junction where you leave the Nature Trail and continue up to the middle carpark on Te Mata Walk. Fine views all round.

Cross the road here and follow the ridgeline Peak Trail as it sidles along the roadway and eventually zigzags up to the 399-metre summit itself – trig, carpark, seats and a glorious panorama. Continue down the Peak Trail as it follows a long open grass spurline and winds down to the stately and silent redwood grove. There is a shelter here, and several track choices.

Continue along the Peak Trail briefly to the Nature Trail again then, turning west, follow this track as it climbs steps up through the pine forest and swings around to a good lookout. The track then crosses the Chambers Walk (more redwoods here), and it is a steady but short climb up to the Kiwani carpark. A very good walk indeed.

CAPE KIDNAPPERS
Pointed peninsula and garrulous gannets

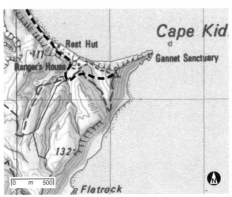

Detail: end of Cape Kidnappers walk

TRACK
Beach walking and a farm track up a hill at the end. A low tide in the middle of the day is essential, and if you start 3 hours after high tide you will not feel any pressure. The colony is closed from July to October to allow early nesting.

WALK TIME AND DISTANCE
5–7 hours (18 km) return. The distance along the shoreline can seem daunting, so come prepared with food and drink and take regular breaks.

THREE- TO FOUR-HOUR RETURN WALK
Black Reef colony return.

ACCESS AND FACILITIES
From Highway 2 at Clive, drive on to the Clifton motorcamp, where if you are prepared to pay the princely fee of 50c you can use the motorcamp carpark and save yourself 300 metres of walking (600 metres if you count the return).

You do not have to walk to Cape Kidnappers. There is tractor transport along the beach, or you can hire quad motorcycles.

INFORMATION
Guide to Cape Kidnappers Gannet Reserve, Department of Conservation pamphlet. To book transport see the Napier visitor centre.

Cape Kidnappers would be impressive even without the gannets. This is a fine beach walk under white sandstone cliffs that seem to undulate like the surf coming onto the shore. Two-thirds of the way along is the Black Reef gannet colony, which in many ways is more interesting than the main colony. However, the climb up onto the final finger of the cape, and looking down on the plateaus of gannets, are sights to remember.

From Scotsman Point at the Clifton motorcamp you are immediately on the beach, which is a mixture of sandy bays and pebbles, with tidal platforms in places. As the tide goes out more sand is exposed, making it easier and faster walking.

The cliffs tower over you with remarkable striations, and streams break the white walls at several points. Black Reef Point can be a long time coming but it is worth it, with gannets nesting on small sea stacks, seemingly quite indifferent to humans standing and staring a few metres away.

Around the point, the beach route does not take long to pass the wide rock platforms and sandy coves to reach the shelter and toilets at the start of the farm track. This well-marked trail climbs up onto Cape Kidnappers itself, passing the ranger's house and up the final grass slopes to the gannet colonies.

You are right beside the plateau colony and overlook the saddle colony, with a constant stream of gannets zipping overhead and making clumsy landings in an already crowded gannet city. Now it's time for lunch, and if you started smartly enough, keen walkers will have a good hour before the tractor people arrive.

The Black Reef gannet colony, on the way to Cape Kidnappers.

Walker and track on the tussock faces of Te Mata Peak (see page 106).

MONCKTON SCENIC RESERVE
A secret bush glen

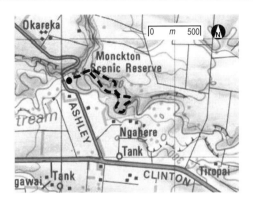

TRACK
Bush track, well-benched at first then more rough. Some climbing.

WALK TIME AND DISTANCE
1.5 hours (2 km) return.

ACCESS AND FACILITIES
From Highway 50 take the Ashley–Clinton road some 11 km to a carpark, shelter and picnic area. There is a rather good swimming hole as well.

INFORMATION
Central Hawkes Bay, Department of Conservation pamphlet.

A small scenic gem, tucked away in the midst of nondescript arable Hawke's Bay — a lush matrix of ferns and trees, and a chattering chorale of birdsong. There is a huge shelter at the carpark and a rather good swimming hole in the Tangarewai Stream, which should be enough to keep the kids occupied during a family picnic.

The walk is not going to wear you out. The bush path is very good at first, as it loops along the attractive mudstone stream. Then it crosses a bridge and gets to a whole lot of steps, after which it becomes a more basic bush track. The forest is a mix of totara, beech, matai and tawa — all sorts.

There are a couple of loop options in a sort of figure of eight, but some of the trails are getting a bit overgrown. At the end there is a blackberry flat and good river views of the slick mudstone river.

That is it, but it is enough.

The picnic shelter at Monckton Scenic Reserve.

SUNRISE TRACK
Red beech to alpine buttercups

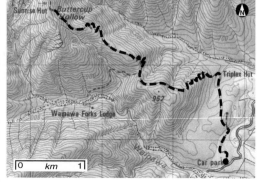

TRACK
A benched bush track that climbs steadily to an alpine hut.

WALK TIME AND DISTANCE
4–5 hours (8 km return). Total climb of 750 metres.

ONE–HOUR WALK
Triplex Hut return, Swamp Track circuit (moss, miro and kahikatea).

ACCESS AND FACILITIES
Turn off Highway 50 at Wakarara Road and travel 18 km to the junction with North Block Road, then 7 km to the Triplex carpark.

A highly accessible track to the tops, passing through a range of forest habitats. At the base there is kahikatea swamp forest, then red beech forest and mountain beech, finishing with alpine flora of daisies and buttercups. A sunny hut is sited beside a small tarn, with a panorama of Hawke's Bay and the Wairarapa.

From the carpark a vehicle track winds around the hillside past the Swamp Track junction to the start of the Sunrise Track. A few minutes later the vehicle track reaches Triplex Hut, which sleeps 12–16. The Sunrise Track climbs slowly through red beech forest, with plenty of native birdsong.

After passing the other end of Swamp Track the main trail climbs up to a small saddle, with mountain beech gradually displacing the red beech as the track puffs up the zigzag. The track is so well graded that it is not as much hard work as you would expect, and Sunrise Hut pops suddenly into sight.

For really good views scramble up to the rock lookout, where you get a prospect of mountains from Waipawa Saddle and on over the tortured scree ridges of the Ruahine mountains.

Wairarapa

MASTERTON CITY WALK –
HENLEY LAKE PONDS
Urban walk to a wetland wilderness

TRACK
Flat walking on gravel paths, stopbanks and mown grass strips. Suitable for baby buggies.

WALK TIME AND DISTANCE
1–1.5 hours (4 km) return.

ACCESS AND FACILITIES
From Dixon Street in Masterton and the carpark at Queen Elizabeth II Park. There are toilets and a large children's play area.

A short, park-like walk alongside the Waipoua River to a series of wetland ponds beside the Ruamahanga River, linking to the Henley Lake Scenic Reserve. This is an unexpected wild area so close to town, with bird-hides and good scenery alongside the Ruamahanga.

From the carpark wander through the manicured gardens of Queen Elizabeth II Park and pick up the gravel path beside the west bank of the Waipoua River, which leads to Colombo Road. Turn left across the river and pick up the east bank track on the other side.

This continues along the stopbanks and paths, reaching the confluence of the Ruamahanga River and circling several wetland ponds that are linked by small waterways. Different tracks meander through this pretty area, with occasional footbridges and a bird-hide overlooking one pond. There is no shortage of ducks.

If you stick to the Ruamahanga River you arrive at the large Henley Lake, where there is a circuit walk around the lake. Then you can pick up tracks back to the Waipoua River on the northern side of the ponds, and retrace your steps to Colombo Road. This time stay on the east bank as far as the footbridge crossing back into QEII Park. A nice little urban trot.

Wildlife ponds, Henley Lake.

CASTLE POINT
An eventful sea coast

TRACK
Beach walking and grass trails up one very steep but short hill.

WALK TIME AND DISTANCE
Castle Point cliff return 1–2 hours (2 km). Christmas Bay return 2–3 hours (4 km).

ONE-HOUR WALK
Lighthouse lookout and reef return 30 minutes, cave return 20 minutes.

ACCESS AND FACILITIES
From Masterton take the signposted Castlepoint road about 50 km to the settlement, carpark and toilets.

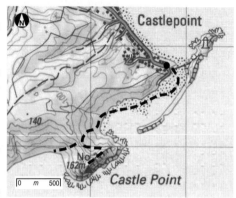

You can see why Castlepoint is popular — it is an eye-catching rock island with a strange claw-like reef, shielding the soft sweep of Deliverance Cove and its immaculate sands. Fishing boats are parked colourfully on the foreshore, and seabirds flock about, taking an interest in the catches of the many anglers who cast off from the reef.

Once you have explored the rock island, lighthouse and reef, another good walk is to Castle Point (162 metres). Follow the beach sands across to the far end of Deliverance Cove and locate the well-worn trail up onto the saddle junction. People with vertigo might not want to carry on up to the high point.

The track sidles across the grassy face of the cliff and although the track is not steep the faces are. It can get wet and slippery after rain. When the track reaches the edge of the ridge it doubles back and wanders up to the top where there are excellent views along the Wairarapa coast. Black-back gulls have a nesting colony on the sheer cliffs of Castle Point.

Back at the saddle, there is a worn side-trail that drops down to the delightful Christmas Cove, a popular sandy bay, and opens up the possibilities of exploring further along the lonely coastline. The further you go the less people there are.

However, from the saddle there is a high-level track back to Castlepoint settlement. It circles around the top of the cliff edge, following the fenced farmland before descending easily through pine trees back to the carpark, the architecturally nasty concrete-block church and the summertime parade of people.

ATIWHAKATU RIVER
Graceful Tararua river track

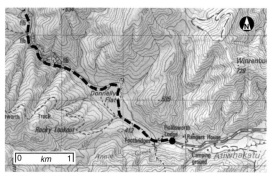

Detail: start of Atiwhakatu River track

TRACK
A well-graded bush track with footbridges.

WALK TIME AND DISTANCE
2–3 hours (8 km) return (to Holdsworth Creek); add 2 hours for the Atiwhakatu Hut (12 km).

If you decide to tackle the gorge, check that the river is average/low. Although you can easily wade through the gorge, it is probably not much quicker than the track these days.

ONE–HOUR WALK
To gorge return.

ACCESS AND FACILITIES
From Highway 2, turn left 4 km before Masterton into Norfolk Road, then take Mount Holdsworth Road (well signposted), and travel 15 km to the road-end and carpark. At the road-end there are picnic areas, toilets, a campground, a caretaker and Holdsworth Lodge, a roomy hut available for the use of trampers, school parties and others (sleeps 30 people).

The Atiwhakatu is a gracious, gentle stream that runs through mature forest in the eastern part of the Tararua Forest Park. The benched track mirrors the swing of the stream, and only climbs away to avoid the short gorge. If you do not mind wet boots, it is well worth returning via the gorge, splashing a pathway of your own.

From the carpark the track crosses the long footbridge over the Atiwhakatu Stream, passes the turn-off to Holdsworth Lookout and Gentle Annie, then continues through to the wide grassy clearing of Donnelly Flat. After another kilometre the well-graded track climbs easily above the short, crisp gorge, with some good river and forest views.

Holdsworth Creek is bridged and the East Holdsworth side-track is marked just on the other side. It is an easy 3 km up a veritable trampers' highway to the knocked-around Atiwhakatu Hut. This may be replaced soon, or renovated, or just removed – whatever, the return beside the sweet-running river is delightful.

TOTARA FLATS
Wide open grassland in the heart of the Tararua Ranges

TRACK
A well-graded bush track up the Gentle Annie, then a rougher track down the Totara Creek with some stream crossings to Totara Flats. Sandflies can get bad at Totara Flats.

WALK TIME AND DISTANCE
6–7 hours (18 km) return.

ONE- TO 1.5-HOUR WALK
Rocky Lookout return.

ACCESS AND FACILITIES
From Highway 2 just before Masterton turn onto Norfolk Road then Mount Holdsworth Road and travel 15 km to the carpark. Ranger station, toilets, picnic area and 30-person Holdsworth Lodge.

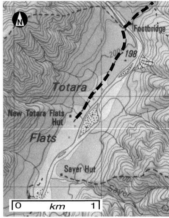

Detail: Totara Flats

INFORMATION
Holdsworth: Tararua Forest Park, Department of Conservation pamphlet.

'Gentle Annie' was the name of a popular sentimental goldminers' ballad of the 1860s, written by the American songwriter Stephen Foster. What it has to do with climbing hills is a mystery, but to get to Totara Flats walkers have to go up the Gentle Annie track. The track then descends Totara Creek to the huge and virtually only open space in the Tararua Forest Park. This is a full-day tramp, and even though it is not difficult it suits the fit and well-prepared.

From the carpark cross the big footbridge, pass the two junctions to Donnelly Flat and start up the designer-trail of Gentle Annie. The well-graded track climbs 300 metres to Rocky Lookout, then a further 150 metres along the ridge to the track junction to Totara Flats on flat-topped Pig Flat.

A well-worn, broad and old cattle track gives away all your hard-earned climbing by dropping 300 metres to the pretty Totara Creek. The track crosses and wanders down this easy-going creek some 3 km to the long footbridge over the Waiohine River. There are several good places to stop for a brew if you do not want to go all the way to Totara Flats.

Over the footbridge there is a short bush walk before you burst out onto a sunny and golden flat, 2 km long. Totara Flats Hut is a few minutes away. On the other side of the river there is a quirky and historic hut that was originally built in 1909 for a grazing lease on the flats held by a man called Sayer. Choice spot.

RIMUTAKA INCLINE
Puffing up an old railway line

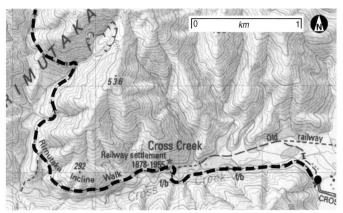

Detail: Wairarapa side of Rimutaka incline

TRACK
A broad, well-graded track that climbs steadily through tunnels to a saddle and descends on the other side. Take a torch. Walkers should be prepared for passing (and whooping) mountain bikers.

WALK TIME AND DISTANCE
4–6 hours (16 km) one way, so a whole day should be allowed. From either the Upper Hutt side or the Wairarapa side it is 3–4 hours return to the first tunnel. This description is from the Wairarapa side, as I feel there is more to see, and the walk can be shortened more easily.

ONE–HOUR WALK
Cross Creek return.

ACCESS AND FACILITIES
Just after Upper Hutt on Highway 2 there is a signposted turn-off at Kaitoke, then it is 1 km to the carpark and signboards. For the Wairarapa entrance drive to Featherston and follow the Western Lake Road some 7 km to a signposted side-road where there is a carpark and signboard after 1 km.

INFORMATION
The Rimutaka Incline, Wellington Regional Council brochure.

The Rimutaka Incline was once the steepest railway in New Zealand, with a 1 in 15 grade, and specialist Fell engines that gripped onto a central toothed rail. The train assembly had four spaced locomotives weighing 200 tonnes, and the maximum speed was 10 kph up, 16 kph down. Often the train moved more slowly than most walkers would achieve today. The incline trains ran from 1878 to 1955, when the Rimutaka railway tunnel was completed. Tunnels, embankments and bridges have remained, and the gorse hillsides are turning into native bush.

From the Wairarapa carpark the track avoids farmland and sidles around into the Cross Creek valley before crossing the stream onto the site of Cross Creek

115

township. There is a shelter here, and many historic photos and interesting anecdotes.

From Cross Creek you are walking on the railway line proper as it gradually snakes up the valley, climbing steadily before Prices Tunnel. The next tunnel is at Siberia, then the line reaches the very long summit tunnel that crosses the range and you pop out on the Upper Hutt side.

It is easy walking with good views as you wander past such places as Ladle Bend bridge, Pakuratahi bridge and the final tunnel at Pakuratahi. The line eases in grade somewhat and drops down past pine plantations to the Kaitoke carpark to complete this grand crossing.

Cabbage tree savannah, Boggy Pond (see facing page).

BOGGY POND
Wetlands and waders

TRACK
An old flat stopbank alongside Boggy Pond. Grass paddocks to Lake Wairarapa.

WALK TIME AND DISTANCE
1 hour (3 km) return (Boggy Pond); 1 hour return (Lake Wairarapa).

ACCESS AND FACILITIES
Take the Martinborough road, Highway 53, and turn down Kahutara Road for some distance to Parera Road; a signpost at the junction reads 'walking track'. After about 2 km you reach a subtle sign on a gate.

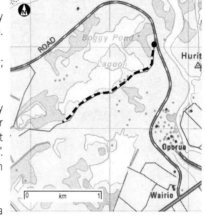

An amiable and unlikely walk along a stopbank that gives a fine vantage point over the wetlands that edge Lake Wairarapa. When this land is not inundated with water it is a peculiar savannah-like flatland of thick reedy grass and cabbage trees. The light is strong, the clouds washed in veiled colours with an almost Vermeer-like intensity.

Finding the start of the stopbank is the main trick. There is no carpark as such, and the small sign does not promise much. The stopbank follows the road at first then turns away, with Matthews Lagoon on the left and Boggy Pond on the right.

The birdlife is diverse, from scavenging pukeko by the roadside to fantails among the scrub and cabbage trees, pied stilts on the swampy edges and a lone harrier hawk patiently working the skies. There is an old anglers' hut on the water's edge about halfway along, and the Boggy Pond is dotted with scaup.

After this the stopbank slips away from the waterline and reaches the return point by a fence and farmland. On the return, the unusual cabbage tree plains around Matthews Lagoon seem to have retained a visual landscape that is uncannily pre-European.

OTHER WALKS
Further along Parera Road there is another signposted walking track across the farmland to Lake Wairarapa itself. It is not well marked across the paddock and you have to thread your way past scrub pockets to the wide-brimmed lakeside.

PUTANGIRUA PINNACLES
Hoodoos and sweeping views

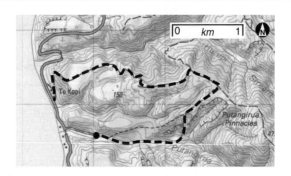

TRACK
Tracks and stream crossings, then a hill climb on bush trails and old vehicle tracks.

WALK TIME AND DISTANCE
3-4 hours (5 km) Pinnacles-Bush Walk-vehicle track-Te Kopi circuit. Total climb 300 metres.

ONE-HOUR WALK
Pinnacles return.

ACCESS AND FACILITIES
From Martinborough it is 35 km past Pirinoa to Te Kopi ranger station and carpark at the Pinnacles. Camping is permitted.

INFORMATION
Eastern Palliser Bay and Putangirua Pinnacles, Department of Conservation pamphlet.

The Putangirua Pinnacles are a striking example of erosion, and the crumbling stones echo eerily in the dry, silent gullies. The best walk is the full circuit, with views of the Pinnacles and Palliser Bay.

From the carpark and picnic area head up the stream, passing the Bush Walk junction, and crossing the gravels where necessary to the Loop Track junction. Wander into the heart of the amphitheatre of pinnacles, largely made of greywacke gravels exposed by rain and floodwaters. Harder layers of rock became 'caps', creating 'hoodoo' pillars. Some of the pillars are estimated to be 1000 years old.

Back at the junction take the steep Loop Track up a spur where you get excellent views of the formations, before the track meets the Bush Walk. Follow up the pleasant ridge trail until it meets an old vehicle track on the ridgeline. This road wends its way back through beech forest, then over open farmland down to Te Kopi ranger station, with superb views of Palliser Bay and the Kaikoura mountains.

CAPE PALLISER TO NGAPOTIKI LODGE
A coastal journey

TRACK
Rough 4WD track all the way, with some climbing. This road is popular with four-wheel-drivers.

WALK TIME AND DISTANCE
3–4 hours (12 km) return.

1.5-HOUR WALK
Stonewall Stream return.

ACCESS AND FACILITIES
From Martinborough take the coastal road past Ngawi and around Cape Palliser, the seal colony and the

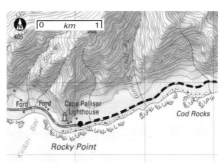

Detail: start of track along Palliser Bay coast

striped lighthouse to the carpark and gate. Some of the last few kilometres can get rough, with at least one awkward ford.

INFORMATION
Rimutaka and Haurangi Forest Parks 274-04 map.

The drive is along a magnificent coastal road, that clings to the soft, cliffy shoreline, and the steep dry hills of the Haurangi Range that plunge down to a shoreline where seals doze. Ngawi is a long row of beached fishing boats, and 'Kupe's Sail' is a naked rock slab. This coast has a raw edge to it, unfinished, untamed.

The walk itself to Ngapotiki Lodge is straightforward, at first weaving past some tremendous potholes, with good views along the coast, where sea spray can make the mountains look misty.

After about 4 km you reach Waitetuna or Stonewall Stream, with its distinctive dry-stone wall stretching from the sea to the hills. Stonewall Stream gushes out onto the shingle fan in a fine waterfall, worth a side trip. Otherwise continue through scrubby flats across two more side-streams to where the road clambers up a vast scree slide. This is the only real hill, and just down on the other side is Ngapotiki Lodge, rather pleasantly situated in a grove of trees.

The hut gets knocked about a bit, and this area is popular with surfers, anglers, four-wheel-drivers and drinkers, and those who combine all four activities. You can see the long reef at Te Rakauwhakamataku Point and a long way along the open, storm-singed Wairarapa coastline.

The old stone fence, looking towards Stonewall Stream.

SMITHS CREEK
A jaunt into the Tauherenikau Valley

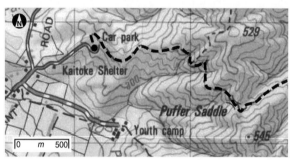

Detail: start of Smiths Creek track

TRACK
A benched bush track over the saddle and down to Smiths Creek.

WALK TIME AND DISTANCE
3–4 hours (12 km) return.

ONE-HOUR WALK
Saddle return.

ACCESS AND FACILITIES
Turn off Highway 2 at Pakuratahi onto Marchant Road, then on to a large muddy carpark. Toilet.

Generations of trampers have slogged up 'The Puffer' track and disappeared into the Tararua mountains for their weekend slog. I was one of them, and I can remember my first bushcraft course at Smiths Creek, when I was a pimply thing on white legs, but a year later I took another bushcraft course – as an instructor! The track has improved as well, and travels gently over the saddle and down to a big, lovely bend in the Tauherenikau River.

The slog up the old vehicle track has been softened with regrowth bush, though it still requires work, and it can be a hot slog on a sunny day – though that is not usually a problem. After 20 minutes you pass the track junction for the Marchant Ridge, and the main track sidles easily around bushy gullies and slips up to the low saddle at the head of Smiths Creek.

No views unfortunately, and the track drops steadily to Smiths Creek itself, then settles in for an easy wander on a good benched track some 4 km down to the Tauherenikau Valley.

There is a nasty concrete-block shelter at the confluence (I helped build it), but it is much better to wander up the Tauherenikau River a short distance to lovely campsites and picnic areas on sunny flats. Woodsmoke, billy brewing, and the remembrance of things past.

QUEEN ELIZABETH II PARK CIRCUIT
Circuits in the sand dunes

TRACK
Well-marked grass and sandy tracks through rolling dunes.

WALK TIME AND DISTANCE
1–1.5 hours (6 km) return.

ACCESS AND FACILITIES
From Highway 1 at Paekakariki, turn down Beach Road then Wellington Road to the southern entrance of Queen Elizabeth II Park. A sealed loop access road leads to the start of the tracks, and there are several sheltered picnic areas. Alternative access at Whareroa Road (McKays Crossing) and carpark.

A different type of walk, through easy, rolling dune country. There are plenty of short or long walk options, or beach walking, with no cars to worry about, and good views of the dark offshore mass of Kapiti Island. The full track is a figure of eight with the middle at the Whareroa Road carpark.

Take the inland track as it weaves through the dunes past an excellent seat and viewpoint. Further along there is another viewpoint before you reach the carpark off Whareroa Road. For the northern dunes pick up the inland track as it crosses a bridge over Whareroa Stream, and there is a fine patch of coastal forest near the Raumati carpark.

The coast track is usually gravelled, and easy to follow, with the option of beach walking all the way to the Paekakariki carpark.

Looking towards Kapiti Island from Queen Elizabeth II Park.

WAIRAKA POINT
Real raw coast

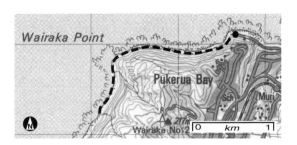

TRACK
Flat narrow coast paths and pebbly beach, ending in a quarry road. A start and end at Pukerua Bay is probably the most attractive walk option.

WALK TIME AND DISTANCE
2–3 hours (8 km) Pukerua Bay to Wairaka Point return.

ONE-HOUR WALK
Sea arch return.

ACCESS AND FACILITIES
Turn off Highway 1 at Pukerua Bay onto Pukerua Beach Road then Ocean Parade and the carpark at the far end.

A tough piece of coast, strewn with driftwood, and kelp washing against the rocks at Wairaka Point. Little blue penguins nest along here and there are small karaka groves, probably planted by the Maori for food and medicinal use. Good views of Kapiti Island.

From the carpark pick your way along the narrow coast trail through the Wairaka Wildlife Reserve, created mainly to protect the rare Whittakers skink. Around the first point there is an attractive sea arch.

From here there is a generally reliable foot trail at the back of the beach, with occasional pebble sections all the way to Wairaka Point. There is an attractive assemblage of small rock stacks that you have to clamber over, and a rusty ladder at one point.

There are good views along the beach from here, and just a little further is a stream and grass clearing, marking the site of an old hermit's cottage. Many walkers might well return from here, for the rest of the route is less interesting, following along the high-backed shingle beach to the quarry works, and the road on to Plimmerton.

Walkers on the rugged coast near Wairaka Point.

COLONIAL KNOB

A blast out of the bush and onto the tops

TRACK
Bush tracks and farm roads with a steady hill.

WALK TIME AND DISTANCE
2–3 hours (7 km) circuit. Colonial Knob is notorious for its wind, so pick your day.

ONE-HOUR WALK
Reservoir loop track return.

ACCESS AND FACILITIES
From the motorway turn-off at Porirua, turn down Kenepuru Drive to Rahia Street, then Broken Hill Road to the carpark

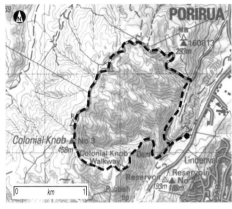

(just before the landfill entrance). There is other access off Rahia Street by Elsdon Youth Camp.

INFORMATION
Colonial Knob Scenic Reserve, Department of Conservation pamphlet.

Threading your way through the industrial estates of Porirua, and nearly into the Porirua tip, is not an encouraging way to start a get-away-from-it-all walk – but persist. Only a short climb and you are way above the suburbs and enjoying the best views of Mana Island and Porirua estuary that you can find.

From the measly carpark at Broken Hill Road, take the main track up to the reservoir junction. Continue through the forest and up past the loop track, which returns back through the Spicer Botanical Park to the carpark. The main bush track climbs up a ridge through some pine trees and reaches open pastureland.

Marker poles march ahead and this is a hard slog up through the grasslands, with the noisy grind of the landfill and factories behind you. The track eases somewhat and you sidle around the main Colonial Knob – 458 metres, with a black and white beacon on top – and go up to the Gulag assemblage of transmitter towers and buildings. But what a view – you look down onto Mana Island, and the far estuary glitters.

As you descend, the marker poles follow the 4WD tracks and pass the junction to the Elsdon Youth Camp exit. Then it is a steep descent down a bush gully with quite a few nikau palms sticking out, and you need to be sharp to pick up the return track to the reservoir.

It is a worn path that zigzags down to a fence and stile, then enters a secret bushy glen, which it follows all the way to the serene reservoir, and on to the not-so-serene carpark.

KOROKORO STREAM & BELMONT TRIG
Full circuit with secret gorge, bush hills and idyllic dam

TRACK
Good gravel paths and some steeper bush tracks and farmland to the trig. A total hill climb from sea level to 457 metres. Watch out for mountain bikes.

WALK TIME AND DISTANCE
4–6 hours (11 km) for full circuit. Farm track sections closed for lambing from August to November.

TWO-HOUR WALK
Korokoro Dam return.

ACCESS AND FACILITIES
Turn off the main Hutt Road by the Petone overbridge onto Cornish Street, where there is a carpark and signboards. Alternative access from Oakleigh Street carpark.

INFORMATION
Belmont Regional Park, Department of Conservation pamphlet.

Detail: start of Korokoro Stream track

There is a bit of everything on this fine circuit, first up a lazy gorge, then past a perfect bush dam and on to the top trig of Belmont. The route can be shortened easily, although it might be smarter to lengthen the day.

The track leaves the ugly industrial conglomeration of buildings in Cornish Street and wanders up the tranquil Korokoro Stream, first through karaka and fuchsia forest, then opening out into a flax and tussock gorge. As you pass the remains of the Mill Dam and cross several footbridges it is hard to credit you are so close to a busy city.

After 3 km you reach the pine trees and track junction at Korokoro Forks. Take the right-hand option and follow up through pine trees and regenerating natives to the Korokoro Dam, which is like an old-fashioned beauty spot.

For Belmont Trig continue up the main track past two junctions and over Korokoro Stream, and climb up through beautiful native forest of rewarewa and tawa. At the bush edge follow the orange marker poles across the farmland and up the Stratton Street track to the trig itself, where the fine views include the Kaikouras and Kapiti Island.

To complete the circuit, take the steep track down through wind-shorn peppertree (horopito) and then out into open country again on the Belmont Ridge. It is a mix of grassy knolls, gorse and mahoe forest, and open country down to Baked Bean Bend, where there is an unappealing grass camping area.

There are nine stream crossings down this pretty waterway to Korokoro Forks, but with some judicious hopping you should be able to avoid wet feet. There is still some way to go before you emerge from the slightly unreal haven of Korokoro Stream and into rushing reality.

MOUNT KAUKAU
Engaging bush tracks leading to a high peak

TRACK
Good bush tracks and some farmland on a steady hill climb.

WALK TIME AND DISTANCE
2–3 hours (3 km) Middle Track and South Ridge circuit.

ACCESS AND FACILITIES
Several access points, but the best are up Woodmancote Road, where there is plenty of car parking beside the swimming pool. A short path links to Clarke Street.

INFORMATION
Khandallah Park, Wellington City Council pamphlet.

This attractive bush reserve nestles behind the suburb of Khandallah, with lookouts over the city, short bush tracks and a good circuit walk that includes the 455-metre-high peak of Mount Kaukau. At Woodmancote Road there is a popular and sheltered area for families, with a children's play area, picnic grounds, toilets, summer swimming pool and excellent cafe (yes, that is a plug).

From the carpark follow the wide Middle Track as it occasionally crosses the gurgling Tyers Stream over several footbridges, past all the track junctions, until it turns uphill. The steps then get a bit remorseless as you climb through a healthy forest of kawakawa, rangiora and rewarewa, with a good and noisy sprinkling of fantails and tui.

The track meets the South Ridge Track, where it sidles quite quickly onto the pastureland. The bristling transmitter tower now looks very close, but the actual summit is marked with a beacon some five minutes beyond. There is a lookout and peak-finding table, and you can see as far as the Inland Kaikoura Range.

A good variation on the descent is to follow the South Ridge Track downhill past the Middle Track, and at the next track junction (where there is a lookout, seat and picnic table) turn left along the benched track as it sidles through dense forest back to the Woodmancote Road play area. A fine circuit.

OTHER WALKS
Nature Walk (10 minutes), Lookout Walk (10 minutes) and the North Ridge Track (an alternative route to Mount Kaukau but steeper; 3–4 hours circuit).

MAKARA HEADLAND
Kai moana and Raukawa Moana

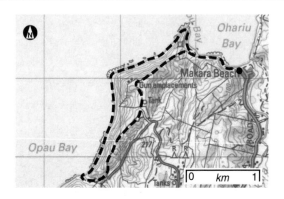

TRACK
A mixture of farm trails and stony beach walking. One decent climb.

WALK TIME AND DISTANCE
3–4 hours (10 km) circuit. A low tide is useful but not essential. The headland part of the walk is closed for lambing from August to October.

ONE-HOUR WALK
Warehou Bay and Point return.

ACCESS AND FACILITIES
From Wellington city drive to Karori and take the winding Makara Road, some 16 km in all. Toilets at carpark.

Raukawa Moana is Cook Strait, and for the Maori at the pa overlooking Makara, Te Upoko o Te Ika, these waters were a good source of seafood, or kai moana. Modern fisherfolk still come here, and kids like to fossick in the rockpools. Paua shell looks vivid on the grey boulders and white-faced herons pick over the samplings with determined delicacy. This walk will give your lungs a good workout, and the sea views are stunning — Cook Strait, Marlborough Sounds, Mana Island, Kapiti Island.

Follow the vehicle track around Makara Beach to Fisherman's Bay (Warehou), then a poled route heads up onto the faint terraces of the pa. The views are good already, and by the time you have managed the steep grass spur up to the old military fortifications you will have reached the highest point on the track circuit — 201 metres.

The gaunt gun emplacements were built hastily in 1942 because of the Japanese scare, but by 1944 were abandoned. There was a full barracks and quarters for the men. The South Island looks remarkably close here.

The marker poles continue to the top of an old sealed road, which makes for an easy descent to Opau Bay. Under the cliffs there is a worn trail that avoids the worst of the boulders and once around Warehou Point you get back onto a good track again, picking its way through all the colourful detritus that Cook Strait sends ashore.

SOMES ISLAND
The heart of the harbour

TRACK
Grass trails.

WALK TIME AND DISTANCE
1–2 hours explore, 2–3 km return.

ACCESS AND FACILITIES
Take a boat or ferry to the main wharf. There are toilets by the western jetty. The island is open from 8.30 a.m. to 5 p.m. daily.

INFORMATION
Somes Island Reserve, Department of Conservation brochure.

In the middle of Wellington Harbour, or Poneke, is the safe haven of Matiu or Somes Island. This rocky outcrop has for centuries been a place of refuge, and imprisonment, but today the island is a refuge for New Zealand's unique native plants and animals. Since the early 1980s a revegetation scheme has replanted the 24.8-hectare island in native plants. There are penguins and many nesting seabirds here already, and tuatara have also been introduced – this is one of the few places on earth where they live.

Local Maori used to shelter here from invading tribes, and in the early years of European settlement the island was used as a quarantine and clearing station for weary settlers. During both world wars the island was used to intern aliens and New Zealanders of Italian and German extraction, and it was an animal quarantine centre until 1995.

From the main wharf the track climbs up onto the plateau, and there is a circular track around the island, overlooking the many little cliffs and rocky bays. Some short tracks visit features like the gun emplacements. Wildlife is thick upon the land and in December the black-backed gull chicks think they own the place.

The light can change from minute to minute, swishing about the island like a

sea itself, and Wellington city seems both close and far away; it is still within cell-phone range, but leave the phone behind, go on, just once. It will be good for your soul.

Silent gun emplacements, Makara (see facing page).

WELLINGTON CITY WALK – INNER CITY
Motorway madness

TRACK
Footpaths, bush paths, steps and quite a bit of up and down. There are many alternative paths.

WALK TIME AND DISTANCE
1–1.5 hours (2 km) circuit.

ACCESS AND FACILITIES
Bolton Street, best carparking on a weekend.

INFORMATION
Town Belt Walks, by Mark Pickering, booklet, now sadly out of print.

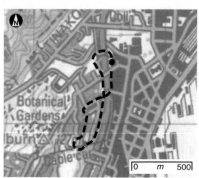

This walk fossicks around the heart of downtown Wellington, enjoying the intricateness of back alleys, bush paths and the tight muddle of streets behind The Terrace, Bolton Street and Kelburn Park. The complexity of city paths in this area is surprising, as is their seclusion from the constant humming motorway. It is a mad place for a walk, but that is its charm.

From the Bolton Street cemetery chapel/museum, take the path past the dell-like 'amphitheatre' onto the footbridge that crosses the motorway. There is a mess of paths on this side of the cemetery, but take the Hart Path on the left, then Powles Path as it plunges into a dark gully, where the graves are permanently lost in the deliberate wilderness of tall macrocarpas and sprouting bush.

Powles Path leads to Easdale Street, then crosses Bolton Street to the sealed path that slips under Aurora Terrace. The healthy plantings of bush along this path include kowhai, karo, manuka, pittosporums, koromiko and many others. There are brick lunch shelters here, which never seem to get used.

Continue to the junction (the other track goes to Clifton Station on the cablecar route and steps under the motorway) and then up some steps and across Everton Terrace to pick up a bush path that climbs into Kelburn Park. At the first junction take the right-hand option, which brings you up to a sealed footpath by the university hostels.

You pop out on Everton Terrace again, walk down this fractionally, and into the furtive Talavera Terrace. At the end of the cul-de-sac take the steps down to San Sebastian Street then up onto Aurora Terrace, and follow it down over the motorway. Just here pick up the pleasant path that leads back to the start at Bolton Street, and that should be the end of your lunch hour.

WELLINGTON CITY WALK – ORIENTAL BAY TO MOUNT VICTORIA
Quick flick to Mount Vic

TRACK
Footpaths, steps, and bush trails. Inconsiderately steep!

WALK TIME AND DISTANCE
1–2 hours (1.5 km) for full circuit.

ACCESS AND FACILITIES
Plenty of car parking by the old pavilion and restaurant (now named, highly originally, Fisherman's Table). A public lookout and seats on top, and public toilets 50 metres away.

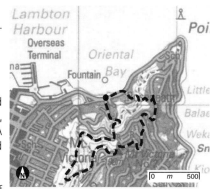

Most people who go to the summit of Mount Victoria drive there. But there is a lot of fun to be had exploring the tangle of steep Mediterranean-like lanes that lie between Oriental Bay and Mount Victoria. Every corner has a different surprise, with hair-raising tramways, quirky bush paths, expensive houses and the satisfaction of a panoramic view from the summit.

From the old pavilion head/pant straight up the steep Hay Street, with the Mount Victoria tower framed by narrow houses, and a sweet gingerbread house at the top. Turn into Telford Terrace and follow the sealed footpath (not signposted) to the junction, and take the uphill option (now part of the Southern Walkway) along a path that climbs to Palliser Road. Note the home-built tramway.

Across the road there is a well-marked track junction and the obvious main walkway track is wide and easy, sidling quite a distance to a lower grass clearing with a prominent white-barked gum tree. Follow up the open spur track as it climbs to a top grass clearing (the pine forest has been confused with numerous unofficial mountain-bike trails) and follow the advice of the 'Mount Victoria lookout' signpost along to road and summit.

On the summits (there are two) is the Byrd Memorial, seats and a quaint 1950s shelter, which obviously has been designed to give no protection from the wind at all. After your breathing is back to normal try this alternative route down through the posh suburb of Roseneath.

Follow the Mount Victoria Road to Alexandra Road, then turn onto Thane Road, into Palliser Road and along The Crescent. That distinctive tangy smell is money. About halfway down The Crescent is a footpath leading down to Grass Street – an astounding 22 zigzags – and you are back on Oriental Parade, where you can choose your cafe.

WELLINGTON CITY WALK – EASTERN WALKWAY
From Breaker Bay to Gallipoli

TRACK
Grass and bush trails in rolling country, then a return on flat coastal footpaths.

WALK TIME AND DISTANCE
2–3 hours (7 km) return.

ACCESS AND FACILITIES
From Seatoun take the Breaker Bay Road to the carpark by the sandy beach.

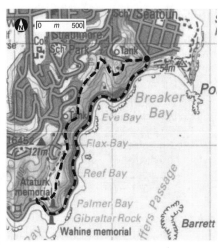

Dramatic coast and history here, as this track links Breaker Bay with the white-marbled column of the Ataturk memorial. There are splendid views all the way along the blowy ridgetop track, and you overlook the Cook Strait ferries as they pass Wellington Heads and the infamous Barretts Reef.

From the carpark at Breaker Bay (which has a sandy beach with a natural rock archway) walk up Breaker Bay Road to the oddly named Pass of Branda and the start of the Eastern Walkway. The track climbs steeply through pine trees at first, then sidles around Beacon Hill itself at a lower level.

At the ridgeline it passes a track junction to Signallers Road and goes up and down past two exits to Sidlaw Street. There is another dip to reach an exit to Bowes Road, then an easy stroll along the wide track to the strangely appropriate site of the Ataturk memorial. The column remembers Kemal Ataturk and Gallipoli, and has the Turkish crescent moon incorporated into its design.

Steps lead down to the carpark by Tarakena Bay and it is only a short distance to the stark *Wahine* memorial. Now it is flat walking along the coastal road back to Breaker Bay, with some quirky and distinctive houses along this restless and expensive piece of shore.

Breaker Bay, near the start of the Eastern Walkway.

RED ROCKS
Sea breezes, seals and the South Island

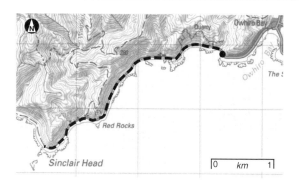

TRACK
Flat 4WD road.

WALK TIME AND DISTANCE
1–2 hours (8 km) return from Red Rocks. Good for mountain bikes.

ACCESS AND FACILITIES
Drive to Owhiro Bay and turn west to the carpark by the old quarry. Cars can continue to the first baches and a second carpark (one ford), but from there on everything depends on road conditions, and the road is not being maintained. The rock 'pass' at Sinclair Head is impassable for cars. The track is okay for baby buggies for a while, but rough in places.

INFORMATION
Red Rocks Coastal Walk, Department of Conservation pamphlet.

This is an invigorating pathway between the sea and the steep southern hills of Wellington, which has been popular for hundreds of years. The Maori used this coast extensively for habitation and food gathering, but today it is city slickers 'getting away from it all' who come to the Red Rocks coast. There are plenty of rock crannies and rockpools to loiter by as you fill your lungs with some of the sweetest air in Wellington — until you smell the seals.

The 'red rocks', or pari-whero.

131

Follow the 4WD track as it passes the second carpark and baches and swings around a bay to the second lot of baches at Waipapa Stream. There is a track junction here for walkers and mountain bikies up onto Hawkins Hill or the old gun emplacements.

It is a short distance along the coast to the strangely coloured red rocks, 'pari-whero', which are pillow lava, and another half kilometre to Sinclair Head, which is a haul-out area for seals. The road dives over a notch in the spur and around a corner of Cook Strait with fine views of the southern coast.

The road continues on to the Karori Stream baches, but somewhere about here either inertia or a gale-force southerly will spin you around for the way home. The interisland ferries slog on to the South Island, which now looks close enough to reach. So please read on.

South Island

FAREWELL SPIT & WHARARIKI BEACH
Sea, space and spit

TRACK
Farmland and beach walking, Fossil Point circuit flat, Wharariki circuit and Hilltop Walk rolling. Mid to low tide is good for both Fossil Point and Wharariki Beach.

WALK TIME AND DISTANCE
2 hours (5 km) Fossil Point circuit; Hilltop Walk 2–3 hours (7 km) one way; Wharariki Beach circuit 2–3 hours (5 km) return. Remember this is a working farm park, and care should be taken not to disturb stock. Some walks will be closed for lambing during September–October.

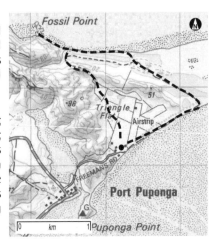

ONE-HOUR WALK
Fossil Point direct return, Wharariki Beach return.

ACCESS AND FACILITIES
From Collingwood in Golden Bay, take the Pakawau and Port Puponga road for 25 km. One kilometere past Port Puponga is a visitor centre, cafe, toilets, viewing telescope, information boards and carpark. The cafe is closed in winter. On the hilltop behind the visitor centre you can see Mount Egmont/ Taranaki, 144 km away.

INFORMATION
Farewell Spit and Puponga Farm Park, Department of Conservation pamphlet.

Farewell Spit has a mythic status, deservedly, for it stretches like a long curved finger of discovery from the top of the South Island. It is well worth the tremendous effort needed to get there. No less impressive is Wharariki Beach, with its armada of offshore islands and magic interplay of rocks and dunes. I am not exaggerating – it is truly a memorable place.

For starters, the Farewell Spit and Fossil Point circuit is a good one. It begins at the carpark and follows the inland curve of the spit until it picks up a vehicle track and crosses through dry manuka forest to the windswept sands by the Tasman Sea. There are wind-torn rocks and tidal platforms at Fossil Point, and a well-marked return track to the carpark.

The Hilltop Walk (if you can arrange transport) is an excellent one-way crossing, wandering up and down beside the big cliffs with a rare view of the whole extent of Farewell Spit. It is mostly open farmland with some coastal scrub.

Wharariki Beach access is 6 km from the visitor centre down the Nguroa Road. Depending on the tides, the best walk is the full circuit, which leaves the carpark along a farm track, past the Dune Lake and then Island Lake, to a track turn-off to the beach and a marvellous descent to this remote bay.

A good track crosses through manuka around Pilch Point onto the main Wharariki Beach, and at low tide there are numerous sea arches and caverns to explore as you wander towards the Archway Islands at the far end. A good track leads through the dunes (Hilltop Walk starts here) back to the carpark, but Wharariki is a hard place to leave, and there are always a few backward glances.

Wharariki Beach — it does not get any better than this!

PUPU HYDRO WALK
Elegant investigation of a water race

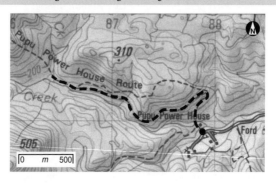

TRACK
Bush track up a hillside, then a flat walk along the water race with boardwalks. Children will enjoy this walk, but some of the drop-offs are steep.

WALK TIME AND DISTANCE
Allow 2–3 hours return (8 km).

ACCESS AND FACILITIES
From Takaka drive 2 km to the Pupu Springs turn-off, and follow the winding road 6 km to the carpark at the end. Two fords.

INFORMATION
Pupu Walk, Department of Conservation pamphlet.

This is an uncluttered walk along an old gold-diggers' water race, which was originally

A narrow boardwalk on the Pupu Hydro Walk.

constructed in 1901 then in 1929 adapted to supply power to New Zealand's smallest power station. The toy-like power system still works, and the water flows brightly along rock channels and around bluffs — a chiselled masterpiece of the goldminers' skills.

At the powerhouse there is a viewing window through which you can see the power turbines, and from the carpark the track crosses a bridge and climbs up a steep zigzag trail to the end of the water race. The penstock is basically a large pipe to carry the water down to the powerhouse.

The stopbank beside the water race is now the walking track, with boardwalks and handrails where the canal gets narrow. Occasionally fluming (aqueduct) carries the water over a gully, and the water race curves cunningly through bush and bluffs for some 3 km before reaching the intake weir at Campbell Creek. A pleasant place to boil the billy, and no doubt the early goldminers did just that.

MILNTHORPE PARK TO COLLINGWOOD
Golden beach and idiosyncratic coastal park

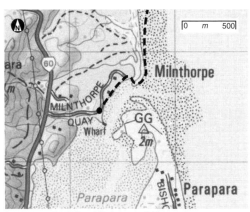

Detail: start of walk from Milnthorpe to Collingwood

TRACK
Flat, easy beach walking, and bush paths through the Milnthorpe Reserve. Low tide not essential but useful.

WALK TIME AND DISTANCE
2–3 hours (10 km) return.

ONE-HOUR WALK
From the wharf take the estuary track, then on to the sand shore around to the beach, back through Milnthorpe Park on 'The Old Coach Road' track through to the Highway 60 carpark, then back down Milnthorpe Quay Road to the wharf. There are many other 1-hour options inside Milnthorpe Park.

ACCESS AND FACILITIES
From Highway 60 turn down Milnthorpe Quay Road to the old wharf beside the Parapara Inlet. Alternatively, take Nelson Street (off Milnthorpe Quay Road) then Kendall Street to the carpark beside the old stone bridge. There are cafes, toilets and a children's play area at Collingwood.

INFORMATION
A local information sheet on Milnthorpe Park shows the layout of the tracks, which is useful because they can be fiendishly difficult to fathom without a map.

Golden Bay – the name sounds good, and real estate agents are grateful it did not remain Murderers Bay, which is what Abel Tasman called it. But it does not take much to sell this place, famous for its benign climate, sweeping sands, and as a last refuge for hippies. This walk is an easy and graceful stroll along a small part of this golden bay.

From the old wharf a good benched track follows the edge of the estuary around to the old stone bridge, which provides an elegant high-tide footway to Milnthorpe Beach. Kids can spend hours playing in the little estuary and soft sands here. Follow the sand shore around to the main beach, which at low tide retreats far out into Golden Bay.

It is easy, flat walking along to Collingwood, an old goldmining town that in 1857 was touted as a future capital of New Zealand. The gold has gone but the cappuccinos remain; after a recharge, head back along the beach to Milnthorpe.

For an interesting variation, take the Redwood Trail into Milnthorpe Park, which plunges you into a rustling dry manuka forest. Tracks and junctions come thick and fast, but one very pleasant route is Redwood Trail, Rimu Flats, Ian's Incline, Elise's Way (nice by the stream here), then Blackwood Trail to Jimmy's Jungle, and Baas Deviation to Nelson Street and Milnthorpe wharf.

Remember, if you do get lost, the park is only 1 km wide between the highway and the sea, so you should make it out by nightfall.

Parapara Inlet, on the Milnthorpe to Collingwood walk.

Limestone rocks on Takaka Hill (see facing page).

TAKAKA HILL
Limestone outcrops on a high plateau

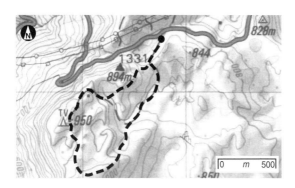

TRACK
A well-marked track but sometimes rough underfoot, with some short hill climbs. Stick to the track to avoid the sinkholes; also remember the altitude of 800–1000 metres and take adequate clothing.

WALK TIME AND DISTANCE
2–3 hours (4 km) return.

ONE-HOUR WALK
To the communication towers.

ACCESS AND FACILITIES
Off Highway 60 on the Takaka Hill road; the start is at a signposted carpark.

Between the flat plains of Nelson and Golden Bay is the high, eerie limestone plateau sometimes known as the 'Marble Mountain'. By Highway 60 the forest has been mostly cleared, exposing a geography of stumps of fluted grey rock, like molars from a giant's jaw. It is a strange place – dry, holey, silent – unlike any other in New Zealand. Well worth stopping and exploring.

At the carpark the track is marked with poles, and it passes the two junctions of the short Bush Walk as it wanders into the rocky land. Low, alpine, scrub-like kowhai and tree daisies grow in unlikely places and every now and then there are copses of the remaining beech forest. The track eventually joins the transmission 4WD road and climbs to the top. There are great views of the Mount Arthur range and the upper Takaka valley.

The trail then wanders about a shattered Armageddon-like landscape, with twisted dead trees and sharp rocks. After this it cuts through a forest grove to reach a junction with the Link Track, which is a shortcut back to the carpark. The main track continues on another long loop but in many ways the Link Track is the better option. It follows the transmission 4WD road and cuts through the heart of this open basin, with good views. Occasional tomo (sinkholes) are extravagantly signposted, positively encouraging you to look in, and the track takes no time at all to arrive back at the carpark beside the cooling bush stream.

ANCHORAGE BAY
A coastal ramble

TRACK
A flat, wide path, with some short climbs along the way. Many track intersections, so it pays to have a good map or brochure.

WALK TIME AND DISTANCE
3–4 hours (10 km) one way (assumes one way on boat).

ONE-HOUR WALK
Tinline Bay return.

ACCESS AND FACILITIES
From Motueka, drive north 5 km to the Kaiteriteri turn-off, then 8 km to Marahau carpark, toilets, information shelter and cafe. A clever option is to take the launch back from Anchorage Bay to Marahau, or vice versa, depending on tides and boat times. There are several launch operators that run daily (in summer) along the coast, and these water taxis add a unique dimension for walkers. This walk assumes you will take the boat, otherwise double the walking time.

INFORMATION
Abel Tasman 273-07; this is probably the best map.

Coastal walking does not get much better than this. A forested shore, a lapis lazuli sea, and tiny slivers of golden sand between. A dozen bays to explore, and many headlands to peer out from. If you do not mind sharing the track, and take suncream and water, you will have a memorable excursion.

From the carpark and cafe cross the Marahau board over the estuary, then follow the track as it hugs the coast for about 2 km to Tinline Bay, a sheltered open clearing with picnic tables and a toilet. A short way beyond is the junction with the inland track, and a good lookout off Guilbert Point.

After this the coastal track ambles along the sea edge 20–30 metres above the shore, past two pretty bays, Appletree and Stillwell. Side tracks lead down to each bay, and there are pleasant picnic areas at both. It is not far from Stillwell Bay to Yellow Point and another tiny picnic area at Akersten Bay.

For the first and last time the track climbs quietly through the manuka forest up to a ridge saddle and a signposted junction. There is a muddle of track junctions here, but tracks to Anchorage Hut are all well signposted. Turn right and follow along the ridge, after a while passing a side track to Watering Cove, which was where Dumont D'Urville filled up his watering casks in 1827.

The main track gives splendid views over Anchorage Bay and drops down to this brilliant sweep of sand, and the hut is just along the beach. Wait for the boat. Daydream.

NELSON CITY WALK – AIRPORT CIRCUMFERENCE
Estuary flights

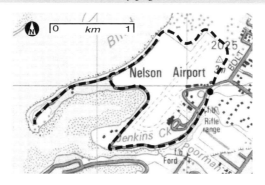

TRACK
Sealed road and grass paths.
WALK TIME AND DISTANCE
1–1.5 hours (4–5 km) return.
ACCESS AND FACILITIES
Drive to Nelson airport and park beside the sign and Oamaru stone sculptures. Reasonably accessible for baby buggies.

This sounds bizarre – a walk round an airfield? You have gotta be joking? No really, Nelson is hardly a busy airport, and this walk has no roads to cross and enjoys extensive views out over the Waimea estuary. In between planes it is quiet, and there are plenty of birds to be seen. If you like bird-watching, walking and aeroplanes – perfect!

From the stone sculptures follow the sealed access road between the perimeter fence and the lapping lagoon inlet. The road swings around a point then loops around another inlet to the shoreline. Here there is an optional side track along a vehicle track that leads right out onto a peninsula, with expansive views of the estuary and its islands.

Back on the main track the route follows the coastal edge and reaches the golf course, then follows the airport perimeter fence alongside worn grass trails. By keeping near to the fence you end up on the main airport road, only 100 metres or so away from the sculpture carpark.

An alternative route at low tide, once you reach the golf course, is to follow the shoreline to Tahunanui Beach.

One of the sculptures outside Nelson airport.

DUN MOUNTAIN
Historic railway line and mountain retreat

TRACK
A well-graded track as it follows the course of an old railway line up a long, steady hill.

WALK TIME AND DISTANCE
Dun Mountain Lower Walkway 1.5–2 hours (6 km) return (from Tantragee Road back to Brook Street).
Dun Mountain Upper Walkway 4–5 hours (12 km) return (from Brook Street motor camp to Third House return).
Dun Mountain Alpine Walkway 8–9 hours (26 km) return (from Brook Street motor camp to Coppermine Saddle and Dun Mountain).

ACCESS AND FACILITIES
From the centre of Nelson city drive up Brook Street to Tantragee Road. Turn down this and almost immediately there is a signpost for the start of the lower Dun Mountain walkway. One kilometre further along Brook Street (before the motor camp) there is another signpost ('Nelson City Council') for the Dun Mountain walkway; this is a closer start for people going to Third House and beyond. There is also a link track from the motor camp up to the walkway.

Detail: start of Dun Mountain walkway

INFORMATION
Nelson 027 map.

This is a long, steady hill walk from an urban environment to an alpine landscape. Built in 1861–62 to extract copper, the historic railway line offers plenty of history and views as it goes up to the strange bare tops of Coppermine Saddle and Dun Mountain. There are many appropriate turnaround points for different levels of walkers, and probably only the keen will reach the summit.

DUN MOUNTAIN LOWER WALKWAY
Take the steep track from Tantragee Street as it zigzags under power lines to reach the old railway formation. There are good interpretation signs about the old railway history as you climb through pine forest and around bush gullies, and some good views. At the crossroads, turn right steeply back down to Brook Street and along the road to the Tantragee carpark.

DUN MOUNTAIN UPPER WALKWAY AND BEYOND . . .
From the signpost follow the walkway for an hour and a solid 300-metre climb up a logging road through pine plantations to a junction with the old railway line. That

was the hard part. Much easier now, the track winds through pleasant beech forest some 4 km to Third House. This large shelter sits in an open clearing, with views back over Nelson.

The next stage is well graded, first passing the junction to Wells Ridge after 1 km, then after another 3 km entering the bare, rocky screes of the mineral belt, and on to the stark Coppermine Saddle. Sometimes the track is built on hand-stacked rocks, one of the few visible remnants of the miners' activities.

If you have still got puff left, take the uphill track to Dun Saddle about 30 minutes further on and you are right on the main ridge itself. Here you can follow an open, cairned route through tussock onto the flat mound of Dun Mountain at 1129 metres. Was it worth it? Look at the view.

Rain clouds over the Dun Mountain track.

Cable Bay and the natural causeway (see page 144).

CABLE BAY COAST
Unique boulder banks and coastal views

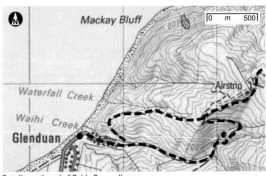

Mackay Bluff

Waterfall Creek

Waihi Creek

Glenduan

Airstrip

Detail: south end of Cable Bay walkway

TRACK
Mostly over rolling farmland, with some mud and climbing. The track is closed during the hours of darkness, and for lambing, approximately September to October.

WALK TIME AND DISTANCE
2–3 hours (8 km) one way.

ONE–HOUR WALK
The Glen loop.

ACCESS AND FACILITIES
The Glen: off Highway 6 down Glen Road to a carpark on Airlie Street.
Cable Bay: off Highway 6 at Hira, down Cable Bay Road. Toilet and picnic area.

INFORMATION
Cable Bay Walkway, New Zealand Walkway Commission pamphlet.

The boulder banks of Nelson are some of the strangest geological formations in New Zealand, being naturally formed by longshore drift. You can see both boulder banks on this walkway, with magnificent views along the Nelson coastline. There is also the history of the telegraphic cable, which came ashore in Cable Bay in 1876 and operated on that site until 1917, when it was shifted to Titahi Bay. If you can arrange transport, do the whole walkway, otherwise start from the Glen.

Walk up Airlie Street to the start of the walkway. The right-hand track, which is less steep, follows a 4WD track and winds around a stream gully and up a steepish hill to a lookout and seat. Grand views of the Nelson boulder bank.

The downhill loop track returns from here, but the main walkway continues past the airstrip (where there are toilets) and downhill to a native forest of tawa, pigeonwood and, further on, beech forest. The track breaks out of the forest onto farmland, with views of Pepin Island, and wanders down through the old cable station complex to the carpark at the south end of the boulder bank. Just here there is an information shelter detailing the history of Cable Bay.

QUEEN CHARLOTTE WALKWAY (PORTAGE TO TE MAHIA)
Sea views on both sides of an open ridge walk

Detail: section of the Queen Charlotte walkway

TRACK
A well-marked hill track through scrub and coastal forest. Remember this is also a mountain-bike track.

WALK TIME AND DISTANCE
3 hours (5 km) one way.

ONE–HOUR WALK
Onahau lookout.

ACCESS AND FACILITIES
Off Queen Charlotte Drive at Linkwater, the Kenepuru Road winds past Mistletoe Bay and Portage. Obviously having transport arranged is important, or a car swap, or else a mountain-bike hidden at one of the road-ends. The carparking is miserly at Torea Saddle, and non-existent at Te Mahia Saddle, though 300 metres down the road there is a large carpark for Mistletoe Bay. At Mistletoe Bay there is a camping area and three DoC lodges that can be hired.

INFORMATION
Queen Charlotte Walking Track, Department of Conservation pamphlet.

The Queen Charlotte Walkway is rapidly becoming one of New Zealand's most popular tracks. It offers almost 55 km of ridge and coastal walking overlooking the glittering turquoise waters and endless peninsulas of the Marlborough Sounds. This walk is a typical snippet of the overall track, with swinging views on both sides of the ridge, a bit of gorse, a bit of forest, and on a hot day more than a bit of sweat. Take plenty of water.

From the stone war memorial the track from Torea Saddle (Portage) is steep, following a bulldozed line that has been softened by manuka forest as it zigzags up the ridge, with extensive views once you get higher. After this the track settles down into a rolling pattern along the ridge tops. You are about 400 metres above sea level here. It can often be hot and dry, but as you near the peak of Te Mahia the track slips through pockets of bush.

Before you drop down to Te Mahia Saddle there is an excellent viewpoint from Mount Onahau (417 metres, with a picnic table) overlooking the complicated waterways of the sounds. Allow 30 minutes return.

Then there is a fast bush descent down to the junction with the James Vogel track. This is a pretty bush walk that goes down to Mistletoe Bay, where there is camping and picnicking at one of the prettiest and most sheltered harbours in the sounds. Otherwise follow the main track directly down to Te Mahia saddle.

Views from Queen Charlotte Walkway (Portage to Te Mahia).

WAKAMARINA GOLD TRACK
Romantic miners' pack-track into the hills

TRACK
Vehicle road at first, then benched miners' pack-track. Some short hill climbs, but mostly easy walking.

WALK TIME AND DISTANCE
3–4 hours (12 km) Devils Creek Hut return.

ONE-HOUR WALK
Doom Creek Hut return.

ACCESS AND FACILITIES
The Wakamarina valley is 10 km west of Havelock off Highway 6, and it is 15 km to the road-end, past the Dead Horse Creek ford, and finishing at the

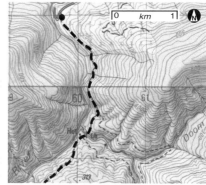

Detail: start of Wakamarina track

Butchers Flat carpark and the attractive and sheltered picnic area. Baby buggies can be taken as far as Doom Creek.

INFORMATION
Nelson 027, Wairau 028 maps

The ripe language and rich character of the goldminers is evident right from the picnic area here. Dead Horse Creek, Doom Creek, Devils Creek – those guys did not mince words. A glance at the map shows Muttontown Stream, Mountain Camp Creek and All Nations Creek, a reference to all the hopeful nationalities that crowded into the Wakamarina in the brief goldrush glory days of 1861. What they left behind were some colourful names and an excellent pack-track that climbs all the way to the top of the Richmond Range.

From the picnic area the route follows a good vehicle track some 2 km to the footbridge and hut at Doom Creek. This is a classic old Forest Service hut, with 6 bunks and an open fireplace.

A pleasant miners' pack-track now meanders upvalley, crossing from scrubby slopes into dappled beech forest, and after 4 km reaching Devils Creek Hut, which sits high above the river gorge on an attractive terrace. From here the main pack-track continues on a remorseless zigzag up to Fosters Ridge Hut, almost 1000 metres and several hours on.

However, from Devils Creek Hut you can explore the river gorge, which is off a side track to the footbridge, and there is also an interesting side-track that deviates to some historic stone huts. Allow 30 minutes return for the latter.

BLENHEIM TOWN WALK – WITHER HILLS
Pasture trails in a working farm park

TRACK
Grass paths in rolling terrain, some farm roads. Well signposted.
WALK TIME AND DISTANCE
1–1.5 hours (4 km) Rotary Lookout and Quail Stream circuit.
ACCESS AND FACILITIES
From Blenheim, off Taylors Pass Road, where there is a carpark.

Wither Hills Farm Park is right behind Blenheim, only a paddock or two from the new housing that is creeping out towards it. It is Blenheim's most popular exercise area for walkers, with several walk circuits and generous views of Blenheim and the Richmond Range mountains. A good burst of fresh air.

Walkers on Wither Hills, with Blenheim behind.

From the carpark it is 100 metres to a good information sign and mapboard of the area, and the Rotary Lookout track slowly climbs through a planted forest up to the striking lookout. This has seats, a water fountain and information panels.

The track continues along the ridge to the water tanks then drops down to Quail Stream, following this insig-nificant waterway through what remains of the exotic forest. A large grass fire on Boxing Day a few years ago devastated this area, and the blackened stumps of trees and burnt-out fence posts can be seen, and probably will be seen for many years to come. A replanting programme has already begun.

The walk finishes off by swinging around the base of the hill and through the blathering sheep paddocks back to the carpark.

WAIRAU LAGOON
Slow time and sweet tides

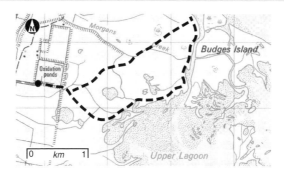

TRACK
Mostly firm-packed earth and sand, and nicely flat.

WALK TIME AND DISTANCE
3–4 hours (7–8 km) circuit. A low tide is useful but not essential. No water, except of the salty kind.

ONE-HOUR WALK
Budges Island return.

ACCESS AND FACILITIES
From Blenheim drive 2 km south on Highway 1 to Harding Road, then 1 km to the carpark and information sign (beside the oxidation ponds).

This is a luminous lagoon and estuary, permeated with understated textures. The glasswort is as intricate as Persian carpet, blending into dozens of subtle colours along the sinuous tidal waterways. Over 70 bird species have been recorded at Wairau, including nesting royal spoonbills. So much of the pleasure in this walk is in the morning or late evening light.

Shortly after leaving the carpark the track divides, and the right fork crosses side channels and wanders along the fringe of the estuary to opposite Budges Island. The charm of the Wairau is its elegant flatness, the absence of structures that block the view. So it is a surprise after an hour when you reach the beached wreck of the *Waverley*, 30 metres long and built in 1883. It was scuttled and later pushed by a flood up this side channel, where it provides a sculptural site for roosting shags.

A short side-trail leads to a view of the Wairau bar, and there are information boards that tell the story of the Maori moa-hunter culture that lived in camps around the lagoon. European settlement began on the Wairau bar in 1847, when an inn was built to cater for the coastal trading ships that had access up the Opawa River to 'Beavertown', the terrible name then given to Blenheim. Apparently the early settlement used to flood regularly.

The return trail cuts across the flat marsh meadows, and in late evening the colours in the sedge turn into a rich rug of reds and yellows.

SAWCUT GORGE
A peculiar alleyway of stone

TRACK

Quite a tough walk, with 15 or 16 river crossings one way and river boulders. Suits the well-equipped. A normal to low river flow is important.

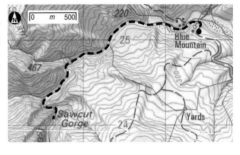

WALK TIME AND DISTANCE

3–4 hours (8 km) return.

ONE-HOUR WALK

Up to Waima Gorge.

ACCESS AND FACILITIES

From Highway 1 turn off to the Waima or Ure River, then it is 12 km of winding road to the Blue Mountain station. You have to continue a few metres past the homestead's front door (which seems odd and intrusive, but the occupiers do not seem to mind) then down a steep gravel driveway to a small parking area by the DoC sign on the river terrace. Please inform the landowners of your presence.

INFORMATION

Kaikoura Walks and Climbs, by Barry Dunnett, booklet; *Grassmere P29* map.

Sawcut Gorge is strange indeed, 50 metres long, 50 metres high and barely 3 metres across in some places. It looks as if a giant's circular saw simply ran through the limestone. The route up the Waima is short, but it has lots of river crossings, some of which are awkward. It would be dangerous to attempt to go to the Sawcut after rain, for this area floods rapidly in a brutal brown gush.

From the carpark follow the vehicle track down to the Waima River to a good and wide ford. DoC has now marked the route with large orange triangle markers and the route keeps to the shingly river, crossing several times past Blue Mountain Stream.

Gradually the river is squeezed between steep walls, and the route keeps remorselessly crisscrossing through the wonderful rock strata. Soon the huge limestone face of the Waima gorge looms over the river, and a well-marked track twists in and out of scrub forest and big boulders past Headache Stream.

The top river crossing is awkward, but after that a good track continues on the south bank past some splendid totara trees to Isolation Creek. Around a few bends in Isolation Creek and the Sawcut appears, a thin slit in the band of rock, the opposite walls almost close enough to be touched by outstretched arms. The creek bed is shingle and it is easy to walk up the length of the gorge.

Note: At the other end of the Sawcut, Isolation Creek continues to wind narrowly and impressively (with some waterfalls) between high cliffs for just over 1 km to the top forks and a wide shingle flat, and there is a 6-bunk hut. Add another 2 hours return for this extra section.

KAIKOURA PENINSULA
Wildlife walk around a peninsula

TRACK
Beach walking and some tidal platforms, with farmland tracks on the return. Generally good underfoot, but a low tide is essential to enjoy this walk.

WALK TIME AND DISTANCE
3–4 hours (5 km) return Shoreline and Clifftop walk circuit. If using the Whalers Bay track 3 hours. The Shoreline Walk is a low-tide route only.

ONE-HOUR WALK
Coastal route to Whalers Bay and return.

Kaikoura Peninsula

ACCESS AND FACILITIES
From Kaikoura township drive past the information centre to Point Kean carpark at the end of the coastal road, where there are information boards, a shelter and barbecue sites. There are toilets 1 km before the carpark. Access can also be gained on the other side of the peninsula, down South Bay Parade to the carpark and recreation area.

INFORMATION
Kaikoura Peninsula Walkway, Department of Conservation pamphlet.

A feature of this walk is that the wildlife is visible, and unavoidable, and at low tide you have to take care not to step on a sleeping seal — they do not like it. There are over 12,000 red-billed gulls (tarapunga) nesting around the peninsula and they can get pesky in spring, with raids on intruders. Shags congregate on offshore rocks, and there are extensive roosting colonies of white-fronted terns. When you include the remarkable tidal platforms and the dazzling white cliffs, it is little wonder the Kaikoura Peninsula walk is a must-do for many travellers.

At Point Kean seals can be sleeping only 30 metres away from the carpark, and at low tide you can wander around the base of the cliffs, exploring small bays and peninsulas on the way to Whalers Bay. There is a shortcut track up onto the clifftop track, but at low tide you can keep following the dramatic shoreline almost to the finger-like Atia Point.

The track crosses the narrow peninsula and follows more extensive tidal platforms (with 'tramlines' running across them) back to South Bay. Here a farm track climbs up onto the clifftop and follows the cliff edges back to the carpark at Point Kean. Welcome views, and a walk that never tires.

MOUNT FYFFE HUT
A 'little' hill looking onto big mountains

TRACK
A good vehicle track made in the 1970s to the hut, and a tussock ridge to the summit. Take plenty of water.

WALK TIME AND DISTANCE
4–5 hours (9 km) to hut return; 6–7 hours (15 km) to Mount Fyffe return. Total climb to hut 1000 metres.

ONE-HOUR WALK
Up to first 'saddle' return.

ACCESS AND FACILITIES
From Kaikoura township take Ludstone Road 8 km to the junction with Postmans Road, then follow Postmans Road 6 km to the carpark, picnic area and toilets.

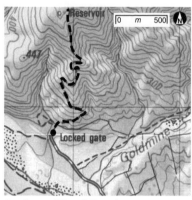

Detail: start of Mount Fyffe track

INFORMATION
Kaikoura Walks and Climbs, by Barry Dunnett, booklet; *Kaikoura O31* map.

This is a big sweat of 1000 metres to a hut perched on the summit ridge of Mount Fyffe. The slog is hard but the rewards are majestic views. Up here the Kaikoura Peninsula looks squashed and small, but the Kaikoura mountains are massive, especially when covered with snow. With an early start and a packed lunch this walk is not as daunting as it seems, and the well-graded road provides an even walking surface.

The walk description is easy. Walk up the road, and keep going until you give up, or get up. It is about an 800-metre climb to Sandy Saddle following the zigzagging road. There is some scrub and forest lower down, but once you gain altitude you are in tussocks and scree slopes.

From Sandy Saddle it is a steady 300-metre climb to the hut, and it does not get any flatter until just before the hut itself, which is a little oasis after the slog uphill.

It has 8 bunks and a woodstove, and there is an old tarn beside it that is usually dried up, but has attractive native herbs fringing it. The view is spellbinding.

For summiters, the vehicle track continues up the barren slopes and rises another 500 metres onto the large beacon on top of Mount Fyffe itself. The views are not measurably better than from the hut, but you are standing at 1602 metres, a long way above the world.

Hot day, snowy mountains, on the way to Mount Fyffe Hut.

HAUMURI BLUFF
Secret coast and sea arch

TRACK
A flat vehicle road, then beach and boulder walking. A low tide is essential.

WALK TIME AND DISTANCE
5–6 hours (10 km) return.

ONE-HOUR WALK
Mikonui Stream return.

ACCESS AND FACILITIES
From Highway 1 at Oaro, turn off on the south bank of the Oaro River and drive through the small

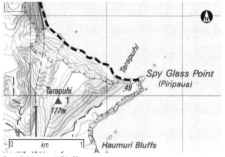

Detail: Haumuri Bluff

settlement. There is some limited carparking here. You can also drive over the railway line (there are no signals) to a locked gate and limited carparking area beside the coast. Baby buggies can be taken along the road to the railway tunnel.

INFORMATION
Kaikoura Walks and Climbs, by Barry Dunnett, booklet.

The sea arch at Haumuri Point is a brilliant white outcrop of fretted limestone. It is not a difficult walk to get there, but you need a low tide at Haumuri bluff and good balance, as there is plenty of rock-hopping involved. Haumuri probably means 'wind at your back', a reference dating from when the Maori used to regularly canoe around this promontory.

It is easy walking along the access road beside the railway line (good mountain-biking too), and past some derelict rolling stock that helps form a melodramatic sea wall. There is a disused railway tunnel on the right-hand side, mostly blocked up, and further along the bays there are stands of karaka trees that were probably planted by Maori as a food source.

Many of the shallow bays have attractive areas for pausing or picnicking, and interesting tidal platforms to explore. At the Haumuri railway tunnel (about 4 km from Oaro) a steep track goes down to the beach, and from here on it is rock-hopping along to the bluff. Seals often come ashore here for a midday doze because they mostly feed at night, and even elephant seals have been seen.

The archway was called Te Pupaki, the crab hole, and it is a wild place, with extensive offshore reef platforms. You can climb above the archway onto the bluff itself, and enjoy a panoramic view of this most excellent coast.

On top of Haumuri Bluff.

153

LAKE ROTOITI
The magic of the dawn chorus

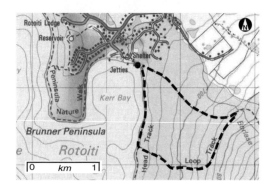

TRACK
Well-graded bush tracks with information panels on the way.

WALK TIME AND DISTANCE
Honeydew Walk circuit 1 hour (3 km); Loop Track 1 hour 30 minutes (5km); St Arnaud Range and Pinnacle Lookout (hill climb) 3–4 hours return.

ACCESS AND FACILITIES
From Highway 63 at St Arnaud, drive to Kerrs Bay picnic and camping area; shelter and toilets.

INFORMATION
St Arnaud Short Walks, Department of Conservation pamphlet.

DoC has made a commitment in selected places to recreate the dawn chorus, and at St Arnaud they are getting close. Intense predator control on this 'mainland island' has created a wall of sound from bellbirds, robins and kaka. This natural music of the forest has not been heard for a long time on the mainland.

You have several walk choices. The negligible Bellbird Walk is just 10 minutes round – fall over a few times and you have done it. The Honeydew Walk is longer, and named after the sweet, almost sickly scent of the honeydew excreted by a scale insect. The bellbirds love this stuff, and they are loud and melodious in appreciation. This walk has excellent interpretation signs all round to explain what DoC is trying to do, and the beech forest is smothered with a carpet of lush moss.

Then there is the longer Loop Track – about 1 hour 30 minutes – and for a big hill climb try the track up onto the St Arnaud Range and Pinnacle Lookout, 3–4 hours return. Whichever track you choose will go through the heart of the predator-controlled beech forest. Do not touch the traps or bait stations unless you are a rat.

BUSHLINE HUT
A healthy hill circuit to an alpine hut

TRACK
Bush tracks and tussock trail on this steep hill walk. Well-marked tracks with snowpoles on the tops, but most of the route is exposed, so you need good weather. Take water.

WALK TIME AND DISTANCE
4–5 hours (5 km) return, total climb 500 metres.

ONE-HOUR WALK
Up the Pinchgut Trail for 30 minutes or so. Excellent views.

ACCESS AND FACILITIES
From Highway 63, 2 km west of St Arnaud, take the West Bay road for 5 km to the Mount Robert carpark and shelter, at the end of a steep zigzag.

This is a walk to remember, and although the steep scree faces of Mount Robert might put you off, the total climb is only 500 metres and the rewards are well worth it – definitely the best views over Lake Rotoiti, as well as a fine outlook along the Angelus Ridge. Bushline Hut, as its name suggests, sits on sunny slopes beside the bush edge in a particularly privileged position.

The beginning of the tramp is horribly steep. The Pinchgut Trail switches back and forth for 500 metres up through a burnt-off scrub face and some remaining beech forest to reach a small box shelter sitting right on the bush edge. The views are superb, and you have done most of the climbing.

It is only a short distance from the shelter to the flat summit and the Relax Shelter Hut (seats only) then on to the track junction to Bushline Hut. A downhill stretch now, past tall snowpoles on a wide, easy ridge, swinging past the private Kea Hut down to the 12-bunk Bushline Hut. Hard to find a better view to have lunch over.

The track that continues down from the hut is known as Paddys Track, and it snakes lazily through open tussock faces for 300 metres before easing into manuka forest and slipping into Robert Stream. There are fine lake views then the track sidles under Mount Robert, slowly making its way to the access road, 100 metres below the carpark.

The zigzag track overlooking Lake Rotoiti, on the Bushline Hut walk.

MURRAY CREEK GOLDFIELD
The gold gone and the tracks silent

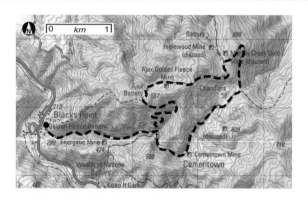

TRACK
Well-graded miners' tracks on the Murray Creek and Royal Track circuit. Some hill climbing.

WALK TIME AND DISTANCE
4–5 hours (9 km) Murray Creek main track and return on Royal Track. The Royal Track is not as well marked and can get overgrown. For experienced walkers only.

ONE–HOUR WALK
Energetic Mine junction return.

ACCESS AND FACILITIES
From Highway 7 at Blacks Point, 1 km from Reefton. There is a museum by the carpark.

INFORMATION
Walks in Murray Creek Goldfield, New Zealand Forest Service pamphlet.

Red beech leaves fall and scatter gold colour on tracks that are a hundred years old, worn smooth by the plodding footsteps of the goldminers. The mining relics are crumbling away and might not impress, but the deep forest and tea-coloured streams take you into a long-lost world. It is hard to believe that these silent forests were once an important and noisy industrial landscape.

The main Murray Track follows a broad pack-track through luxuriant moss and beech forest, passing the junction to the Energetic Mine and the bridges at Cementown. Not much here now, though gold was mined in the Murray Creek from 1870 to the 1930s.

Not long after this, the main track goes into a broad area of manuka forest at Chandlers Open Coast Coal Mine, then reaches the Waitahu Track junction at a saddle. Keep to the main track as it climbs steadily to the Inglewood junction, then it is only a short side-track past the Painkiller Track junction to the iron remnants of the Inglewood Mine.

Now take the Royal Track, which climbs up to another saddle and the remains of the horse whims. These are circular raised embankments where the poor horses walked round and round pulling coal carts.

Quite quickly afterwards there is the Ajax Mine, a chilling 1700 metres deep (think about that — a mile deep, dug by hand!), then the Ajax Battery, which is the most attractive of the gold ruins. The track is not so good after this, and climbs up a furtive mossy gully to another of these strange little saddles. Then it is a long, steady descent almost 300 metres back to the main Murray Creek track.

The remnants of a goldfield, Murray Creek.

LAKE DANIELLS
An easy bush stroll to a lake

TRACK
Mostly flat bush track with a slow and subtle climb.

WALK TIME AND DISTANCE
3–4 hours (12 km) return.

ONE-HOUR WALK
Pell Stream seat.

ACCESS AND FACILITIES
From Highway 7 the Lake Daniells turn-off is 5 km east of Springs Junction at the Marble Hill picnic area. Camping area and toilets.

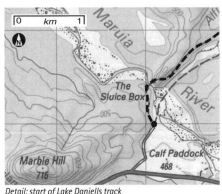

Detail: start of Lake Daniells track

This is a well-made path through dense beech forest to the lapping shores of the lake — a track anyone can tackle, with plentiful native birdsong and a crisp-cut gorge through the Sluice Box.

From the carpark, the track turns a corner and reaches the footbridge over the well-named Sluice Box, where the Maruia River cuts through hard granite with a rush and flurry. Then the track sidles through groves of red beech, occasionally crossing matagouri river flats before reaching the Pell Stream confluence, where there is a seat.

The track starts to climb gently, and slips from the Alfred River valley into the attractive Frazer Stream, which drains Lake Daniells itself. The red beech changes to silver beech and the stream twists through moss banks, almost silent.

The lake is a surprise — a large, sequestered body of water, tucked under bush hills with a short jetty pointing out into it. Often you can hear kaka, with their creaky-door call, flapping wildly from one side of the lake to the other. A hut provides a good lunch shelter and the return walk is gentle.

Lichen, Lake Daniells.

LEWIS PASS TOPS
An accessible track to tarn-studded tops

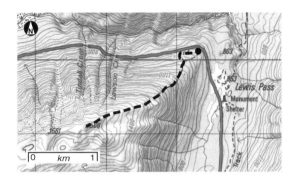

TRACK
A beech forest tramping trail up a short, sharp hill. On the tops there is a worn trail and pole markers to the first high point, but beyond that you need a map, compass and a good day.

WALK TIME AND DISTANCE
3–4 hours (5 km) return.

30-MINUTE WALK
Lookout track circuit.

ACCESS AND FACILITIES
Off Highway 7, literally on Lewis Pass itself. The carpark and track are easy to miss and is accessed off a short, steep, rutted road. There is better carparking about 200 metres down the highway on the Canterbury side.

INFORMATION
Lewis M31 map.

Short on distance but high on height, this is a fast track to the alpine tops of the Lewis Pass. The views are splendid, and in season there are carpets of alpine flowers such as celmisias and gentians.

The track does not muck about, climbing quickly through open, rocky country to a seat and junction with the lookout track. Then it is a steady 300-metre climb through old gnarled silver beech then mountain beech to the

A snowpole marker, looking towards Cannibal Gorge on the Lewis Pass tops.

159

clean-cut bush edge. Only now does the track take a breath, and a worn trail climbs up through the open tussocklands, with a steady 200 metres to the first obvious unnamed peak, which I have named 'Panorama Peak'.

The views are good, and the double-peaked Mount Gloriana up Cannibal Gorge looks as a mountain should look. Beyond that is Faerie Queene, and all around are the rolling, graceful tops of the Lewis Pass. Further on there is a sprinkling of tarns, and anywhere along this ridge you can have lunch straddling the main divide itself — one foot on the West Coast, the other in Canterbury.

Cloud clearing from the wide valley of the Hope River (see facing page).

HOPE RIVER
Classic Southern Alps valley walk

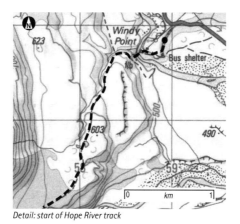

Detail: start of Hope River track

TRACK
A rolling track with one hill climb over tussock slopes, then through beech forest. Well marked.

WALK TIME AND DISTANCE
4–5 hours (18 km) return.

ACCESS AND FACILITIES
From the Lewis Pass, Highway 7, turn off to the Hope River/Windy Point carpark and shelter. There is an information board here, and a logbook further along the track.

The Southern Alps are the grandest feature in the South Island, stretching from Nelson Lakes to Fiordland, and this walk up the Hope River is typical of the scale of the scenery. The valley is wide, with beech forest cloaking the sides of mountains well over 1500 metres high, particularly majestic with snow on them. On the way there's a wee gorge, and a soft carpet of moss under the bush canopy – plenty of space and plenty of solitude.

From the shelter follow a short vehicle track past the huts at Windy Point, then down and over a long footbridge suspended across the gorge of the Boyle River. After that the track climbs steadily, some 150 metres up over farmland terraces to the bush edge. Good views downvalley.

You are now meandering along in fine, dense beech forest for most of the way to Halfway Hut, staying about 100 metres above the river on a flat bush terrace. Every now and then you get superb views from grassy clearings of the Hope River and the mountains beyond.

The 6-bunk hut stands at the far side of a major matagouri clearing. It is a logical place for lunch – sunny and sheltered – and about 30 metres away there is a dribbling thermal spring, which is disappointing if you are in search of a hot bath. That will have to wait until you get home.

Canterbury

HANMER SPRINGS
Woodland walks

TRACK
Well-formed trails in gentle rolling country. Note that forestry operations can close tracks at any time of the year.

WALK TIME AND DISTANCE
2–3 hours (5 km) return Woodland and Dog Stream Walk.

ONE-HOUR WALK
Woodland Walk circuit.

ACCESS AND FACILITIES
Hanmer Springs is off Highway 7, 130 km from Christchurch. The Hurunui Information Centre is right beside the Hanmer hot pools, with detailed information boards and pamphlets. There is an extensive network of mountain-bike trails in the Hanmer Forest, some utilising existing walking tracks.

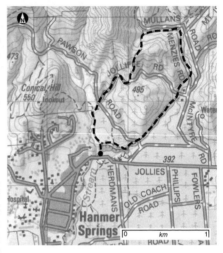

INFORMATION
Hanmer Forest Recreation, Department of Conservation pamphlet.

'Forest' in Hanmer means either native beech or pine plantations; the two types mix together with sometimes incongruous and sometimes lovely results. This forest is a strange beast, commercially operated yet at the same time available for recreation. The Hanmer Springs community is trying to establish the forest as a permanent public park.

This walk is a reasonably flat circuit from the Woodland Ponds with a return down the Dog Stream track, but there are many permutations and you should be able to design a circuit to suit yourself.

From Jollies Pass Road beside Dog Stream there is a good track up steps and past a small, pretty waterfall to the two ponds and flax wetland. This is a tranquil enclave. Head north along the Woodland Walk, pass the Majuba Track junction and follow the Timberlands Trail. This starts in redwood forest and links with the Joliffe Saddle Track.

The track wanders over a low manuka saddle and provides a cross-country link to the Dog Stream track near Mullans Road. A good track wanders through beech forest alongside Dog Stream, and this can be followed all the way back to the Woodland Walk. There are numerous track junctions (and track options) but stick close to the stream and you will be okay.

OTHER WALKS
Dog Stream Waterfall and Spur Track circuit, Chatterton River Track and ascent of Mount Isobel.

MOUNT THOMAS
Beech forest and alpine views

TRACK
Good bush tracks in a steady climb to the ridge, where there is a flattish trail through the tussocks to the summit. Keep alert for track junctions.

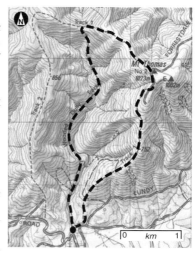

WALK TIME AND DISTANCE
4–6 hours (7–8 km) return to Mount Thomas summit.

ONE-HOUR WALK
Wooded Gully and Loop 2 circuit.

ACCESS AND FACILITIES
For Mount Thomas drive north from Rangiora across the Ashley River, then take the road to Lowburn and Glentui until you reach Hayland Road (just before the Garry River). It is well signposted. At the road-end is a well-sheltered and exceedingly pleasant picnic and camping area, with extensive grass terraces on several levels. Toilets, picnic tables and information board.

Mount Thomas is excellent day-trip country, and the peak has a fine view over the plains. There are various ways up the mountain but the Wooded Gully is the most attractive. It is well graded, with plenty of drinking water from the side-streams, but it is a deceptively long and convoluted track as it sidles up the valley, with some ups and downs as it crosses side-creeks.

If you can drag yourself away from the charming picnic area, follow the Wooded Gully track over the footbridge, and pass both intersections with the Loop 1 track. Slightly further is the junction with the Loop 2 circuit, which is a good option for 1-hour walkers. The Loop 2 track drops down to the stream at a nice bush picnic site.

The main track starts to climb slowly, passes the junction with Red Pine Track, then drops down to the stream. It climbs a bit, crosses another side-stream and settles into a steady long zigzag up the bush face to the ridgeline.

From this saddle you can amble along through mountain beech onto the tussock grasslands and alpine herbfields to the Mount Thomas beacon. The view is excellent: the Port Hills, the Kaikouras and the Puketeraki Range. Track 1 is the fast, slalom way down.

OTHER WALKS
Options to the summit of Mount Thomas include Track 1 or Track 2 up different spurs, and there are several shorter track options including Red Pine Track.

CASTLE HILL
Sculptured shapes in the high country

TRACK
Worn grass paths. Take care as you explore, for sudden drops can appear from nowhere. The area is also popular with rock climbers. Baby buggies can be taken on the first part to the cliffs.

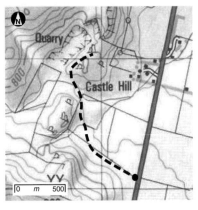

WALK TIME AND DISTANCE
1–2 hours wandering, 2–3 km. Carry your own water.

ACCESS AND FACILITIES
Castle Hill is easily visible from Highway 73 between Christchurch and Arthur's Pass, and access is via the 'kissing gate' and signboard before Castle Hill Station. You park any old how on the grass verge, and be warned: the cars on the highway are travelling fast.

INFORMATION
Kura Tawhiti: treasure from afar, Department of Conservation pamphlet.

The setting of Castle Hill is superb. It is surrounded by an arc of high country mountains, tipped with old snow, where cirrus cloud swishes across the brilliant blue sky and invariably heralds the famous hot Canterbury nor'wester. Several generations of travellers have been attracted to the limestone formations of Castle Hill; the Maori found seasonal shelter here, and left charred moa bones and rock drawings. Quite a bit of quarrying went on too (fortunately not marring the main outcrop) and a little of the limestone found its way into Christchurch Cathedral.

From the gate follow the worn trail past the matagouri scrub to the base of the cliffs. The size of the stones is deceptive from the road and it is only when you walk among them that their true scale emerges.

You can scramble in any direction, with stones looming up in animal-like groups, or standing alone and vaguely resembling huge mushrooms. By skirting the lime quarry and the fenced reserve you can climb up 150 metres onto Castle Hill itself. A prominent clump of pinnacles stands on top, the tallest of which are 10 to 12 metres high.

Nearly all the rock shapes have an uncanny resemblance to something else: sheep, camels, Easter Island statues, whatever the imagination suggests. Among the rock labyrinth is an ephemeral tarn, an archway, several holes and curious canyons — eerie, silent and evocative.

OTHER WALKS
Cave Stream, a short underground tunnel of 360 metres, is signposted 15 minutes further along the highway from Castle Hill. You need torches and one experienced person for the cave, but the entrance and exit are easy to visit.

LAGOON SADDLE
Gold tussocks and gracious wetland

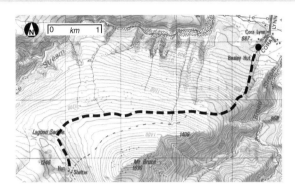

TRACK
A well-marked and steady hill climb through beech forest and onto a tussock bench.

WALK TIME AND DISTANCE
4–5 hours (10 km) return.

ONE-HOUR WALK
To bushline return.

ACCESS AND FACILITIES
Off Highway 73, between Christchurch and Arthur's Pass; turn at the Cora Lynn Wilderness Lodge sign and follow the road to a carpark. The last piece of road to the hut is too steep for most cars.

There is a well-known oil painting by Jim Sutton called *Bruce Stream*, a bare, hot picture of a dry river and a peeling bridge in a nor'wester. After 40 years nothing has changed. The bridge is still there, and the hot, dry land is stark and familiar, yet this walk reveals some of the subtlety and beauty in these mountains. It climbs up through beech forest and across a tussock downland to a perfect wetland, almost a picture in itself.

There is a classic old 6-bunker Forest Service hut at the Cora Lynn road-end, and from the hut a good track climbs up through beech forest and straggly pine trees about 300 metres to the open tussock slopes below Mount Bruce.

The poled route now sidles along a tussock bench, then steers past Lagoon Saddle and eases down through the bush to the A-frame lunch shelter. This track continues as part of the Cass–Lagoon track.

However, it is worth the detour up onto Mount Bruce, an insignificant bump at 1630 metres, but what a view: from the gorge of the Bruce Stream, to the graceful greys of the Waimakariri River and on to the mountains of Arthur's Pass. R.W. Bruce was one of the early owners of Cora Lynn.

It does not take long to get down to Lagoon Saddle itself, a parkland intermixture of tarns, cushion plants, mosses, beech groves and alpine grasses. This is a very fragile area, so please walk lightly.

AVALANCHE PEAK
A rocky, rewarding peak

TRACK
A well-marked tramping track through beech forest, then a poled route over the tops.

It is recommended that you check the weather forecast at the Arthur's Pass Visitor Centre, and log in your intentions. There is a long history of accidents in this area, particularly with inexperienced walkers.

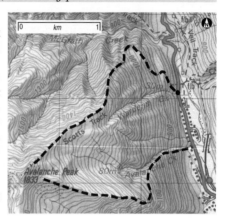

WALK TIME AND DISTANCE
5–6 hours (6 km) return to summit; total climb 1100 metres.

TWO- TO THREE-HOUR WALK
Bush edge return.

ACCESS AND FACILITIES
Arthur's Pass is on Highway 73, 155 km from Christchurch. There are two cafes, a store, petrol, toilets and a public shelter, and the National Park Visitor Centre. The easier track to Avalanche Peak starts 500 metres north of the visitor centre.

It is a tough day-tramp to the summit of this peak, but many people get immense satisfaction from just reaching the bushline or the top basin. There are alpine flowers in late spring, and sensational views. You do need clear weather, as cloud will ruin the views and there is some route-finding higher up.

There are two track options, but most people start up the gentler track north of the village and come down the steep track that exits by the visitor centre.

It is a steady climb leading up a rough and ready track through beech forest and mountain scrub, almost 500 metres to the alpine tussocks, with good views along the way. The track does get a little easier, but still follows the strong spur some 400 metres to the summit, although it is well poled and cairned on the way up. Mount Rolleston looks awesome, and you can also peer into the narrow Crow Valley.

The alternative spur down is basically due east of the summit, and again cairned and poled. It is relatively easy travel down to the bush edge, then the track does a steep descent beside a dizzying sequence of waterfalls before reaching the visitor centre and carpark.

OTHER WALKS
There are good walks in the Bealey Valley, to the Punchbowl Falls, the Dobson Nature Walk, Otira Valley and Temple Basin Skifield Walk.

WAIKARI ROCK DRAWINGS
Dry land and fine drawings

TRACK
Old flat railway line, then worn grass foot and sheep trails over rolling farmland.

WALK TIME AND DISTANCE
2 hours (3 km) return.

ONE-HOUR WALK
Along the railway and up the fenceline to the hilltop.

ACCESS AND FACILITIES
From Highway 2 at Waikari township, either beside the Yorkshire Teapot tearooms or down the Hawarden road 1 km to the signpost.

INFORMATION
Maori Rock Art, by Paul Thompson, book.

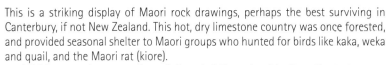

This is a striking display of Maori rock drawings, perhaps the best surviving in Canterbury, if not New Zealand. This hot, dry limestone country was once forested, and provided seasonal shelter to Maori groups who hunted for birds like kaka, weka and quail, and the Maori rat (kiore).

Whichever end you start the walk from, it follows the old railway line 200 metres to a signposted stile. The track then follows the grasslands beside the fenceline, climbing some 150 metres, with a good hilltop viewpoint over the limestone outcrops.

Continue down the fenceline into the limestone valley, part of the Timpendean farm, which is private property.

A sign turns you right and it is a few minutes to the obvious rock overhang and the Maori drawings. Wire netting keeps out sticky fingers. Some of the drawings have been touched up with house paint, and there is a confusing array of overlaying shapes, figures and drawings that are believed to be around 600 years old.

What are the drawings for? Doodles? Religious icons? A guidebook for hunters? Graffiti? Marking property or territorial rights? Art? The comic strips of their time? Whatever the artists' intentions, the drawings are enthralling.

The Punchbowl Falls from the Avalanche Peak track (see facing page).

TIMARU CITY WALK – SALTWATER CREEK
Coastal lagoon and a view of Mount Cook

TRACK
A real mix of beach travel, sandy 4WD and stopbanks. Baby buggies are okay along the stopbanks but some of the sand trails might be awkward.

WALK TIME AND DISTANCE
1–2 hours (6 km) return.

ACCESS AND FACILITIES
From Highway 1 in Timaru take High Street then South Street to a large carpark beside the Caledonian Grounds.

INFORMATION
Timaru Walkways, Timaru District Council pamphlet.

Leftover land makes good walkways. No one wants the land anyway, and every city has some: the sides of railway lines, bush gullies, mangrove swamps, industrial land, flood plains and stopbanks, and that favourite scorned area, estuaries. Well, the wheel has come full circle, and these little pieces of land are now valued for recreation, and councils up and down the country have been creating urban walkways out of the most unpromising material.

At Timaru the council has managed to turn a neglected creek, a forlorn beach, and the scrags of perimeter land around a rubbish dump into a fine walkway. On the weekday morning that I visited, the Saltwater Walkway was busy with joggers, walkers and people exercising their dogs. It seems to me that if you provide good facilities, people will use them.

From the carpark cross the outlet, assuming it is sanded up, and follow the poles through the scruffy scrub country on the beach. Alternatively you can walk along the beach. After a while the track reaches a massive footbridge, and as you follow the stopbank upriver you wander along the lagoon. You may see Mount Cook on a fine day.

After you reach Highway 1 you can return via the stopbank beside the rubbish dump (you cannot see it, I promise) then follow trails into Redruth Park and over the railway line back to the carpark. There is also the option to walk along South Beach to the lighthouse.

OTHER WALKS
Dashing Rocks, Centennial Park, Patiti Point and beach.

LITTLE MOUNT PEEL
Bush and alpine spur up to a Canterbury summit

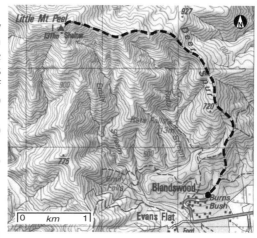

TRACK

A well-marked and steady climb through bush, with boardwalks across the tussock. Little Mount Peel is exposed and gets plenty of snow in winter. A day-tramp rather than a walk.

WALK TIME AND DISTANCE

5–7 hours (6 km) return to Little Mount Peel.

TWO–HOUR WALK

Tarn return.

ACCESS AND FACILITIES

Turn off Highway 72 and travel 12 km past the Peel Forest Visitor Centre to Blandswood Road, and follow this some 2 km as it climbs steeply to a small carpark. Peel Forest store and tearooms have all supplies.

INFORMATION

Peel Forest Park, Department of Conservation pamphlet.

There is not much left of any native forest in South Canterbury, and most of it is in Peel Forest. Some massive totara live on the fertile flat below Little Mount Peel, and this walk climbs up through the bush to a high alpine peak, with an eye-opening view of the patchwork plains.

From the Blandswood carpark take the Deer Spur track, which passes the junction with the Fern Walk and climbs steadily up through a mixed forest of fuchsia, broadleaf, lemonwood (tarata) and mahoe, with a glossy carpet of ferns.

There are occasional views of the plains as the track passes the junction with Allan's Track, and some southern rata trees (look out for the crimson flowers at Christmas time). The track then enters the upper alpine shrub belt, which consists of turpentine, flax and dracophyllums.

A tarn on the way up Little Mount Peel.

The tarn, which is at an altitude of 900 metres, might be something of a disappointment if it has not rained for a while, leaving little more than a sodden bogland. However, there are some splendid specimens of spaniard with razor-sharp flowering stalks, often reaching over a metre in height.

The track winds up the spur onto the tussock, with extensive boardwalks higher up. The last 150 metres is a steeper, muddier climb to the small, sharp top of Little Mount Peel. There is a beacon on top and a wee shelter 20 metres below (enclosed, with seats and water).

OTHER WALKS

There are various other walks in Peel Forest including Acland Falls (1 hour return), Dennistoun Bush Walk (1.5 hours circuit), Fern Walk (1.5 hours one way) and Kahikatea Walk (1 hour circuit).

The beach at Saltwater Creek (see page 168).

Boardwalk over the wetland of Travis Swamp (see facing page).

Christchurch

CHRISTCHURCH CITY WALK – TRAVIS SWAMP
Superb suburban wetland

TRACK
Good gravelled tracks or boardwalks. Baby buggies are fine on the sealed paths.

WALK TIME AND DISTANCE
2 hours (8 km) return for walk from Angela's Stream to Anne Flanagans Track. In time a perimeter track will be linked right around the Travis wetland, taking 1–2 hours; the aim is for it to be completed in 2003–04.

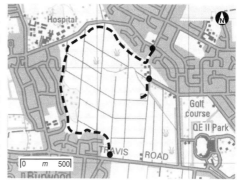

ONE-HOUR WALK
Angela's Stream return.

ACCESS AND FACILITIES
Angela's Stream is off Travis Road, with carparking on the broad grass verge. Access for Anne Flanagan is from the carpark in Mairehau Road.

INFORMATION
An information kiosk along Beach Road, off Mairehau Road, seems to float in its own pond. It has interpretation panels as well as a short walk to a bird lookout platform. In time this will be part of the perimeter walking track.

My, how things change! At one time everyone wanted to drain Travis Swamp, and no one wanted to live next to it. Now the Christchurch City Council has been busy sculpting ponds and waterways, and people are scrambling to pay expensive prices for a house with a view of this local treasure, where over 60 different bird species have been recorded, and more pukeko than you could throw a stick at.

There is good carparking off busy Travis Road and the sealed pathway wanders alongside Angela's Stream, busy with waterfowl. Large, posh homes from the Travis County subdivision come close to the track but do not overwhelm it, and it is a peaceful walk along to Clarevale Reserve. The track follows a boardwalk to a bird-watching viewing platform, and then continues on boardwalks through to open grass swales with good views. Now the Anne Flanagan Track, it passes a seat lookout (and carpark off Mairehau Road) before swinging round the northeast corner of Travis wetland to an accessway that leads to the Inwoods Road/Mairehau Road junction. You have to return the same way, or walk Mairehau/Frosts/Travis roads around to Angela's Stream. By the time you read this, however, the council may well have joined up all the gaps – and it will make a superb wetland for both wildlife and walkers.

CHRISTCHURCH CITY WALK – BEXLEY SALTMARSH
Salty circumference around an estuary

TRACK
Gravel paths, stopbanks and grass verges on this flat walk. Pretty good for baby buggies, though some of the cycle barriers can be a nuisance.

WALK TIME AND DISTANCE
1–2 hours (6 km) return.

ONE-HOUR WALK
To Owles Terrace return.

ACCESS AND FACILITIES
The Kibblewhite Street carpark can be accessed off Estuary Road then down the no-exit Kibblewhite Street. Seats.

This is a graceful circuit of the lower Avon River estuary as it winds past the suburbs of Bexley and New Brighton. Shags commonly roost along the shingle banks, and the mudflats are busy with white-faced herons and pied stilts, and in winter perhaps spoonbills and white herons, which is all the more surprising since the whole saltmarsh is ringed by frantic roads.

Walk upstream on the stopbank, past the embankment seats and along the pale red saltmarsh. The Avon is broad here and includes the elongated Naughty Boys Island, its curious name derived from two boys who were killed in a sand tunnel they were digging in 1962. In Kibblewhite Street you can see a two-storey red-tiled house, which was built in 1906 by Professor Bickerton as a seaside house with a gazebo. Bickerton was a colourful and appropriately salty professor at Canterbury College, who taught the young Ernest Rutherford.

The track skirts through pine trees and wanders past a fishing platform on the way to Owles Terrace and the Pages Road bridge. Across the bridge, walkers can follow the riverside downstream on easy paths to Bexley Reserve. Ponds have been artificially made and there is a fine seat lookout, with a compass set in stone on the ground; a contemplative place.

Now go south. The track follows the stopbank as it runs between the saltmarsh and rural fields, and reaches Bexley Road. Keep to the grass sward alongside the busy road to Bridge Street and cross the bridge back to Kibblewhite Reserve.

Wetland ponds of the Bexley saltmarsh, with a view of the Port Hills.

CHRISTCHURCH CITY WALK –
SCARBOROUGH HEAD
TO TAYLORS MISTAKE
A breathtaking place

TRACK
Narrow headland trail with some up and down. Can get slippery and muddy after rain.

WALK TIME AND DISTANCE
2 hours (4 km) return.

ONE-HOUR WALK
Scarborough and Nicholson Park circuit.

ACCESS AND FACILITIES
Drive up Scarborough Road to the carpark beside Nicholson Park. Picnic area and toilets.

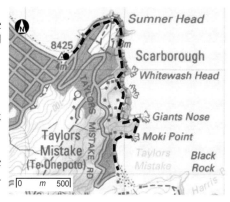

A short, powerful walk. Modern homes perch on top of the lava cliffs, no less improbably than the garrulous colonies of little spotted shags. Seagulls wheel and spiral in an aerial ballet, and the sea surges against the severe cliffs. At Taylors Mistake there are a dozen baches huddled in unlikely positions just above the tide line, a world away from the penthouse palaces 100 metres above them.

From Nicholson Park cross the road and take the broad berm down to the sudden cliffside. The left track goes to Sumner via steps and Whitewash Head Road, but the right track heads to Taylors Mistake.

The track drops quite quickly down steps and sidles in and out of various gullies and short spurs. The views of the cliffs are dizzying, and you can see the guano-splattered ledges where the spotted shags roost. In places the track drops quite close to the sea, and there are one or two unofficial side 'tracks' to the shore itself, but be careful.

The track climbs around the snub peninsula known as the Giant's Nose, and swings around to Hobson Bay. Here are deviously ingenious baches, slotted picturesquely in cliff corners, and some seem isolated at high tide. You can either follow the high-tide track, which sidles through the baches, or at low tide drop down to the beach. It is an easy walk along the sand and rocks at Hobson Bay to the main Taylors Mistake beach.

You can return up Taylors Mistake Road, but it is narrow, with no footpath. Much better to return on the same track — once you have caught your breath.

OTHER WALKS
Scarborough Head and Nicholson Park circuit, and Godley Head circuit.

HALSWELL QUARRY
Historic quarry track and sculptural surprises

TRACK
Gravel paths and mown grass strips, some short hill climbing. The flat tracks are reasonable for baby buggies.

WALK TIME AND DISTANCE
1 hour circuit (Rim Track), 1 hour return (Farm Track); both 2 km return.

ACCESS AND FACILITIES
Drive to Halswell and the Akaroa–Sparks Road junction then take Kennedys Bush Road to the signposted turn-off; 10 km from Christchurch city. Extensive picnic areas, walking tracks, sculptures, toilets and information centre.

INFORMATION
Halswell Quarry Christchurch, Christchurch City Council pamphlet.

This fine park has been formed out of an old council-run quarry and is a unique combination of botanical gardens and historic quarry buildings; a quiet, involving landscape, with plenty of discoveries and surprises on the way. Sculptures from other cultures are scattered among the garden trails, with ponds, seats and lookouts.

The main Rim Track starts from the carpark, goes up past the interesting assemblage of old quarry buildings and gradually follows the outer rim of the quarry. There are lookout points and interesting interpretation panels on the way. At the top, the faces of the rock quarry have striking rock patterns, and there are expansive views over the park, the plains and the southern mountains beyond.

The down track passes a 10-minute side-trail up to Kennedys Bush Road, then goes through the shady Findlays picnic area and back to the carpark.

Other tracks include the Farm Walk (1 hour), a circuit around the other side of Halswell Quarry up to a high point with fine views. There are also many shorter rambles (10 minutes) among the sister city gardens that are being developed: Seattle, Adelaide, Christchurch (England), Songpa-Gu (Korea), Sansu (China) and Kurashiki (Japan).

Some of the historic buildings at Halswell Quarry.

COOPERS KNOB
A classic skyline walk

TRACK
A mix of bush tracks and tussock trails over rolling country. Occasionally rough underfoot, and a rock scramble to the top of Coopers Knob.

WALK TIME AND DISTANCE
2–3 hours (8 km) one way (Coopers Knob to Cass Peak/Sign of the Bellbird).

ONE–HOUR WALK
Coopers Knob return.

ACCESS AND FACILITIES
This track is part of the Crater Rim Walkway and follows along the Summit Road. It can be accessed at many different points, but this description starts from Ahuriri Bush and assumes that you have arranged transport to pick you up at Cass Peak/Sign of the Bellbird. Toilets and picnic area at the historic stone resthouse, the Sign of the Bellbird.

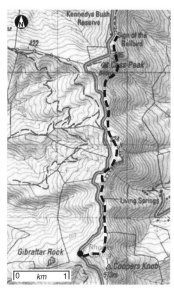

This track follows the twist and twine of a volcanic ridge, slipping past rock tors and overlooking bluffs down to the lovely blue-green cleft of Lyttelton Harbour. There are extraordinary views from Mount Cook to the Kaikoura mountains, and despite the rugged terrain there is not a lot of climbing. On a fine day you would not wish to be anywhere else.

The track starts inconspicuously near a small carpark beside Ahuriri Bush, passes through an elegant and dark patch of lancewood and fuchsia trees, then follows the fenceline to Coopers Knob, where it separates into the main track and a shortcut. Both end up with rock scrambling to reach the trig top.

This is the highest point on the Port Hills (573 m) and the views are stunning. Lake Ellesmere and Kaitorete Spit are in the foreground, then the whole panorama of the Southern Alps, including Mount Cook (just to the left of Mount Somers), Mount Arrowsmith and Mount D'Archiac.

From Coopers Knob pick up a broad vehicle trail that follows along the ridgeline almost down to the road. Skirt through a small bush reserve and around a prominent rock outcrop to another bush remnant, then the track climbs out along a rugged line of bluffs, with sweeping views on the way.

Cass Peak is 546 metres high, with the obvious meteorological mushroom on top. The main track drops past a hang-gliders' launching pad then sidles on the dramatic east face of Cass Peak, past a stone seat around to the Sign of the Bellbird.

SIGN OF THE KIWI
Unrivalled views and original tearooms

TRACK
Well-marked bush tracks and tussock trails, with an easy hill climb of Mount Sugar Loaf.

WALK TIME AND DISTANCE
1.5–2 hours (3 km) circuit.

ACCESS AND FACILITIES
From Christchurch drive up Dyers Pass Road to Dyers Pass and the carpark beside the Sign of the Kiwi. An excellent lookout, but be warned: the crossroads can get busy with traffic on weekends.

INFORMATION
The Sign of the Kiwi has information brochures, and they do teas, milk shakes and ice-creams.

This is a short, civilised, circular walk on the Port Hills, which explores bush reserves on the Lyttelton Harbour side and outstanding views on the Sugar Loaf side; and you can end with a cup of tea or an ice-cream in the 1917 stone resthouse.

The start of this walk is over the crossroads, opposite the Sign of the Kiwi, where there is a stile and a sign saying 'Mitchells Track'. This bush track sidles slowly through a substantial hillside of native bush with dominant mahoe, lancewood, broadleaf and lemonwood (tarata), and some tuneful bellbirds and grey warblers. There is an excellent lookout over the deep blue gash of Lyttelton Harbour.

It takes about 30 minutes to amble up through the bush reserve and past the Smyth seat to the junction with Cedric's Track. This track climbs gently uphill across tussocks and around to the large Sugar Loaf carpark, and it is worth the 20 minutes or so extra to walk up the sealed road to the Sugar Loaf summit and television tower. At 496 metres you get superb views, and you can look along the length of the volcanic escarpment of the Port Hills.

Back down at Sugar Loaf carpark pick up the other half of Cedric's Track, which lollops down to the Sign of the Kiwi.

OTHER WALKS
Coronation Hill Walk (1 hour return) and the H.G. Ell Track to Victoria Park (1 hour one way).

Mount Sugar Loaf, on the Sign of the Kiwi walk.

Previous page: Tidal channel, Wairau Lagoon.

Left above: The memorial shelter to the pioneer women, at the top of the Bridle Path.

Left below: Godley Head, Christchurch.

Opposite: Red Tarns.

Above: Picture-perfect Lake Matheson.

Below: Sea stacks and swimmers on the Motukiekie coast.

Opposite: Kea and rainbows at the Fox Glacier carpark.

Above: Lake Kaniere mist.

Left: Akers Point.

Opposite: Sand sculpture at Sandfly Bay.

Following page: Rock drawings, Waikari.

MOUNT VERNON
From suburb to summits

TRACK
Dry tussock trails and farm vehicle tracks up a long hill. The 4WD tracks also get used by mountain bikers.

WALK TIME AND DISTANCE
4–5 hours (9 km) Mount Vernon summit return.

ONE-HOUR WALK
Plane table return.

ACCESS AND FACILITIES
Off Centaurus Road and Hillsborough Terrace to a large carpark and signboard.

This is a superb day-walk circuit, easy to access from the city, and exploring many facets of the Port Hills. There are tussock downlands, rock outcrops, plane tables and seat lookouts, an historic Maori trail and two memorial poles to lost children.

Start from the carpark, and at an immediate track junction follow the zigzag up the hill to the spur, then follow the spur track to a plane table. Good views from here already. Continue up the spur track to where it joins the farm vehicle road, and settle into a slow, steady slog all the way up to Summit Road. On the way you can glimpse the isolated pocket of native forest called Dry Bush.

At Summit Road there is the Lamar wheelchair and pushchair track, a short, tidy circuit with plane tables and seats. There is also a memorial pole to John Lilley, aged 8, one of two children who died in a snowstorm in 1883. The other pole to 10-year-old William Mason, is just off the side of the Rapaki Track. The poles were placed on the sites where the bodies were found.

The farm road continues up to the summit of Mount Vernon itself, with great views everywhere, and from here pick up the Crater Rim Walkway and follow it

down to Rapaki carpark. This rock was an icon to Maori as well as today's rock-climbers, and marked the way of the Rapaki Track from Otautahi (Christchurch) to the Rapaki settlement in Whakaraupo (Lyttelton) harbour.

Now it is a four-wheel-drive road and a broad, easy walk past the second memorial pole to where the valley track starts. This leads gently down to the Hillsborough Terrace carpark.

Walkers on the valley track, Mount Vernon.

177

BRIDLE PATH & CASTLE ROCK
Historic footpath and striking rock outcrop

TRACK
Gravel track up a steep hill, then a worn path through tussocks up to Castle Rock.

WALK TIME AND DISTANCE
2–3 hours (4 km) return.

ONE-HOUR WALK
Seymour seat return.

ACCESS AND FACILITIES
From Christchurch city it is about 7 km to the gondola, and just beside it is the Bridle Path carpark. Picnic tables and water fountain.

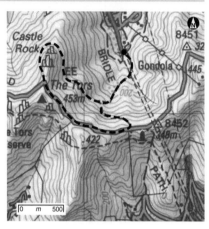

The Bridle Path was surveyed and constructed in a feverish hurry over the Christmas period of 1850–51, and finished in the second week of January 1851. Originally the main road from Lyttelton to Christchurch was to go via Evans Pass, but progress was excruciatingly slow. After a year the 'Sumner Road' was still uncompleted, and with the settlers due to arrive in December there was an urgent need for some sort of pathway to the plains. It was a tight finish. The Bridle Path was surveyed in November 1850 and the *Charlotte Jane*, the first of the four immigrant ships, arrived on 16 December.

From the carpark the track climbs steadily past seats and up a broad zigzag. At the Seymour stone seat, named after one of the first four ships, the Castle Rock side-track is signposted the Kahukura Track. This beaten trail winds up under Castle Rock, climbing steadily, with expansive views over the estuary and the Kaikoura mountains. It reaches a top track junction, and by turning right you can do a circuit of the rock itself, which has distinctive volcanic strata and is popular with rock-climbers.

Once you reach Summit Road follow it down to the top of the Bridle Path and its historic shelter to the pioneer women. The plunge back down to the carpark will be steep, but at least you will be unhindered by Victorian crinolines.

GODLEY HEAD
Cliff coastline and precarious baches

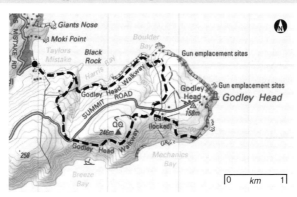

TRACK
Broad, well-graded tracks on an open tussock peninsula. You will need a torch for the tunnel.

WALK TIME AND DISTANCE
4–5 hours (9 km) for circuit (including tunnel).

ONE-HOUR WALK
Boulder Bay return.

ACCESS AND FACILITIES
From Christchurch city drive 14 km to Taylors Mistake beach. Picnic area and toilets at Taylors Mistake.

Penguins like this coast and so do people, and this is a popular walkway that has a swag of good views and some curious facets of history, including a military tunnel. The Maori knew Godley Head as Awaroa or Otokitoki, while another early name was Cachalot Point, probably named by the crew of a French whaling ship. 'Cachalot' is French for sperm whale.

Taylors Mistake is a fine sandy beach, with baches clumped under the cliffs, hanging as perilously as a shag's nest. From the beach the track follows a coastline eaten out into bays and caves (some of which were inhabited once) and cuts cleanly around headlands to where a few baches snuggle down at Boulder Bay. Nesting sites for spotted shags and the white-flippered little blue penguin are found along this coast.

It is a steady climb from Boulder Bay up to the top of the peninsula, where the track crosses Summit Road to the carpark and toilets. The tunnel track descends past the remains of old military buildings (also a side-track to a coastal lookout), then zigzags sharply down to the 110-metre tunnel, which you can walk through to the two searchlight 'pillboxes'. Splendid headland views, and on a fine day a popular place for fishing.

Back on the main ridge, follow the track as it rambles along the side of the tussock peninsula, past a lookout, and down to Breeze Col. It then descends dramatically to the bay. Several mountain-bike trails have been constructed on the peninsula, and these can be utilised by alert walkers.

GOVERNORS BAY COAST
Coastal wandering

TRACK
Old flat road for most of the way, then an optional bush trail. Excellent for baby buggies on the road.

WALK TIME AND DISTANCE
2 hours (6 km) return (Allandale to Sandy Bay).

ONE-HOUR WALK
Sage Reserve return.

ACCESS AND FACILITIES
There are several entry points but carparking at many of them is awkward. There is no carparking at the Governors Bay jetty, only a few places at Sandy Bay, not much at Church Lane carpark, but plenty at the attractive Allandale picnic area, right by the shoreline.

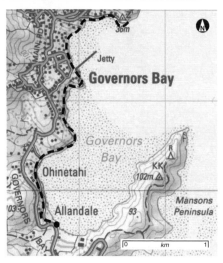

This is an easy-going shoreline walk, rambling along the old coastal road with refreshing views out over Lyttelton Harbour and the humped rolling peaks of Banks Peninsula. The walking is surprisingly private once you leave Allandale carpark, and you get glimpses of houses up on the terraces, including the fine old stone mansion of Otakaikie.

Just past Church Lane there is a short (rather overgrown) 10-minute track through the Sage Reserve, which is mostly kanuka forest. On around the point, the road swings past some swirling rock patterns in the soft cliffs, and it is very peaceful beside the oystercatchers and shags picking over the mudflats. Governors Bay has a long finger of a jetty, and the road ends here.

However, a good bush trail fossicks around the circumference of Governors Bay, past boatsheds and bushy backyards to the carpark at Sandy Bay. If you want to continue, there is a benched track past the old jetty and a side-track heads down to a bay with baches tucked under the cliffs. The tide platforms are extensive at low tide, and an access track zigzags up a precarious spur to the main road.

The old jetty at Governors Bay.

ADDERLEY HEAD
Headland of history

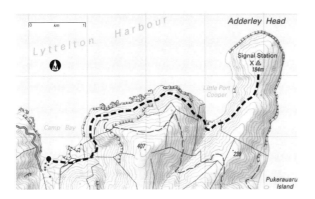

TRACK
Farmland trails and old pack-tracks. Permission to cross the farmland must be obtained beforehand from the owners at Camp Bay, and a small donation is requested for the Red Cross. The track is not marked; some navigation skills are needed and there are bluffs if you stray from the obvious line.

WALK TIME AND DISTANCE
3–4 hours (8 km) return.

ONE-HOUR WALK
30 minutes along the coast.

ACCESS AND FACILITIES
From Diamond Harbour on Banks Peninsula, drive to Purau Bay then take the highly scenic Camp Bay Road as it twists along Lyttelton Harbour to the picturesque Camp Bay, about 40 km from Christchurch. The tiny schoolhouse at Little Port Cooper is locked but can be hired overnight. Contact the Stapleton-Smythes for schoolhouse and access.

Adderley Head was one of the first points of land the early European settlers saw when they arrived to settle Canterbury in 1851. It became important in their history, for a quarantine camp was established in Little Port Cooper and a signal station built on the headland to guide the early sailing vessels into the harbour on the other side of the world.

From the Camp Bay farmhouse follow the vehicle track around towards the first headland, then at a gate and fence drop down some 20 metres to pick up the line of the old pack-track. This worn path is quite easy to follow and in places you see the original stone walling. It sidles along the dramatic coastline under bluffs, and around the steep hillsides to the historic schoolhouse at Little Port Cooper.

This is a protected bay, with a few wildflowers and old trees dating from the time there was a substantial population living and working here. From the bay obvious pack-tracks angle up towards Adderley Head, and continue on to the tiny stone signal station that now serves as a cosy shelter. Wonderful all-round views.

SIGN OF THE PACKHORSE
A hut in lonely limbo

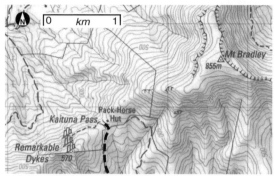

Detail: north end of Packhorse Hut track

TRACK
The track is well signposted and poled, following vehicle tracks up a steady hill climb.

WALK TIME AND DISTANCE
3–4 hours (6 km) return.

ONE–HOUR WALK
Up the valley onto the spur 30 minutes.

ACCESS AND FACILITIES
Access to the Packhorse Hut is off the Christchurch–Akaroa road, Highway 75, into the Kaituna Valley, then off an unsignposted short side-road about 7 km along the Kaituna Valley road.

The Sign of the Packhorse is perched in a fine romantic situation, alone on the tussock pass that looks from Lyttelton to Kaitorete Spit. It was built in the 1920s, when walking became popular on the peninsula with a well-established circuit. The Sign of the Packhorse was part of a network of hostels', and early photos show a homely place, with curtains at the windows and flowers on the table. At the hostels it cost walkers a shilling for a bed, a shilling for a meal, and lunch (thick bread and butter with cheese) was sixpence.

The track is well signposted and poled, and sidles past the farm, following vehicle tracks up a bush-filled valley then climbing onto a big spur. There are extensive patches of scrub forest in the Kaituna Valley and you can hear quite a few native birds, including kingfishers and bellbirds. Kanuka trees are dominant here, with lots of kowhai as well.

After a while the track stops climbing up the spur, and sidles on a farm track past Parkinsons Bush Reserve to the saddle and old stone hut. The hut has bunks and mattresses, a woodstove and a rainwater tank. In summer the water supply cannot be relied upon, unlike the views.

OTHER WALKS

The Packhorse sits in the centre of a web of tracks. For the fit, a poled track leads behind Mount Bradley and on to Mount Herbert, the high point of the peninsula. It is shorter, and not difficult, to go directly on to Mount Bradley. Another poled route continues down from the Packhorse Hut, past the Remarkable Dykes (an outcrop of volcanic rock) and then on to Gebbies Pass, 2–3 hours one way.

Tussock saddle with Mount Bradley beyond, part of the Sign of the Packhorse walk.

Little Port Cooper, on the Adderley Head walk (see page 181).

SUMMIT CREST
A wild way on a high ridge

TRACK
Farm tracks and 4WD roads. The walking is generally easy and rolling, but there are quite a few climbs as the route follows a rather zany course along the main ridge. The route is poled, and follows legal paper roads for the most part.

Detail: Montgomery Park section of Summit Crest walk

WALK TIME AND DISTANCE
3–5 hours (10 km) one way from the Port Levy/Little River road saddle to Montgomery Park. You will have to pre-arrange transport, as the road-ends are a long way apart.

ONE-HOUR WALK
Waipuna Saddle return.

ACCESS AND FACILITIES
From Little River take the tortuous Western Valley Road up to the Port Levy saddle, a dramatic site.

These Banks Peninsula tops are wild, and the crouched shapes of the totara trees give a fair idea of what the weather can be like up here. The three hillside reserves of Mount Fitzgerald, Mount Sinclair and Whatarangi-Totara have surprising subalpine plants — like mountain holly and spaniard. Pick a fine day and you will have a fine walk.

From the saddle it is 1 km through stands of stunted totara to point KK (738 m), then a brief drop down to Waipuna Saddle and an easy swing around tussock slopes up to Mount Fitzgerald (826 m). The route drops down to a saddle then up to Mount Sinclair (841 m), about 3 km.

The tree 'graveyards', particularly on the eastern slopes of Mount Sinclair, are striking; both beautiful and ugly at the same time, with intricate patterns etched into the stumps.

There is a big descent from Mount Sinclair to the tiny Whatarangi-Totara Reserve, then the track crosses open grasslands to an unnamed rocky peak (700 m) overlooking Montgomery Park. The track is poled into, and through, Montgomery Park, and this dwarf of a reserve has some giant totara trees. Quite astonishing; you simply do not expect such a size of tree in such a tight space.

Tree graveyards on Summit Crest.

ONAWE PA
Historic Maori peninsula

TRACK
Beach and grass trails up to a low summit. A low tide is essential.

WALK TIME AND DISTANCE
1 hour (3 km) return.

ACCESS AND FACILITIES
Drive to Duvauchelle on the Christchurch–Akaroa road, Highway 75, then turn onto an unsealed coastal road for 1 km to the carpark.

From a distance the Onawe Peninsula looks like a greenstone pendant dangling in the smooth waters of Akaroa Harbour. It is now a peaceful place, and the quiet lapping tides make it an island at high tide. But this was no defence for Ngai Tahu Maori who occupied this pa site when Te Rauparaha's warriors approached in 1830. The slaughter was immense, and was followed by a cannibal feast on the beach. Today there is no trace of this conflict except, fancifully, in the red-stained and writhing rocks that are exposed at low tide.

From the carpark a short vehicle track drops down to the pebbly beach. There are striking rock patterns in the tidal rocks. Onawe is connected to the mainland by just a thin, razor-like ridge, which broadens out into a wide and rising grass slope to the beaconed summit 100 metres above sea level.

A good trail climbs up to this summit, which is further than it looks, and the outlook is fine. Some false trails look as if they lead down from the summit to the shoreline at the head of the peninsula, but these are for goats, and keen goats at that.

Manuka forest and thick grass now largely obscure the details of the pa site, but nothing can obscure the magnificence of the harbour landscape.

Coming down from Onawe Pa.

AKAROA TOWN WALK
Backyard exploration of an historic town

TRACK
Footpaths and grass trails. Some short hills.

WALK TIME AND DISTANCE
1–2 hours (2 km) circuit.

ACCESS AND FACILITIES
85 km from Christchurch on Highway 75. There are cafes, a visitor centre, museum, toilets, beach, wharfs and shops in Akaroa. Plenty to do.

INFORMATION
Good visitor centre in Akaroa.

Akaroa is a charming town, started by French settlers in this most English of provinces. Historic cottages, overflowing with roses and wisteria, can be found up and down the narrow bylanes of the town. Views are unexpected and everywhere on this backyard trail, and to round off the walk there are numerous cafes supplying a quality of *café au lait* the early settlers could only dream of.

On Rue Lavaud the signposted walks to Stanley Park start just before the bakery and the track pleasantly ambles up from the sea, with a good view back over the harbour. One end of the top track emerges onto Le Lievre Lane, which can be followed to Watson Street down to Rue Balguerie.

Just up and opposite is Settlers Hill Road, a steep climb with tracks that lead into L'Aube Hill area. Either will do, and both lead down to the green, secluded site of the Old French Cemetery, the earliest known European burial site, dating from 1842. It is easy now to continue down to Pompallier Street and Rue Lavaud, and follow this back to the whiff of croissants.

OTHER WALKS
Garden of Tane (20–30 minutes), Purple Peak (4–5 hours), Britomart Memorial (10 minutes), and Woodills Loop Track (1–2 hours).

A quiet morning in Akaroa.

HINEWAI RESERVE
A forest being reborn

TRACK
Good bush trails, and the track signposting is superb. There are information boards and pamphlets available at most carparks, and first-time visitors to Hinewai should study the maps carefully.

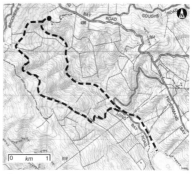

WALK TIME AND DISTANCE
4–6 hours (8 km) for the full Hinewai circuit. Fire is the major threat to this reserve, so no fires, billy boiling or smoking at any time. No dogs allowed. Conservation is first at Hinewai; people come second.

Many tracks not shown

ONE-HOUR WALK
West Track, Big Kanuka Track, South Track and climb up East Track to the visitor centre.

ACCESS AND FACILITIES
From Akaroa take Long Bay Road up to the Summit Road junction (known locally as the Cabstand), then turn down Long Bay Road to the main entrance and carpark. For Otanerito Bay, continue down Long Bay Road all the way to the lower carpark near the Otanerito homestead. 90 km from Christchurch.

INFORMATION
There is a visitor centre with interesting displays on Hinewai Reserve and what is being achieved here. Please take boots off before entering. Toilets.

Hinewai Reserve is now one of the most extensive walking areas on Banks Peninsula. Almost 12 km of well-marked tracks run through this unique 1000-hectare bush reserve, which is privately owned and managed by the Maurice White Native Forest Trust, but open to the public. Regenerating forest runs virtually from sea level to the summit, and gives an insight into how an ecologically managed area can be successfully restored.

From the visitor centre take West Track along to the Big Kanuka Track and South Track. The attractive Hinewai Falls is worth a look. At Boundary Falls continue down the easy Valley Track past a cascade and a big kahikatea to the Otanerito road.

For the beach cross the road and follow the trail beside the stream and farmland to Otanerito Bay. The bay is sandy and sheltered, with big sea-cliffs guarding the entrance, and a sprinkling of private baches around it.

Return to the road again and the Valley Track junction. From here it is a solid climb up through the tall kanuka forest of The Stones Track to the junction with Lisburn Track. This track follows up the pleasant Waterfall Gully and sidles round to Lothlorien lookout.

Lisburn Track merges with Broom and Manatu tracks, with good views over upper Hinewai. At the junction with South Track, follow Beech Terrace Track to Tawai Track and West Track, which sidles easily back to the visitor centre.

MOUNT JOHN
Perspiration for a perfect panorama

TRACK
Pine forest trail up a steady hill, then dry tussock slopes.

WALK TIME AND DISTANCE
2 hours direct return from summit; 3–4 hours (8 km) for full circuit.

ONE-HOUR WALK
To lookout above larches, or easy lakeside return.

ACCESS AND FACILITIES
From Lake Tekapo township take the road to the lakeside motor camp and continue to the carpark just before the ice-skating rink.

INFORMATION
Lake Tekapo Walkway, Department of Conservation pamphlet.

Mount John sticks up like the proverbial sore thumb above the Mackenzie plain, in its isolation acting as a marker post for Lake Tekapo. There is a perfect panorama from the summit, from Mount Cook to Lake Alexandrina and Lake Tekapo, then back over the arid Mackenzie Country to Burkes Pass and Mackenzie Pass.

It is not that far to climb, about 300 metres, for Lake Tekapo is already at 800 metres and Mount John summit is at 1031 metres. So you could fit in a quick jaunt to the summit on the way to Queenstown. However, you cannot quite get all the way, for the summit is fenced off for the astronomical observatories.

From the carpark the track climbs steadily through the larch forest and reaches a junction with a loop track that circles the summit. Already the views are good. If you are walking the full circuit, take the track on the Lake Tekapo side and climb up to the lookout where the views are even better. Mount John is surprisingly flat on top and Himalayan chukar (introduced as a game bird) are sometimes spotted on the top slopes.

Continue on the summit loop then take the track down the long easy spur some 2 km to where the track drops sharply down to Lake Tekapo itself. Staying 50 metres above the lake, the track sidles around the base of Mount John, back to the skating rink and carpark.

The top stile on the Mount John track, with Lake Alexandrina behind.

LAKE ALEXANDRINA

Solitude at a high country lake

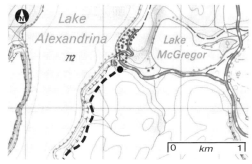

Detail: north end of Lake Alexandrina track

TRACK
An easy anglers' casual track across dry tussock country. Some mud.

WALK TIME AND DISTANCE
1–2 hours (5 km) one way; 3–4 hours (10 km) return.

ACCESS AND FACILITIES
From Highway 8 (6 km south of Lake Tekapo) take Godley Peaks Road 3 km to a turn-off to the south end of the lake, or 8 km to the middle of the lake and Lake McGregor. There are baches at both road-ends, and toilets, camping and information boards at Lake McGregor.

There is something subtle and silky about Lake Alexandrina, which sits in an old glacial gouge alongside its much bigger and more blustery sister. The bach owners have discovered the sheltering ways of this lake, power boats are not allowed, and the crested grebes patrol the willowy edges in calm, persistent ripples. This is a land that takes many seasons to appreciate, and the colours are harsh: blue-grey waters, yellow shores, black mountains.

From the Lake McGregor road-end the best route is to climb straight up from the carpark about 50 metres to a flat-top hill. A stile crosses the fenceline, whose main purpose is to stop four-wheel-drivers trashing the tussock.

Along here the unmarked trail wanders down to the lakeside again, and the footpath settles into some definition as it rounds the point and goes down to the beaches at the south end of the lake. This is another feast of bach architecture, and unless you have had the foresight to organise transport you will have to wander back the same way.

The serene Lake Alexandrina.

HOOKER VALLEY

A perfect and popular mountain walk

TRACK

A well-marked track, easy and mostly flat at first. Later it becomes rougher, with some clambering. Two dramatic footbridges and the sidle by the Hooker River gorge can unnerve some walkers.

WALK TIME AND DISTANCE

3–4 hours (10 km) return to ice lake.

ONE-HOUR WALK

Return walk to second swing bridge.

ACCESS AND FACILITIES

Detail: start of Hooker Valley track

From Highway 80 turn off just before Mount Cook village and go to the large carpark and camping area under White Horse Hill. Picnic tables and toilets.

INFORMATION

Walks in Mount Cook National Park, Department of Conservation pamphlet.

The Hooker Valley is the perfect frame for Mount Cook. The dark and dirty V-shaped valley, with its rumbling moraine walls, is precisely mocked by the pristine and soaring A-shape of Mount Cook. This short walk is packed with interest and drama, and

walkers have been making this mountain pilgrimage for over a hundred years. So you will not be lonely on the track, unless you go off-season or early in the morning – hotel breakfasts rarely start before 7 a.m.

The track starts from the White Horse camping area and passes the original site of the Hermitage and an alpine memorial, and groves of matagouri with some spectacular *Aciphylla* (or spaniard) plant, with their huge, prickly, flowering stalks. The track zigzags down to the first swing bridge across the milky-blue Hooker River.

The second footbridge over the Hooker River, heading up the Hooker Valley.

Good views continue upvalley, past the Mueller Glacier terminal lake, and the track cuts along a gorge with a spectacular swing bridge. You can often find native edelweiss in the cliffs here. After the bridge you turn a slight corner of the valley and get some photogenic views of Mount Cook, and in summer there can be a profusion of Mount Cook lilies (or properly buttercups).

Stocking Stream shelter was named for walkers in the nineteenth century who would take off their shoes and stockings here. There are toilets and a plane table, which is stuck rather oddly on top of a rock. After a flat section with some boardwalks the track crests a slight rise and you reach the ice lake, the terminal lake of the Hooker Glacier. There might be small icebergs drifting in the lake.

Hooker was named after William Hooker, an eminent English botanist and the father of Joseph Hooker, Mount Cook was named after the explorer Captain James Cook also a distinguished botanist, but to the Maori the peak is Aorangi (or Aoraki to South Island Maori), sometimes translated as 'cloud piercer' — and you have to admit, it's a better name.

RED TARNS
Secluded alpine wetland

TRACK
A hill walk, sometimes steep, but well marked. Gravel path at first, but it gets rougher in places. Beyond the tarns the track becomes a worn route over boulders up to the Sebastopol ridgeline.

WALK TIME AND DISTANCE
2–3 hours (4 km) return to tarns. For Sebastopol ridgeline add 1 hour.

ACCESS AND FACILITIES
Start from the public shelter on the Mount Cook village loop road, not far from the shop and beside Governors Bush. Toilets and information panels here.

INFORMATION
Walks in Mount Cook National Park, Department of Conservation pamphlet.

The Red Tarns are a quiet escape from the tourist hubbub of Mount Cook village – a crystal sprinkling of ponds, like two clear eyes in the stony face of Sebastopol. In summer the waft of flax, turpentine wood and totara berries can be quite heady, and soothing – a meditative refuge.

At the public shelter, signs direct you along a gravelled path beside a bubbling creek, then out of the village to a long footbridge over the Black Birch Stream. The track then starts to climb steeply through the alpine scrub, crossing occasional gullies on its way to the lip of the basin. It is a 500-metre climb to the tarns, where there is a seat and a plane table. The tarns get their name from the red pondweed that grows in them. On a still, sharp day you get a perfect reflection of Mount Cook.

A rough track with cairns continues on to the Sebastopol ridgeline, with excellent views. Allow another 1 hour return from the tarns.

BALL HUT ROAD
Road to nowhere

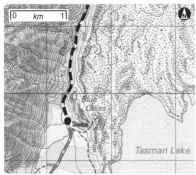 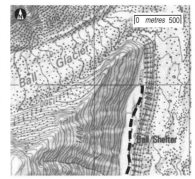

Details: start and end of track

TRACK
Flat, easy walking initially on a gravel road, then a 4WD track, then a trampers' track on a moraine terrace.

WALK TIME AND DISTANCE
4–5 hours (18 km) return to Ball Hut.

ONE-HOUR WALK
Celmisia (daisy) Flat return.

ACCESS AND FACILITIES
From Highway 80 just past Mount Cook airport, turn onto the Tasman Valley Road and drive to the Blue Lakes carpark, shelter and toilets. Sometimes you can take a car 2 km further to Celmisia Flat, but that is pushing it.

INFORMATION
Walks in Mount Cook National Park, Department of Conservation pamphlet.

Blue Lakes, beside the Ball Hut road.

An unusual walk in many ways, this is not everyone's cup of tea. It is a long bash up a four-wheel-drive road, with steep, rotten hillsides of the Mount Cook range on one side and the huge, grinding rock factory of the Tasman Glacier on the other. It can be hot work too, with little shade, which makes you wish for a mountain bike.

But you are following in the footsteps of history. In February 1882 the Reverend W.S. Green and his Swiss guides Emil Boss and Ulrich Kaufmann slowly trekked along this moraine wall, camping by the streams and searching for a route to the unclimbed peak of Mount Cook. They almost made it too, but for 'a mere matter of detail', a lack of daylight and 10 metres short of the summit.

Later the Ball Hut road was built and in the early 1890s a climbers' hut (one of several) was established at the far end, with parties in the early part of the twentieth century having to walk *up* onto the glacier. But this region is a textbook study of rock processes and rapid erosion. The Tasman Glacier retreated and shrank under its mantle of rock, and the moraines' walls crumbled and took away the hut and parts of the road.

The road now peters out into nowhere, some 6 km from Blue Lakes at Husky Flat. Even poncy four-wheel-drives cannot struggle over these boulders, but there is a worn foot trail that threads along the terrace and reaches an unexpected oasis of grass and alpine shrubs beside the small Ball Hut shelter.

About 500 metres further on the moraine wall itself ends at the top of a nasty eroded access valley nicknamed 'Garbage Gully' by generations of climbers. But the view is anything but rubbish.

BEN OHAU
Little hills have big views

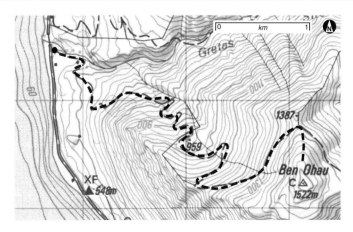

TRACK
An old farm 4WD track zigzags most of the way up a very big climb, with the last 150 metres to the summit across screes and tussock.

WALK TIME AND DISTANCE
4–5 hours (6 km return); total climb 1000 metres.

ONE–HOUR WALK
Good views of Lake Ohau, but the Mackenzie is still hidden.

ACCESS AND FACILITIES
You will need a good road map, and a topographical map for the walk.

From Highway 8 north of Twizel look for 'Glen Lyon Station' signs, and follow the Pukaki and Ohau Canal roads (all sealed). Eventually you get to Lake Ohau and the seal ends, and the narrow road twists along past huge dry-stone road walls. These were built during the Depression as a work-relief scheme. You also pass a skein of alpine Halls totara forest, another of the reasons why this area is precious.

There is nothing to indicate the start of the Ben Ohau track, not a carpark or a sign, though the farm road and mountain are obvious. DoC is intending to do more work on this route.

INFORMATION
Day Walks of the Mackenzie Basin and Waitaki Valley, Department of Conservation pamphlet.

In Scotland 'ben' means mountain, although you might not consider Ben Ohau to be much of a mountain. It sits beside giants on the edge of the Mackenzie basin, a mere mole on the body of the Southern Alps. Nevertheless at 1550 metres it is not a hill to be sneezed at, especially when you start to walk up it. It is a 1000-metre climb to the summit, so this walk suits the dedicated hill-walker, giving him or her a good stiff workout.

There is no sign at the gate by the derelict barn, and you follow the farm road past an old musterers' hut and rustling beech forest by Greta Stream. This is the last of the shade, the road then zigzags powerfully up the mountainside spur and up to a small saddle.

From the saddle the route leaves the road and cuts up the scree and tussock slopes to the high point. Carry lots of water and have lunch on top. And expect a breeze — 'O hau' means wind.

But the reward is a view of four lakes — Ohau, Pukaki, Benmore and the artificially made Lake Ruataniwha. At least that is what they say in the pamphlet — you may be more lucky, but I saw only fog.

An old shepherds' hut at the start of the Ben Ohau farm track.

FREEHOLD CREEK
From easy to alpine

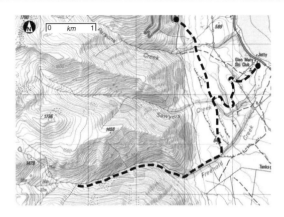

TRACK
A good signposted path through rolling tussock and scrub, followed by a steady hill climb in beech forest on an old logging line.

WALK TIME AND DISTANCE
5–6 hours (18 km) return from bushline (from Ohau skifield road), 4–5 hours (12 km) return from Glenmary ski huts.

ONE-HOUR WALK
1 hour return will get you to Sawyers Creek from Glenmary ski huts. Or 1 hour one way from the Ohau skifield road to exit at Glenmary, a nice cross-country trip.

ACCESS AND FACILITIES
From Highway 8 take the Lake Ohau road to either the Glenmary ski huts or 4 km further to the turn-off to Ohau Lodge and the skifield road. Follow this road 1 km to a ford and the start of the track. Signposted.

INFORMATION
Day Walks of the Mackenzie Basin and Waitaki Valley, Department of Conservation pamphlet.

There is a bit of everything on this walk, which suits both the unfit and the keen. You start on soft sunny slopes and somehow end up in big, bluffy country, the real heart of the Southern Alps.

From the Glenmary ski huts the track follows an old four-wheel-drive route up through tussock and matagouri terraces to a well-signposted junction with the main track from the Ohau skifield road. There are open landscapes, with Lake Ohau dominating the view, and the Ben Ohau Range across the way.

The track crosses the footbridge over Sawyers Creek and follows across tussock terraces to the beech forest at Freehold Creek. You slip into a green, bouldery valley, and after a little climbing reach a footbridge over the creek. This is another good return point, say 2 hours total from the road-end.

Now the track gets a little more serious as it climbs up through the forest past a large camping area and on to the sudden fringe of the bushline. If you are game enough, a cairned trail leads quite clearly into the alpine basins to the top forks, with waterfalls gushing down the side-creeks, and well-fed alpine plants in every cranny.

If you are still keen (and within your time budget) it is not that far up to a large, broad saddle, but there is no track up to this. You have strayed into wilderness.

CLAY CLIFFS
Beautiful badlands

TRACK
Easy farm road, but scrambly under the pinnacles themselves. Watch for falling debris.

WALK TIME AND DISTANCE
1 hour (2 km) return.

ACCESS AND FACILITIES
Access is 3 km north of Omarama off Highway 8, turning onto Quailburn Road, then Henburn Road, and driving a few kilometres to a farm gate and signpost. Access is

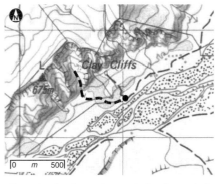

permitted when the sign says 'open', otherwise the farmer's permission is needed.

The gravel road is fairly bumpy for the next few kilometres to another gate and sign close by the Ahuriri River. The road continues beyond here, to a carpark right under the clay cliffs, but there is some point in parking by the river and walking that last 1 km to get a feeling for the strange character of this formation.

These cliffs are not 'clay', but the name does have excellent alliteration, and calling them gravel or silt cliffs just would not be the same. The Maori called them 'Paritea', which means 'white or coloured cliffs', and the early morning light brings out the subtle colours and textures of the sediments.

Erosion of the soft sediments by water has left deep ravines, with striking pinnacles wearing little caps of turf. The cliffs are 30–50 metres high in places, and just falling away. Some tracks have been made, but these all get undermined by the constant movement of the rocks.

On a hot, glaring day there is something spooky about the shady silences inside these chasms, with the tinkling sound of pebbles bouncing and falling off the sides,

and the unexpected whoosh of pigeons in the air. You often come away with a distinct sense of relief, possibly because you are grateful nothing has fallen on top of you, or perhaps there is something unnerving about seeing geological processes in such an accelerated form.

The badlands of Clay Cliffs.

CHARMING CREEK
Old tramway through a granite gorge

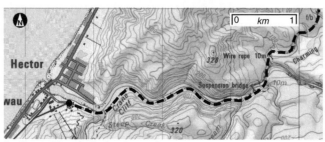

Detail: start of Charming Creek walkway

TRACK
Flat gravel track on an old tramway. Reasonable for baby buggies for a while.

WALK TIME AND DISTANCE
2 hours (6 km) Ngakawau Gorge return.

ONE-HOUR WALK
Irishmans Tunnel return.

ACCESS AND FACILITIES
From Westport drive 35 km to Ngakawau; the walkway is signposted just before the river, 200 metres to the carpark.

INFORMATION
Charming Creek Walk, Nelson District Walking Committee pamphlet; *Buller Walks*, Terry Sumner, booklet.

There was never a more apt name for a walk. Charming Creek has tunnels, walk verandahs, waterfalls and many other features all packed in on a dense trip into the cramped and gloomy spaces of a gorge, closely overhung with sombre native forest. Excellent information boards detail the coal-extracting operations in the area.

From 'The Bins' terminus you quickly follow the slick dark waters of the Ngakawau River through the S-bend of Irishmans Tunnel (a mistake in alignment), and through another 'tunnel' which is in fact a natural rock arch. The granite gorge is at its narrowest here, as the tramway crosses the long suspension bridge with spectacular views of the Mangatini Falls.

There is another 50-metre-long tunnel, a boardwalked verandah, then the confluence of Charming Creek and Ngakawau River. The river always carries a thin line of foam and creates elaborate swirls and patterns as it joins the Charming. Just around the next corner is Watsons Mill, where there is a toilet and shelter, and after the bridge a short casual trail goes down to the picnic rocks by the dark tea-stained river. A salubrious spot for lunch.

From here on, the walkway changes character as it leaves the gorge and enters a chewed-over forest of mine debris, relics of the old steam sawmill, a sulphur hole and the Papa Tunnel. If you continue right through, either arrange transport at the other end, or allow 2 hours return (10 km extra).

DENNISTON INCLINE
The remains of a mighty enterprise

TRACK
A bush track up the original bridle path hill to Denniston township, with steps at the top.

WALK TIME AND DISTANCE
4–5 hours (10 km) return.

ONE-HOUR WALK
One Mile Log return.

ACCESS AND FACILITIES
From Westport travel 14 km on Highway 67 to Waimangaroa, then take Conns Creek Road to the carpark. If you continue

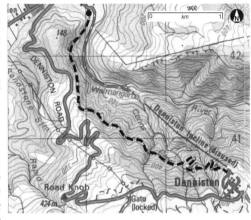

along Conns Creek Road you reach the historic site at the actual base of Denniston Incline.

For the top access, follow the signposted Denniston road as it climbs the 700-metre plateau, then down a side-road to the carpark and lookout over the top of the incline. One Mile Log carpark is on the Denniston road and offers a shorter walk to the top. Obviously if you can arrange transport to drop you off at the top of the incline, the walk time is halved.

INFORMATION
Denniston, New Zealand Walkway Commission pamphlet; *Stepping Back,* Mark Pickering, book.

The Denniston Incline was built in 1878–79 and operated until 1967. When it was built it was proudly considered New Zealand's biggest and best engineering project.

Water-operated brakes slowed the coal-laden wagons (in a descent that was 1 in 1.20 over the 548-metre drop) and helped pull up the empty wagons. Once 250 miners and their families lived and worked on this bleak plateau, and ultimately 12 million tons of coal were taken from Denniston.

At first the walk goes through regenerating forest and past the old

The top of the Denniston Incline.

brickworks site, climbing 2 km up to One Mile Log. After this the forest becomes more substantial, with tall rimu and red beech. This bridle track was built in 1884 when the hazards of riding down on the incline wagons became all too obvious — namely, when someone died.

After two-thirds of the climb there is a short side-track to Middle Brake, where you can get an idea of the uncomfortable steepness of the incline. There is an old viaduct below Middle Brake but it is unsafe to go on; indeed, the incline is generally too steep and insecure to walk on.

On the main track, the last part zigzags up stone steps to the lonely and rusting machinery at the top of the incline. On misty days the place seems haunted, which perhaps it is — haunted by memories.

OTHER WALKS
Coalbrookdale Mine (1 hour).

Old coal wagons, Charming Creek (see page 200).

CAPE FOULWIND
The smell of seals and the sea

TRACK
Benched gravel track at first, then muddy, cattle-plugged farmland.

WALK TIME AND DISTANCE
1.5–2 hours (4 km) one way.

30-MINUTE WALK
Seal colony return.

ACCESS AND FACILITIES
From Westport it is 12 km down the Carters Beach road to the large carpark, information boards and toilets at Tauranga Bay. There is a cafe at the other end of the bay.

The winds howl and crack their cheeks on this corner of the West Coast, and in 1770 Captain Cook called it 'foulwind'. The name has stuck and so have seals, to one of the most publicly accessible seal colonies in New Zealand. Other attractions include the colony of friendly, thieving weka at the carpark, and the glorious golden sweep of Tauranga Bay.

From the carpark an excellent track climbs up onto the headland and leads down to the lookouts over the seal colony. At breeding time the colony is spectacular, with as many as 100–150 pups. The New Zealand fur seal is found only in New Zealand waters and off the south coast of Australia, and the seals arrive to give birth in November and December. By March the numbers of pups are at their peak, and a lively lot they are.

From here on the track gets a lot muddier, and can get churned up by the cattle. After a short sidle and climb you reach a plaque and a perspex-enclosed astrolabe, which was of the type Abel Tasman used when he first arrived in New Zealand in 1642. He named this point 'Clyppygen Hoeck' or 'rocky corner'.

After this the track sidles around more farmland to the lighthouse. The best route is down by the shore, walking along the banking of the old railway line, which was used for moving quarried rock. Straggler seals often haul ashore here, no doubt trying to get some peace and quiet from the noisy quarrels at seal city. Sound familiar?

Tauranga Bay.

THE BALLROOM & FOX RIVER
Deep river to a vast natural overhang

TRACK

A good benched track to Fox River ford, continuing on the south bank to the Dilemma Creek junction. Only one river crossing separates the two tracks, but from near the Dilemma Creek junction there are several deep river crossings on the way to the Ballroom.

This walk is suitable for experienced walkers and trampers. It should not be attempted in wet weather, as river levels can rise quickly and dangerously. Get good weather information from the visitor centre at Punakaiki.

WALK TIME AND DISTANCE

4–5 hours (9 km) return.

ONE-HOUR WALK

Fox River ford return.

ACCESS AND FACILITIES

From Highway 6 beside the Fox River take the short side-road to the carpark. There is a toilet at the Ballroom.

At Punakaiki there is a good visitor centre, cafe and craft shop, as well as a motor camp.

INFORMATION

Paparoa National Park Visitor Centre at Punakaiki. *Paparoa National Park 273-12, Punakaiki K30* maps.

This is a deep gorge that cuts into the heart of the karst syncline of Paparoa National Park. You can get a long way into this heartland with only one straightforward river crossing, but to reach The Ballroom you will get wet knees (at least). This is a wilderness walk, with tall forest, and limestone rocks that have been shaped into sculptures by the emerald river.

The marked track starts as a stopbank that becomes an old gold-diggers' pack-track, and crosses two low bush spurs via old miners' cuttings. It crosses a dry side-branch of the Fox River where the granite boulders glitter with quartz, and shortly afterwards reaches the first Fox River ford.

(The Fox River cave track continues along a benched track, becoming gradually rockier, then steeply follows up a creek bed to the entrance of the cave, which can be explored for a short distance. Take a torch.)

Fox River.

For The Ballroom cross the river at this easy point and join the well-benched south bank track that continues most of the way to the Dilemma Creek confluence. The Fox Gorge is striking, and every twist in the river breaks open new angles of rock and light.

At Dilemma Creek the rock walls have formed a sharp prow, splitting the two rivers. The track has now ended, and you have to start fording the Fox River. Some of the fords can be deep but the river is usually slow-moving. It is about six to eight crossings upstream to the high natural rock shelter called The Ballroom. This is a massive overhang curved over a grassy flat, and you could fit a few houses under here comfortably. There is no record of any ancient balls ever being held here, but it is a lovely idea.

PANCAKE ROCKS & TRUMAN TRACK
Strange rock formations on a rugged coast

TRACK
Pancake Rocks: well-made gravel paths; baby buggies can be taken some of the way round this track.
Truman Track: well-made gravel paths and some beach walking.

WALK TIME AND DISTANCE
Pancake Rocks 30 minutes circuit; Truman Track 30 minutes return. Both 1–2 km return.

ACCESS AND FACILITIES
Drive to Punakaiki on Highway 6 (60 km from Westport, 45 km from Greymouth), to the

information centre, cafe, tearooms, toilets, shop and large carpark. The Truman Track is 2 km north at the signposted carpark.

INFORMATION
Paparoa National Park Visitor Centre at Punakaiki.

Sea caverns under the Pancake Rocks.

The Pancake Rocks are a peculiar rock formation, with limestone rocks layered in elegant towers. The BBC imposed digital pterodactyls on these rocks for their *Walking with Dinosaurs* television series — and it did not look odd. Surf surges into the caverns, and with the right sea running can blast up through the blowholes underneath the rocks, creating a memorable short walk.

Opposite the visitor centre the track starts through coastal bush then dense flax (harakeke) and cautiously circumnavigates a surging sea chamber. There are good information signs at the many lookouts. These rocks were formed by sedimentation of shell debris, accumulated and compressed over millions of years, and then uplifted. Shrubs cling to the very edges of the blowholes, which have names like 'Sudden Sound', 'Chimney Pot' and 'Putai' (seaspray). On a clear day you can see Mount Cook in the far distance, though often the Paparoa coast seems to 'smoke' from the heavy spray of the pluming sea.

TRUMAN TRACK

Slightly north of the Pancake Rocks, this track plunges down through a coastal jungle of rimu, matai and entanglements of vines like kiekie and supplejack. Walk through the final flax belt and you are on an exposed rock shelf above the sea.

The broad tidal platforms are stained with colours, and sea stacks take the brunt of the West Coast surf. Seals haul ashore up and down this coast, and little blue penguins nest here. Nikau palms can stick up like weird feather dusters.

Steps go down to a gorgeous beach, where shallow sea caves have been carved out and glisten with subtle colours of lichen and moss. The sea fairly barrels into this tight little bay, but at low tide it is possible to scramble around the greasy rocks to the next bay. It is an ancient, relentless shore.

MOTUKIEKIE COAST
Low-tide exploring past sentinel sea stacks

TRACK

Beach walking and low-tide scrambling. A low tide is essential, and the surf should not be too big either. If you follow the route right through, wet feet are a probability.

WALK TIME AND DISTANCE

1–2 hours (5 km) return. The gold-diggers' terminology on this coast is confusing, since Nine Mile Bluff is at Ten Mile Creek. And the distance between Nine Mile Bluff and Twelve Mile Bluff is not three miles (or 5 km) but 2 km! The frequency of gold-diggers' 'shanties' in the 1860s, serving 'cold tea' along this coast, may have contributed to the confusion.

ONE–HOUR WALK

Twelve Mile Bluff return.

ACCESS AND FACILITIES

Off Highway 6, just past Greigs settlement at the rest area carpark. For Nine Mile Creek beach and carpark, there is an unmarked gravel side-road that leads past a bed-and-breakfast place to a rough carparking area by the beach.

INFORMATION

The Southern Journey, by Mark Pickering, book.

The Paparoa coast highway is wild enough, but out of the car it just gets wilder. This walk explores a cliff-hanging coast, with sea stacks at Motukiekie and a hole in the rock at Ten Mile Creek. Dodging the surf will keep you fit and is exactly what the early travellers had to do. Motu means 'island' in Maori, and kiekie is the rambling, salt-tolerant vine that makes the cliffs such a jungle.

From Greigs walk across the wide exposed sands onto the tidal platforms that swirl out to the sea like solidified ribbons of seaweed. Close to Twelve Mile Bluff large conglomerate boulders have tumbled onto the shore, some coloured terracotta and as fine as Roman mosaics.

Motukiekie is a sensational stand of sea stacks, topped by some tenacious plant life that manages to survive on the spume-soaked headland. Around the corner there is a short sandy beach, and another headland to clamber over where the rocks have slumped, then a passage across tidal platforms to Ten Mile Creek and a surprise — a large hole in a rock. Local legend says the early goldminers scrambled through it to avoid the high tide.

To get to Nine Mile Creek beach and carpark you will get wet feet across Ten Mile Creek, then there is a short rocky clamber over big boulders and under a cliff. You have to hit a low tide right on the button to get through, but then it is an easy, broad beach. There is a safe escape up Ten Mile Creek to the highway.

CROESUS TRACK
Classic pack-track to the tops

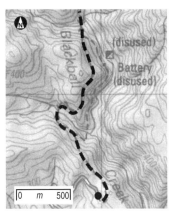

Detail: start of Croesus Track

TRACK
A well-graded goldminers' pack-track to the bush edge, with a short off-track wander up onto Croesus Knob itself.

WALK TIME AND DISTANCE
7–8 hours (18 km) return from Croesus Knob (including a side-trip to the stamping battery).

ONE-HOUR WALK
First Hotel site return.

TWO-HOUR WALK
Second Hotel site return.

FOUR-HOUR WALK
Garden Gully stamping battery return.

SIX-HOUR WALK
Ces Clarke hut return.

ACCESS AND FACILITIES
From Blackball township drive 1 km on Roa Road and turn onto the Blackball road, which winds through forest for 4 km to the Smoke-Ho! carpark. The road is narrow and can get rough, though it is usually suitable for cars.

INFORMATION
Croesus and Moonlight Walks, Department of Conservation brochure; *Ahaura K31* map.

This walk is a wonderful leg-stretcher, following an historic, perambulating track that never loses interest. Indicated above are several shorter return walks for people who do not fancy the full workout, but don not be put off by the times. The walk is on an excellent gradient that makes the hill seem far gentler than it really is, and if it is a fine day you really have to try for the top – Mount Cook is truly awesome.

Take the track from the Smoke-Ho! carpark as it passes a logbook and stay on the top track option to the First Hotel site, in a large, grassy clearing. There are good easy grades up to the Second Hotel site (past Perotti's Mill junction), and up past a couple of lazy zigzags to the Garden Gully junction. This side-track crosses a saddle down to the old Garden Gully Hut then climbs up a side-creek to arguably the best-preserved stamping battery on the coast.

The main Croesus Track zigzags steadily upwards past the old Top Hut, reaching the bush edge at the Ces Clark Memorial Hut. Dedicated to a ranger who died on the track, this was the first mountain hut to be opened by a prime minister (David Lange, in August 1986 — and no, he did not walk).

Fine views already, but once out into the tussock basins the views get better and better, especially if you can manage the final fling up onto Croesus Knob itself. On top is the remains of the aerial cableway for the Croesus Mine, and his proverbial wealth is still not as good as the views.

NELSON CREEK & GOW CREEK TUNNEL

Tricks of track and tunnel

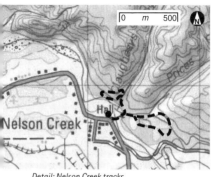

Detail: Nelson Creek tracks

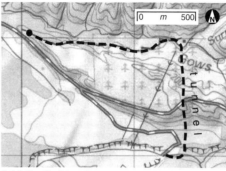

Detail: Gow Creek tunnel

TRACK
Bush trails with streams running through the tunnels. Mostly flat.

WALK TIME AND DISTANCE
Nelson Creek: 1.5 hours (4 km) full circuit (Tailrace Walk and Colls Dam Walk).
Gows Creek Tunnel: 1 hour (2 km) return.

ACCESS AND FACILITIES
From Highway 7 just past Ngahere turn onto the Nelson Creek Road for 6 km to Nelson Creek. Carpark and toilets.

INFORMATION
Nelson Creek Walks, Department of Conservation pamphlet.

A short walk through a fascinating landscape of tunnels, tailraces and tailings, created by goldminers in desperate need of water. Ground sluicing was the dominant technique used at Nelson Creek, but too much water was as much a nuisance as too little. The miners dug tunnels to gain a healthy pressure of water to attack the gold-bearing gravels and trap the heavier gold in riffle boxes, but they also cut tailraces and sludge channels to drain water and the excess tailings away. You can see their hard work and admire their skill.

From the carpark the track starts spectacularly — through a tunnel! Then it is over a long suspension bridge and around to the Tailrace Walk, past the turn-off to Colls Dam, Callaghans and the Tunnel Walk.

The Tailrace Walk is a 20-minute circuit around a number of carefully incised tailraces. Back at the junction with the Tunnel Walk have a look at the beginning of the tunnel. This discharges a small stream into Nelson Creek, and you can walk down it, though you will need a torch. There is a large swimming hole at the Nelson Creek end.

Lastly, go back to the Colls Dam Walk and enjoy this peaceful circuit past Colls Dam then continue round, crossing numerous other tailraces.

GOW CREEK TUNNEL
This is an impressively engineered tunnel, 1 km long, dug with just pick and shovel.

Obviously you need a torch, but in average flows this is a straightforward (with maybe wet knees) trek down the tunnel to come out beside Nelson Creek.

Drive from Nelson Creek the short distance to Gows Creek Road, then follow this reasonable gravel road past the Colls Dam carpark and park after 2 km where the road forks at a dip in the road. The top road is obviously suited only for four-wheel-drives and unless you possess one it is better to walk about 1.5 km to where Gows Creek disappears into the 1-km-long tunnel.

Back at the road forks, the lower and better road continues across farm terraces, then drops steeply to a bridge over the Left Branch of Nelson Creek with a locked gate on it. The exit for the tunnel is 20 metres upstream from this bridge. However, it is better to park up on the terrace, near the metal roller, as there is no turnaround point by the bridge and it is a pain trying to reverse up the hill.

South Westland

GOLDSBOROUGH TRACK & TUNNEL LOOP TRACK

Mossy creeks and the art of tunnelling

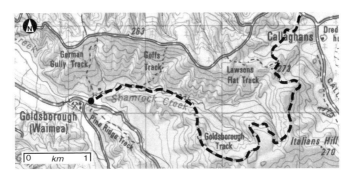

TRACK

An even-graded pack-track in bush, with river crossings and wet feet to reach the miners' tunnels.

WALK TIME AND DISTANCE

2–3 hours (6 km) return.

ACCESS AND FACILITIES

Turn off Highway 6 at Awatuna onto the Stafford–Dilmanstown road and follow this some 10 km to a large carpark, picnic area and campground.

INFORMATION

Goldsborough Walks, Department of Conservation pamphlet.

The great 1865 goldrush was the foremost historic event on the West Coast, and changed the landscape irrevocably. At Goldsborough the land has been completely trashed by generations of goldminers who shifted creeks, stacked pyramids of rocks, and inadvertently created an artistic labyrinth of tunnels. They did things with the pick and shovel we would not attempt with a bulldozer, and the Goldsborough Track is a marvellous testament to their endeavour.

The track initially follows Shamrock Creek quite closely in regrowth bush, then crosses the creek beside a bluestone cliff. Over a low spur there is a side-track back down to Shamrock Creek.

There are two tunnels, the first just 100 metres downstream, over smooth boulders in the mossy riverbed. It is a beautiful piece of work, built to eliminate a bend in the river so as to assist the miners in flushing out the tailing debris.

Upstream 5 minutes is an even better tunnel, some 30 metres long. Both tunnels are well-fashioned examples of the gold-diggers' art, with crypt-like arched ceilings in the green, cloistered riverbed.

OTHER WALKS

The Goldsborough Track continues for another 2 hours to Callaghans Road and the Manzoni Claim, with its huge man-made tunnel.

The Tunnel Loop Track starts 5 km before the Goldsborough carpark, off the Stafford–Dilmanstown road. It is not well signposted (as the Tunnel Terrace Walk), but the kids will love it. It starts through a water-race tunnel, loops around old stone stacks of tailings past the entrances to other tunnels, and pops out on the road through the clever finale of a tunnel; 10 minutes of frolicking fun.

An elegant, mossy tunnel on the Goldsborough Track.

KANIERE WATER RACE
Easy walking along a goldminers' water race

TRACK
Well graded and gravelled all the way. Baby buggies can be taken to the hut and road.

WALK TIME AND DISTANCE
3–4 hours (9 km) one way.

ONE-HOUR WALK
Ward Road return (5 km).

ACCESS AND FACILITIES
Drive to Lake Kaniere, where there is a carpark and picnic area by the control gates. The power-station end starts with a significant hill climb and is not as interesting.

INFORMATION
Kaniere Water Race Walkway, Department of Conservation pamphlet.

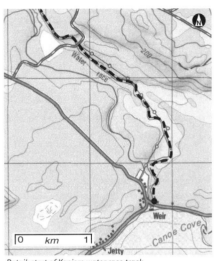

Detail: start of Kaniere water race track

The Kaniere water race was built in 1875 to provide water to boost the flagging Kaniere goldfield. The water flowed but alas not the gold, so by 1916 the race was utilised for power supply instead, and it has stayed that way. The fully automated

The track alongside the Kaniere water race.

Kaniere power station is one of the smallest in the country and supplies between 100 and 125 houses in Hokitika. The water race walk is easy going, through bush forest and past tunnels, with the constant sweet accompaniment of the rippling race.

From the control gates by Lake Kaniere the first part of the walkway goes through cutover manuka forest with some emerging kamahi. Freshwater mussels can be seen in the race, and it is a cruisey 3 km to Wards Road and the old Racemans Hut.

The bush gets thicker and taller for the next section, with ferns underneath the rimu and miro. The race disappears briefly into three tunnels and you get good views of the river below, before eventually reaching Tunnel Hill, where a 2-km tunnel takes the water race through to the power station. The track picks up a rather uninteresting bulldozer trail then drops down quickly to a gravel road, which is followed down to the carpark.

OKARITO LAGOON
Pack-track to wilderness lagoon

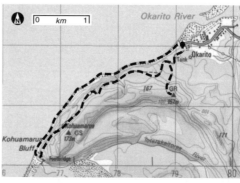

TRACK
Good bush pack-track one way, easy beach walking the other. A low tide is essential.
WALK TIME AND DISTANCE
3–4 hours (6 km) return.
ONE–HOUR WALK
Okarito Trig return.
ACCESS AND FACILITIES
From Highway 6 at 'The Forks' it is 13 km to Okarito, where there is a campground, information post (in the wharf shed), signposted walks and a boat-launching ramp. Tide tables at the beach noticeboard.
INFORMATION
Okarito Walks, Department of Conservation pamphlet.

This is a 150-year-old bush pack-track that once sturdily carried goldminers to the Three Mile Lagoon, but now carries walkers. The views of Mount Cook and Tasman across the tea-stained waters are just jaw-dropping, and on the beach return there may be sleeping seals on a shoreline that rarely gets disturbed. Okarito was a gold town that lasted from 1865 to about 1868 — three glorious, mad, drunken years, all gone now except for the pack-track.

From the sign by the roadside (before the beach carpark) the pack-track climbs up to a track junction with the Okarito trig. If the day is fine this is a most worthwhile side trip, on up to a lookout platform with views of Okarito in the foreground and the long horizon filled with the snowy peaks of the Southern Alps.

The main pack-track rolls along to Three Mile Lagoon, sometimes coming close to the cliff edge, with a good crop of ferns and mosses beside the track. It drops

Mount Cook from Three Mile Lagoon.

sharply to a junction, the left-hand fork going to a long bridge over Three Mile Lagoon. The other fork goes on to the wide beach. The lagoon entrance is often blocked by a sandbar.

With a low tide the beach walk is pretty easy, and quicker than the pack-track, with not much rock-hopping and the constant surf rolling in. Occasionally a seal hauls ashore, but often it is just the gulls that take an interest in you, on this restless, rollicking coast.

ROBERTS POINT
Tough track to an historic glacier outlook

TRACK
An adventurous up-and-down bush track with some slimy rock-slab work, a scramble up a ladder, three suspension bridges and a boardwalk bolted into the rock. All in all, not for the faint-hearted.

WALK TIME AND DISTANCE
4–5 hours (9 km) return.

TWO–HOUR WALK
Hendes seat and hut shelter.

ACCESS AND FACILITIES
From Highway 6, take the Glacier Access Road some 3 km to the Douglas Bridge carpark.

INFORMATION
Franz Josef Visitor Centre. *Roberts Point*, Department of Conservation pamphlet.

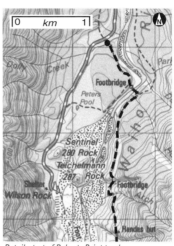
Detail: start of Roberts Point track

This track was the main tourist track to the Franz Josef Glacier in the 1930s, hence the old lunch shelter at Hendes Hut. Since then the glacier has retreated dramatically, leaving the lookout rather in limbo. Seventy years ago you were only metres above the glacier, but today imagination has to fill some of the gaps. But do not let me put you off — it is still a fantastic viewpoint.

From the carpark you cross the flat bush to the historic Douglas Bridge, then cross Hugh Creek as the track winds up and down (a staircase at one point) through dense rata and kamahi forest before climbing abruptly up to a swing bridge across Arch Creek.

The track sidles across bare schist rock and scrubby slopes to a well-situated seat and the old Hendes Hut shelter. Immediately there is a nerve-racking descent down a boardwalk bolted into the rockface. Then the track climbs and crosses the dramatically incised Rope Creek on a swaying swing bridge.

It is a steady climb over greasy rocks, then a rather tedious sidle with no views at all, and you begin to wonder if the track will go on and on and when — Roberts Point arrives abruptly. Initially you might be disappointed, for you cannot see down onto the foot of the glacier. But once you have sat awhile you become absorbed in the scenery and the tremendous scale of the Franz Josef icefall as it cracks and groans down its severe rock corridor to the sea.

The view from Roberts Point.

LAKE MATHESON
Reflections around a pristine lake

TRACK
A high-grade flat track and boardwalk around a lake. Most people go clockwise.

WALK TIME AND DISTANCE
1.5–2 hours (2 km) return.

ACCESS AND FACILITIES
From Fox Glacier village drive 5 km to the signposted carpark, where there are toilets and a cafe, a pleasing novelty.

INFORMATION
Fox Glacier Visitor Centre. *Lake Matheson*, Department of Conservation pamphlet.

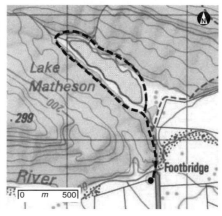

In the last century Lake Matheson would have been called a 'beauty spot', and that is still true, as 20 coach tours a day confirm. The backpacker buses try to get in early for the famous 'view of views' and the tranquil waters that giveth off the perfect picture. God, however, does not always supply the perfect weather, and cloud has ruined many a fine reflection, but the lake is still pretty and pristine.

The track crosses the Clearwater Stream bridge and goes to the first viewpoint, but you need to go to the head of the lake and climb up to the View of Views platform to get the 'classic' tablemat and calendar view. On the way the rich rainforest is made of tall kahikatea, rimu and matai, with a lush understorey of shrubs and ferns.

A few minutes on from the View of Views there is a side track to Reflection Island, a particularly pretty perch beside the lake. The famous reflections partly result from the brown coloration of the water, which is caused by organic matter leached from the humus on the forest floor. The calm surface of the lake accentuates any bird sound. The main track then moves away from the lake and follows the forest around to farm paddocks with splendidly isolated kahikatea trees.

FOX GLACIER
Kea and ice

Note: position of glacier and track can alter

TRACK
A well-marked track follows over old moraine humps and a scree slide to the foot of the glacier. There are two walks to glaciers on the West Coast, the Franz Josef and the Fox, and one is as good as the other. Since I have included the Roberts Point track at Franz Josef, this walk balances the options.

WALK TIME AND DISTANCE
1 hour (2 km) return.

ACCESS AND FACILITIES
From Highway 6 by the Fox River, follow the signposted glacier road to the carpark. This road is often subject to change and closure due to river floods.

INFORMATION
Fox Glacier Visitor Centre.

The glaciers are retreating again. After some interesting advances in the late 1990s the Fox and Franz Josef glaciers are following the centuries-old pattern of shrinkage, but there is still a lot of glacier to go. The scale of the mountains, the sheer cliffs and the crumbling tongue of the glacier make for an awesome short walk. And the kea are never in retreat.

The drive in alone is worth the walk, crossing the Fox River floodplain and winding under the severe cliffs of Cone Rock. At the carpark there are usually kea, which cock their heads obligingly as the cameras click.

The well-marked track climbs over a series of humps, which are actually lumps of old glacier ice covered in rock. The views are good already as the trail winds over the scree slope and crosses the stream by a footbridge.

You cannot touch the ice, for obvious reasons — a large lump might fall on you (it has squashed one or two incautious people) — and the glacier tongue is roped off. Still, you can feel the icy air rolling off the glacier, and photograph an object that, if you came back the following month, would have already moved on.

PARINGA CATTLE TRACK
Historic route over the mountains

TRACK
Good benched track, but can get wet and muddy underfoot. Flat to Blowfly Hut, then a steady but graceful climb up to Maori Saddle. This is a big day-trip, so start early.

WALK TIME AND DISTANCE
6–7 hours (24 km) return to Maori Saddle Hut. Total climb of 500 metres.

TWO–HOUR WALK
Blowfly Hut return.

ACCESS AND FACILITIES
Off Highway 6, signposted 5 km short of Lake Moeraki.

INFORMATION
Haast F37, Landsborough G37 maps. *Haast-Paringa Cattle Track*, Department of Conservation pamphlet.

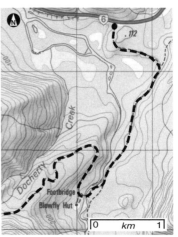

Detail: north end of Paringa Cattle Track

An historic cattle road, climbing into the high mist and memories of another time. It was once a Maori trail, then a cattle road until the early 1960s, and you can still see an old roadman's hut and the remains of the telegraph line. Now it is a splendid walking track, with your only companions the ghosts of roadmen past, and the squawking of kaka.

From the Lake Moeraki end the track is muddy at first then connects onto a good pack-track that sidles through bush over to the big suspension bridge over the Moeraki (or Blue) River. Blowfly Hut sits in a clearing. I did not notice the blowflies but I can vouch for the sandflies.

From here the excellently graded track starts its slow perambulations up to Maori Saddle hut. The forest is rich in rimu and silver beech and the birdlife is equally profuse. Kereru, tomtits, fantails, bellbirds and kaka add sound to a rarely silent forest. Old totara posts on the trackside indicate the telegraph line, and the flat stones in the creeks were laid to make the passage of the cattle easier.

After an hour you reach the narrow Whakapohai Saddle, and a little later there is a side-track up to a mica mine. The main track climbs steadily, meandering past several side-creeks (Thompson, Stormy and finally the Whakapohai itself), then descends a little to the spacious hut at Maori Saddle. The hut stands in a cleared beech glade and has 12 bunks and a woodstove. It is a cosy place for lunch, especially as rain is not unheard of in this locality, and you have a long, easy romp downhill to look forward to.

SMOOTHWATER BAY
Wet feet to a secluded bay

TRACK
A good, easy pack-track, then a river to follow. Wet feet are unavoidable – it is part of the joy.

WALK TIME AND DISTANCE
3–4 hours (7 km) return.

ONE–HOUR WALK
To Smoothwater River return.

ACCESS AND FACILITIES
From Highway 6 follow the sealed road some 45 km to Jackson Bay, where there is an information shelter and toilets.

INFORMATION
The surreal shelter at Jackson Bay has good historical information on the bay's settlements. *The Southern Journey*, by Mark Pickering, book.

At the bottom of the West Coast is Jackson Bay, where today there are a few houses, a wharf and some fishing boats. An old pack-track goes over to Smoothwater Bay. Both bays were sites for ill-fated government settlement schemes – Irish, English and German at Jackson Bay, mainly Scandinavian at the Waiatoto River, Italian at Okuru River, and Polish at Smoothwater Bay.

What a beautiful land to fail in, and fail they did. Isolated and poorly equipped in a wretched climate, the colonists slipped away to somewhere more favourable (and presumably drier). The well-marked track starts from Jackson Bay, following the old pack-track that was probably started by the Polish settlers in 1875. A gentle climb and fall.

The Smoothwater River is a wide, shining path, rarely more than knee-deep, and you walk on soft, easy gravels. On a sunny day splashing down the river is delightful.

The thick bush is full of birdsong and it is about 1.5 km down to the coast, crossing the stream maybe eight or ten times.

The beach is a curvaceous curl of sand; at low tide you can explore along either shoreline, with the route to the Stafford rewarded by sea stacks and strange rock 'flowers' – but that is another story. At Smoothwater Bay there is a grass terrace overlooking the bay, where both you and the sandflies will no doubt enjoy an excellent lunch.

Lonely Smoothwater Bay.

221

BENMORE PENINSULA
Simple and surreal

TRACK

A well-signposted circuit gravel track, but with more climbing than you might expect.

WALK TIME AND DISTANCE

1–2 hours (6 km) return. 15 minutes return to 'house boat bay' and point.

ACCESS AND FACILITIES

Carpark. Lookout and seat halfway.

INFORMATION

Day Walks of the Mackenzie Basin and Waitaki Valley, Department of Conservation pamphlet. A topographical map is useful for understanding the complex geography.

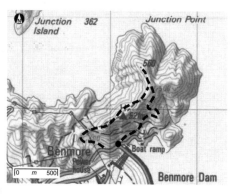

Humans do remarkable things to landscapes. Obliteration is popular, as is good old-fashioned stuff-it-up, but every now and then we manage to pull off something remarkable and make the landscape look more beautiful than nature intended. Lake Benmore was created by the huge Benmore dam (1956–65), and behind it spread an intricate waterway into these old Otago valleys, softening the harsh rock with a surreally stunning blue.

The peninsula juts out into the lake and the walk starts at the lookout carpark above the dam. There is a short sloping track down to a houseboat in the bay, but follow the main track as it climbs up on a steady grade. There is quite a bit of climbing involved (and some steps), before you leave the pine forest and come out on an alpine scree knob.

Lake Benmore.

Here, everything is satisfying contrasts. The brooding hills have long spur lines that get swallowed into the blue lake, and the fir trees on the peninsula turn gold in autumn. Even the power lines do not seem out of place, and spin along the sides of the mountains like gossamer threads of a crazed but methodical spider.

The track continues along to another lookout, then down to a saddle, and completes a well-composed circuit back to the carpark.

DEEP STREAM & GUNNS BUSH
Two easy tracks in harsh country

Detail: Gunns Bush

Detail: Deep Stream

TRACK
Deep Stream: an easy, well-graded gravel track.
Gunns Bush: a well-marked bush trail with one small hill.

WALK TIME AND DISTANCE
Deep Stream: 1 hour (2 km) return.
Gunns Bush: 1–1.5 hours (in part a circuit).

ACCESS AND FACILITIES
Deep Stream: from Highway 83 cross the Aviemore Dam and take the lake road north 1 km.
Gunns Bush: Gunns Bush is signposted from Highway 1 just south of Makikihi, about 15 km inland. There are various ways there, but one route from Highway 1 is to take Lower Hook Road, then the Waimate–Hunter road and Upper Hook Road past the youth camp to the carpark.

INFORMATION
Day Walks of the Mackenzie Basin and Waitaki Valley, Department of Conservation pamphlet (for Deep Stream).

DEEP STREAM
This is a short and sweet track that you wish would go further than it actually does. After a dramatic entry into the Deep Stream canyon, the track sidles high then drops down onto a scrubby flat where it dribbles into nothing. Ah well, still the canyon was worth it, with the vivid contrast between the electric blue of Deep Stream, the naval blue of Lake Aviemore and the soft, washed blue of the sky.

GUNNS BUSH
Tucked under the Hunter Hills are a number of small bush reserves, lonely, isolated remnants of what was once an extensive foothills forest behind Waimate. Gunns

223

Bush is perhaps the best of these reserves, with a dark, mossy interior and an unexpectedly rich and vibrant fern field under the forest.

The track follows alongside the cheerful brook, and you have to ignore the pine plantations on the spurs above you and enjoy the dense fuchsia forest and its strange (almost Middle Earth-ish) mossy understorey. At the loop junction the track climbs steadily, then dips down and around back to the river again, retracing an easy path through this spectacular outdoor fernery.

Deep Stream.

The view over Bushy Beach from the penguin hide, Graves Walkway (see facing page).

GRAVES WALKWAY
People and penguins on parade

TRACK

A flat, well-benched track, and some beach walking. Note that the low-tide track and the clifftop path are prone to erosion; maintenance has proved difficult and these tracks are sometimes closed.

WALK TIME AND DISTANCE

1–2 hours (4 km) return. One section of the shoreline route needs a low tide to get past, however there is a high-tide clifftop alternative track.

ACCESS AND FACILITIES

From Oamaru take Tyne Street turning into Arun Street, then taking Waterfront/Breakwater Road for 1 km to the carpark by the breakwater. The south access is along Tyne Street to the top of the hill, then via Bushy Beach Road to the carpark.

At the harbour end of the track there is a grandstand for viewing the twilight penguin parade of little blues (korara) that scuttle across to the fenced-off burrows under the cliffs. Little blues weigh about 1 kg, with a height of 25 cm. There is a warden and a charge for the parade.

INFORMATION

Graves Walkway, Department of Conservation pamphlet.

This is a short, charming coastal track that features good views, pillow lava at low tide, a secluded beach and the home of the world's rarest penguins — the yellow-eyed or hoiho. A striking bird, half a metre high, with yellow feathers around the eye and a yellow crown, the penguins weigh between 5 and 8 kg. The 'Grave' in the name of the walkway refers to W.G. Grave, a local man who developed this walking track for Oamaru people. It was opened in the 1930s, and despite its short distance the track has so much interest that it feels longer.

The well-graded track cuts around headlands, where a side-trail leads up to old gun emplacements and a lighthouse, and continues up to a lookout on the hill. This is the clifftop return track if the tide is against you. Otherwise the main track drops down to a small, sandy beach where there are tidal platforms and pillow lava visible at low tide.

The track restarts at Cape Wenbrow, and goes around the orange sands of Bushy Beach. Here a track climbs up to the carpark or the bird-hide on a prominent ridge.

Both the little blue and the rare yellow-eyed penguin nest here, and the best time to watch for penguins is in the morning or late evening as they cross the sands. The birds will not come ashore if they see people on the beach. All penguins are vulnerable to disturbances throughout the breeding and moulting seasons, so follow the advice on the information boards, and watch from a distance at the specially made hide.

KATIKI BEACH
A beach of boulders

TRACK
Flat, easy walking. A good low tide important.

WALK TIME AND DISTANCE
1–2 hours return, rambling around. Various, 4–8 km return.

ACCESS AND FACILITIES
Alongside Highway 1 there are several rest areas. The two either side of Back Creek are good starting points, then you can walk 4 km south, seeing most of the interesting rock formations. North from Back Creek is a wild sandy beach, with Waimataitai Lagoon at the far end.

INFORMATION
Moeraki and Katiki Point, Department of Conservation pamphlet.

Detail: section of Katiki Beach

The coastline between Oamaru and Dunedin has many surprises, which the average punter who stays on the main highway will never enjoy. Highway 1 resolutely avoids the interesting places, so that Kakanui, Moeraki township, Katiki Point, Shag Point, Trotters Gorge, Matanaka Farm Estate, Huriawa Pa and the Seacliff hospital site are all gloriously bypassed. For many people only the tacky cafe at Moeraki boulders gets a visit, and they will speed on past Katiki Beach not realising it has its own mini-parade of Moeraki boulders.

On the beach itself there is no sign or sound of the highway, and from Back Creek it is easy walking on the gorgeous wide sands. Initially there are small, isolated boulders, but further on there are some large hollowed-out boulders.

At the cliffs you get an interfusion of tidal platforms and boulder shapes, with mini-domes encrusted with sea-moss. Around another headland the wide, easy sands continue to the rest area.

These strange boulders are called concretions, and they are not unique to Moeraki. There are good examples at Waimarama Beach in Hawke's Bay, in North Canterbury and at other sites around the country. They are formed by the precipitation of calcium carbonate around a small nucleus, like a piece of wood or shell, and can take millions of years to form. Because they are harder than other rocks, the surrounding mudstone gets washed away and the boulders become exposed, as on this lovely beach in Otago.

226   *Boulders on Katiki Beach.*

DUNEDIN CITY WALK – ROSS RESERVOIR
Mossy glen and still reservoir

TRACK
Flat at first, then a short hill walk on a good gravelled track. Well signposted at junctions.

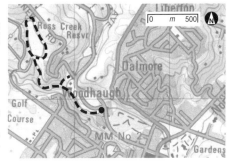

WALK TIME AND DISTANCE
1 hour (3 km) return.

ACCESS AND FACILITIES
From central Dunedin turn off George Street into Malvern Street, then Woodhaugh Road. Alternative access off Rockside Road.

INFORMATION
From Sea to Silver Peaks, by Graham Bishop and Antony Hamel, book.

An easy urban walk into a rich, fern-filled gully and up to the serene pond of the Ross Reservoir. This historic dam is one of only two working nineteenth-century dams in the country; the other is also in Otago, in the Eweburn. The Ross dam was built in 1867 of local stone and puddled clay, to supply the rapidly growing city of Dunedin, flushed with gold and hope. The pretty valve tower became a showpiece on picture postcards of the time. The walk is a satisfying woodland promenade only 2 km from the city centre, and it would be true to say that it has remained popular for well over a hundred years.

At Woodhaugh Road, where there is reasonable carparking, the track follows the Water of Leith past a boulder trap, then across a footbridge and on up past a quarry to the track junction with Rockside Road. There are some excellent information panels on the way. The broad track now gets very shady and green as it climbs up along the deep, mossy creek and on to the dam up to the seldom-rippled reservoir.

There is a circuit track around the lake, and the valve tower is worth a look. What is surprising is that after leaving the bustle of downtown Dunedin the view from the dam is almost completely rural.

OTHER WALKS
It would be relatively easy to connect the Ross Reservoir tracks with the Dunedin Botanic Gardens, via Woodhaugh Gardens. Indeed, there are pleasant path connections and student backstreets that could be linked all the way alongside the Water of Leith to the University of Otago.

The valve tower, Ross Reservoir.

DUNEDIN CITY WALK – ORGAN PIPES & MOUNT CARGILL

Classic hill climb

TRACK
A hill walk on a good gravel track, but steep only at the beginning. Well signposted.

WALK TIME AND DISTANCE
2–3 hours (4 km) return.

ONE-HOUR WALK
Organ Pipes return.

ACCESS AND FACILITIES
From central Dunedin drive into the North-East Valley up North Road, which blends into Norwood Street then Mount Cargill Road, almost to the ridgeline saddle. There is a pitiful carpark.

INFORMATION
From Sea to Silver Peaks, by Graham Bishop and Antony Hamel, book.

Mount Cargill has a central position in Dunedin's geography and psychology, helped no doubt by the massive 104-metre television tower. The mountain can be seen from many parts of the city and the peninsula, and the name – a reference to Captain William Cargill – taps deeply into the city's pioneering past. So it is a 'must do' walk, but it is also a very good walk with fabulous views and only one disappointment – the Organ Pipes.

From the carpark there are steep steps, then the track settles down as it passes a rock cave before zigzagging up to the foot of the rock outcrop called the Organ Pipes. Curious yes, but overrated, and they seem rather small. Large, segmented volcanic chunks are piled below the outcrop; indeed, some of these segments have been utilised thriftily to make the steps for the track.

The track is steady from here to a saddle and a side-track to Buttars Peak (617 m), with a good view on top. The native scrub is growing well up here and the views are getting less, with emergent totara and tall mountain cedars.

There is a flat section then a junction with the track to Bethunes Gully. The views in the tussockline are now very good, and the track sidles around the base of Mount Cargill and turns quickly to the summit.

This is not a beautiful place. There is an ugly assemblage of concrete boxes and unlovely metallic structures, but at the other end of the summit from the tower there is a rock outcrop that makes a fine rest area. On a fair day you need an hour to absorb the view, because practically everything can be seen.

SANDFLY BAY
The bay where sand flies and seals lie

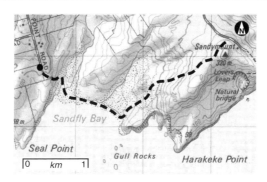

TRACK
Easy down to Sandfly Bay on farmland and sand dunes, but a steady hill climb up to Sandymount carpark.

WALK TIME AND DISTANCE
1–2 hours (4 km) one way to Sandymount.

ONE-HOUR WALK
Sandfly Bay return.

ACCESS AND FACILITIES
About 18 km from Dunedin. Take Highcliff Road on Otago Peninsula (which leads to Larnach's Castle) and follow it to Pukehiki, and shortly afterwards take Sealpoint Road to a small carpark at the road-end. Signposted. There is alternative access via Highcliff Road, then Sandymount Road to a high carpark. From here there is walking track access to Sandymount, The Chasm and Sandfly Bay.

INFORMATION
From Sea to Silver Peaks, by Graham Bishop and Antony Hamel, book.

There is a strong sense of welcome as you cross the farmland towards Sandfly Bay. The headlands' two strong arms seem to reach out to you, and the sand and sea glitter. The farm track drops quickly downhill and you can let yourself go at the top of a huge sandhill, with a glorious romp down to the beach plain.

There is much to see. The wind manufactures small ventifacts, rocks shaped curiously by the abrasion of wind-blown sand, and everywhere the sand is patterned in absorbing and delicate shapes. Sandfly Bay is named after the wind, not the insects.

A small fur-seal colony exists on the far western end of the beach, and there are yellow-eyed penguins. There is a small observation hide behind the dunes, though the birds are rarely seen except at dusk and dawn. No dogs allowed.

Just at this end of the beach a thinly poled route climbs up through the sculptured sand dunes to the scrub line. The obvious route follows a fenceline and a 250-metre climb up to the carpark, and the bay looks lovely.

TUNNEL BEACH
Sea cliffs, sea stacks and whimsy

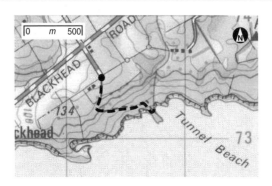

TRACK
A downhill walk on a farmland grass track, followed by a steady uphill walk to the carpark. A low tide is useful.

WALK TIME AND DISTANCE
2 hours (2 km) return.

ACCESS AND FACILITIES
From Dunedin follow Highway 1 to Green Island, then turn onto Green Island Bush Road across Blackhead Road to the small carparking area. Take care not to block the turning area for other users. The track is closed from August to October.

If you are rich you can afford some eccentricity, and some privacy. Captain Cargill had a tunnel built through this sandstone headland in the 1870s to give his family exclusive access to their own private beach.

But now even we peasants can get there, and what a place it is — a powerful carved coastline of arches, sea stacks and sandstone cliffs, where the honey rock colours contrast with the wild blue sea.

From the carpark it is a steady downhill to the top of a broad sea arch, and views along the coast to other sea stacks. The tunnel has concrete steps and drops steeply to the surging bay. I do not fancy swimming here myself, and it is not recommended, but what a beautiful and battered shoreline.

The only down side is the 150 metres of climbing to regain the carpark.

The cliffs at Tunnel Beach.

Central Otago, Catlins & Southland
SUTTON SALT LAKE
Sliver of skinks and a sort of inland sea

TRACK
Well-marked tussock trail, mostly flat.

WALK TIME AND DISTANCE
1–2 hours (4 km) return.

ACCESS AND FACILITIES
From Highway 87, turn down Kidds Road and travel 2 km to the signposted carpark.

INFORMATION
Sutton Salt Lake Scenic Reserve, Department of Conservation pamphlet.

You cannot equivocate with a place like 'Central'; either it satisfies the soul or it repels you. Here, even the sky has its own peculiarities, with vast cauliflower cumulus building over the Rock and Pillar Range. And the salt lake is peculiar too, as far away from the sea as you can get, yet rainwater runs over these arid rocks and brings out tiny traces of salt that over years have accumulated and encouraged the odd situation of salt-tolerant coastline plants fringing the lake.

The track is circular, threading through a tussock plain and schist rock outcrops that every now and again hold a shiver of light where a skink had been basking. The occasional falcon flicks high above, and if the lake has water in it (sometimes it dries up) there will always be a pair of paradise ducks — I guarantee it.

The lake soothes this desperately dry land, and if it is hot, you will probably want to quench your thirst!

A lonely walker at Sutton Salt Lake.

POOL BURN GORGE (CENTRAL OTAGO RAIL TRAIL)
An open air history book

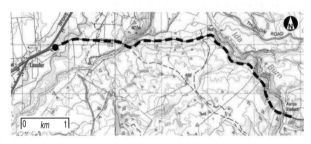

TRACK
Easy and flat, with a gentle climb on a gravelled track.

WALK TIME AND DISTANCE
3–4 hours (14 km) return.

ONE-HOUR WALK
40 minutes return to Manuherikia River bridge.

ACCESS AND FACILITIES
From Highway 85 at Lauder a signpost and a short road lead to a picnic area, passing a toilet on the way. Lauder's other main claim to fame is that it has the (officially) coldest recorded temperature in New Zealand — -25° Celsius — but in compensation temperatures can also reach the high thirties during the summer — if that is compensation.

Old railway lines make excellent walking tracks, and the Central Otago Rail Trail is one of the best. It was designed for mountain bikers and it is doubtful that you will want to walk the whole of it, but this is one of the best bits. The trail wriggles alongside the pretty Pool Burn gorge, negotiating two bridges and two tunnels on the way, and you pass through a landscape that is rarely seen.

An historic railway bridge on the Pool Burn Gorge trail.

The start of the rail trail is well-signposted, just past the gun club, and it is about 1 km to the Manuherikia River bridge. This is a fine iron bridge, with an information panel detailing its history.

It is then a further 3 km to the Pool Burn gorge and the first tunnel. You could get away without a torch, but the tunnel has a kink in it where both ends are hidden, and you literally cannot see your hand in front of your face. You have to use it as a guide against the wall.

The second tunnel is 1 km further on, and straighter, and then it is a short distance to the Pool Burn bridge, the highest on the entire rail trail — quietly spectacular. A short distance further on the gorge ends, and there are views over the flat, soothing land.

The lenticular rocks seem to mimic the saucer-like clouds, and this is a good meditative location in which to admire a land that has no equal in New Zealand.

Note: There is some confusion as to whether this gorge is the Pool Burn or the Ida Burn gorge. The topographic map clearly marks it 'Ida Burn' but the Central Otago Rail Trail brochure calls it 'Pool Burn'.

BUTCHERS DAM & FLAT TOP HILL
Wild lands and wild thymes.

TRACK
Some hill walking in tussock and scrublands.

WALK TIME AND DISTANCE
Optional 1–2 hours (3–4 km) return.

ACCESS AND FACILITIES
Off Highway 8, a few kilometres south of Alexandra. Carpark and information sign.

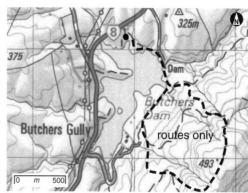

This track gives you quick, easy access to a typical Central Otago landscape, and it also incorporates Butchers Dam, a clean curve of concrete with a trickling waterfall from the overflow of the lake. After the dam you are on your own, and various old farm tracks wind up onto Flat Top Hill.

Larger trees have given up the struggle with Otago's blighting extremes of temperature, so the place is barren, with the odd result that birds have to nest in rock crannies. The rock tors have an almost human-like quality in the way they arrange themselves, in both community and solitary groups. Sometimes a face seems to peep out, or eyes seem to stare. These are the ghosts of shepherds and gold-diggers who moved through here, their hopes soon turned to stone.

Botanically, Flat Top Hill is interesting, which is why the Department of Conservation owns it. There are 180 native vascular plants and several rarities, including a native forget-me-not. However, what mostly thrives here is the ghastly briar, the sickly scented thyme, and the downright weird woolly mullein.

All are passengers on the human cargo, and all no doubt have their defenders, although briar needs no defence. I cannot think of a worse weed anywhere. It is a pricklesome, useless, infesting plant that will in time entangle the clean, free ways of this land, so that eventually no one will be able to reach the skyline.

Butchers Dam.

CATLINS RIVER TRACK
Silver river through an emerald forest

TRACK
Often flat travel on a forest trail beside the river, but some climbs over spurs and back up to the carparks.

WALK TIME AND DISTANCE
3–4 hours (9 km) one way from Wallis to the Tawanui camping area. 1–2 hours (4 km) one way from Wallis to Franks Creek carpark. Full Catlins Wisp to Tawanui 5–6 hours. The signposted times seem pretty

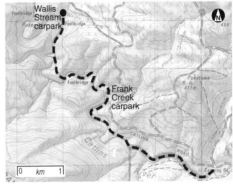

generous to me. If you take the Wallis to Franks Creek option you could walk back along the forestry road, which is quite easy and pleasant walking; about 3–4 hours for the round trip.

ACCESS AND FACILITIES
From Highway 92 turn onto Catlins Valley Road at Houpapa, about 8 km south of Owaka; well signposted. Follow the signposts some 6 km to the Tawanui camping area, where there are toilets and picnic tables. From here on the roads are forestry — gravel and narrow but well maintained. It is about 7 km from Tawanui to the turn-off to the Wallis Stream carpark, and a steep 500-metre descent to the carpark itself. This last stretch can get muddy and a 4WD might be useful after rain.

INFORMATION
Walks and Tracks in the Catlins, New Zealand Forest Service booklet. This wonderful booklet (published in 1983) is probably impossible to get hold of, but you never know your luck, someone might reprint it. Otherwise try libraries.

The inland geography of the Catlins is a munched up, crazy paving of bush reserves, farmland, gum plantations and leftover logging areas. Some of the best forest left is alongside the Catlins River, which spins a silver thread through a mossy and green-bearded beech forest. The river is popular with anglers, and provides welcome seclusion from some of the Catlins' more squally weather.

At Wallis Stream the track passes the junction with the upstream track to the Wisp (great name!) and follows gently alongside the river. Here and there the river slicks over rock cascades, and the silver beech forest is healthy and mature.

After 1 km the track climbs steadily over a side spur then drops down to a long footbridge over the river. Another 1 km or so brings you to another swing bridge and a track junction. It is a short climb up a gully to the main Catlins road.

Otherwise, continue downstream, with mostly easy travel apart from one short climb, some 5 km to the Tawanui camping area. A soothing walk.

PICNIC POINT & KINGS ROCK
Estuary and exploration

TRACK
Flat walking to Picnic Point on the beach or gravelled bush track, but there is a hill on the way to Kings Rock with some mud on the way. A low tide is almost essential to enjoy the estuary and rock platforms.

WALK TIME AND DISTANCE
2 hours (4 km) return to Kings Rock.

ONE–HOUR WALK
Picnic Point return.

ACCESS AND FACILITIES
From Highway 82 at Papatowai store (a remarkable place, selling everything including most foods, good wine, takeaways and 91-octane petrol) drive

through the bach backstreets down to the foreshore and picnic area. There is a children's play area up the road a wee way.

INFORMATION
Walks and Tracks in the Catlins, New Zealand Forest Service booklet.

The Catlins is a coastline that demands exploration, and rewards it. A quick drive through the area on Highway 92 will miss the magic of the place entirely. You will not see much coastline, or enjoy the wonderful Southland light that squabbles over it and illuminates it. At Papatowai the Tahakopa River swings out into the bay and has manufactured a small, brilliant estuary at Picnic Point.

From the carpark wander out onto the low-tide sands of the estuary and head south. After less than 1 km is a seat commemorating local landscape painter Edna Robinson. There are some excellent tidal platforms here. From the seat a very good bush track almost good enough for wheelchairs, leads back to Papatowai.

However, just past the seat is a track junction, and to go to Kings Rock the track starts to climb quite steadily through dense coastal forest. You get occasional glimpses of the coast, then the track reaches a fence and farmland, and a poled route leads down a gully back to the shoreline.

Kings Rock is obvious, and there are other rock platforms to explore. It does not look quite possible to return to Picnic Point via the rocks at low tide — but you could give it a go.

The beach at Picnic Point.

WAIPAPA BEACH & SLOPE POINT
The quicksand and the dead

General view from Waipapa Point to Slope Point

TRACK
Mostly flat on a 4WD sand road, beach travel and sand dunes, but take a topographical map. It is useful to have a low tide, and there is some quicksand.

WALK TIME AND DISTANCE
2–3 hours (10 km) one way.

ONE-HOUR WALK
Waipapa Creek return.

ACCESS AND FACILITIES
From Invercargill turn off Highway 92 at Fortrose onto the coastal road to Waikawa Bay. It is about 10 km to the signposted turn-off to Waipapa Point and 20 km to the signposted turn-off to Slope Point. Follow the Slope Point road to the end, 2 km past Slope Point track, to a turning area where the road ends by a 'Four Wheel Drive Vehicles Only' sign.

INFORMATION
F47 Tokanui map.

A raw and restless coastline, with a long, wild beach and stark bits and pieces of human history — a cemetery built for a shipwreck, the bucket chain of an old gold dredge, a solitary lighthouse. This is not a comfortable walk, for Slope Point is the southernmost point of the South Island and gets blasted by winds that often have bits of Antarctica in them. But if you want something a bit different, this will suit you.

At the four-wheel-drive sign follow the sandy road (a legal line) as it cuts through gorse some 2.5 km out to Waipapa Stream. If it is low tide you can probably sneak across the outlet without getting wet feet, but chances are you will have to take your shoes and socks off and wade across. Did I mention the quicksand?

It is strange stuff, not especially threatening, as it lies in a narrow margin of 1–2 metres alongside both sides of the stream. The sand looks solid but your feet puddle into it like porridge. Remember, the streambed is solid; there is no quicksand under the free-flowing water, so that is a safe haven. Otherwise, for the cautious, walk upstream on the dune banks and cross higher up.

One hundred metres past Waipapa Stream is the remains of a gold dredge, tucked behind the main sand dunes out on a flat and pondy area. All that is left is the bucket chain, which has obviously been restored to some extent, but it is rather evocative, and worth hunting about for.

Waipapa Beach stretches a long way in front now, some 4 km to Lake Brunton,

237

An old gold dredge, Waipapa Beach.

which may also have soft sand or quicksand by its outlet. About 1 km from the outlet there is a slightly lower part of the sand dunes, and if you cross this area you should find the Tararua Acre. This is a cemetery built to hold most of the 131 victims from the SS *Tararua*, which hit Otara Reef off Waipapa Point in 1881. It is a bleak, lonely scene, matched by the loneliness of the little wooden Waipapa lighthouse, 2 km further along the beach. This was built in 1884 specifically because of the terrible *Tararua* tragedy.

OTHER WALKS – SLOPE POINT

Off the Slope Point road there is a short signposted walk across farmland to the southernmost point of the South Island. There is a nice sign to take your photo by. Thirty minutes return walk.

Kahikatea wetland, Thomsons Bush (see facing page).

INVERCARGILL CITY WALK – THOMSONS BUSH
City forest and river views

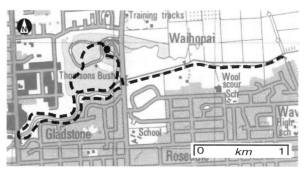

Not all tracks shown

TRACK
Flat, firm gravel or grass in Thomsons Bush, but some muddy patches. Stopbanks are generally mown grass. Baby buggies can be taken along the pathways in the bush and on the Waihopai River stopbanks.

WALK TIME AND DISTANCE
1 hour return from Thomsons Bush, down the north stopbank and back along the south stopbank; 2 hours (3 km) return along the south stopbank to Racecourse Road.

ACCESS AND FACILITIES
Carpark and picnic tables with a children's play area.

Thomsons Bush is the closest piece of native forest to the Invercargill town centre, but it is in a shabby state – no information signboards, litter everywhere, some voracious weeds like ivy and bramble crawling over the understorey, and the bush reserve is obviously the most popular place for Invercargill residents to take their dog for a poop. The whole place is in desperate need of a good management plan.

I am hoping there is one, for this reserve has enormous potential, with graceful wetland areas and tall kahikatea bush walks that link up with the embankment trails alongside the Waihopai River. If you start from the carpark you can cross the footbridge over what must be an original channel of the Waihopai River before the stopbanks persuaded it otherwise. Then wander along the various footpaths – wander because there is no signage – until you reach the edge of the bush, where a mown trail goes around the perimeter.

Follow this on to the stopbank of the Waihopai River and walk west to North Road then back alongside the other stopbank to Queens Drive and Thomsons Bush again. Good river outlooks. Across Queens Drive the southern stopbank will take you 2 km across rural paddocks, and if you wish, right through to Racecourse Road.

FOVEAUX WALKWAY
A blast at Bluff

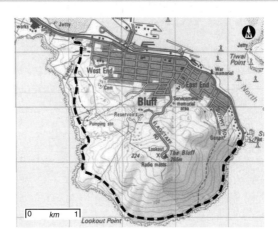

TRACK
Mostly easy, flat travel, on bush and farm tracks. Some mud.

WALK TIME AND DISTANCE
2 hours one way, 3–4 hours return. 3km one way.

ONE-HOUR WALK
Glory Track junction return.

ACCESS AND FACILITIES
Drive from Invercargill to Bluff township, through to the Stirling Point carpark, signposts and the termination of Highway 1. There is a cafe and restaurant (open 7 days) overlooking the carpark.

It is a rare day without wind on this track, something to do with the gale-force personality of Foveaux Strait. The trees get bent, and the sea thrashes along the coast. In compensation there are brilliant light bursts along the squally horizon, and a pretty healthy forest with bellbirds and fantails enjoying the bracing climate.

From Stirling Point the track follows through coastal forest, past the Glory Track junction, then out of the shelter of the bush. Around the corner the coast gets even rougher and rockier, and some parts have an uncanny resemblance to the Western Isles of Scotland. The dark shape of Stewart Island is omnipresent, and squalls blur the horizon.

There is farmland to cross at the end, and the track loses its way somewhat as it follows a fenceline and thick grass over the narrow-neck peninsula and down to Highway 1. It is 4 km plodding on the road through the hardy Bluff township back to Stirling Point. Alas, Fred and Myrtle Flutey are no more, but the Paua House is still glorious.

WANAKA TOWN WALK – WATERFALL CREEK (OR MILLENNIUM WALKWAY)
Wander along a lapping lakeside

TRACK
Well-marked gravel trails, a few small climbs.

WALK TIME AND DISTANCE
2–3 hours (12 km) return.

ONE-HOUR WALK
Waterfall Creek return.

ACCESS AND FACILITIES
From Roys Bay on the foreshore of Wanaka town, or at Waterfall Creek carpark and boat ramp. Picnic area and toilets at Roys Bay.

INFORMATION
Wanaka walks and trails, Department of Conservation pamphlet.

A pleasant, easy walk with plenty of turnaround points, depending on your inclination. The perfect doddle for knackered skiers and jaded socialites. But do not bother searching for the 'waterfall' of Waterfall Creek, which is hidden up the mountainside. Perhaps that is why this recently upgraded track has been renamed the 'Millennium Walkway'.

The first part of the walk follows the gentle lakeside and is well sheltered by willows along to the carpark at Waterfall Creek. Over the bridge the trail winds through a delta of wildflowers, including the blue viper's bugloss, pink briar and the grotesquely impressive yellow woolly mullein.

The track climbs a little above the lake and winds along with views of Ruby Island, concluding at a peaceful viewpoint.

OTHER URBAN WALKS IN WANAKA
Mount Iron (1.5 hours return), lake outlet walk (1 hour return).

Crystal lake edge on the Waterfall Creek walk.

LAKE DIAMOND
Steep tracks to glittering views

TRACK
Well-worn and marked tussock trails up a steep, short hill.

WALK TIME AND DISTANCE
2–3 hours (3 km) return.

40-MINUTE WALK
Lake Diamond lookout return.

ACCESS AND FACILITIES
From Wanaka, about 16 km on the Mount Aspiring road to a roadside carpark and signposts. This track is closed during the winter months, June, July and August. Toilet at Lake Diamond.

INFORMATION
Wanaka walks and trails, Department of Conservation pamphlet.

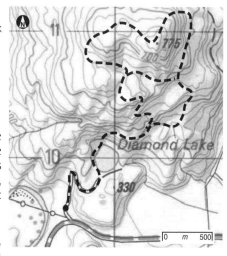

After you have done the shorter walks around Wanaka this is a very good step up. It is almost a 400-metre climb to the high point, with a panorama of views over Lake Wanaka and arguably the best view of Mount Aspiring you will ever see.

Walk up the road to Lake Diamond, which is fringed by willows and raupo, then follow the steep track under rock slabs to the lake lookout. Just past here the track divides, and a map signboard shows how the tracks follow a figure-of-eight pattern through the tussocks.

Keep to the outer curves as the track climbs up through various rock bluffs, passing the link track, and then (and this is the best bit) sidling around the side of the tussock platforms to expose a stunning view of Mount Aspiring.

Then there is just a short walk up to the high point of 775 metres, and Lake Diamond glitters a long way below. This is worth enjoying, for easy trails descend through the nonchalant sheep back to the lake lookout and carpark.

The top of the hill and the view to Mount Aspiring, Lake Diamond walk.

ROB ROY GLACIER
Adventurous walk to ice and spectacle

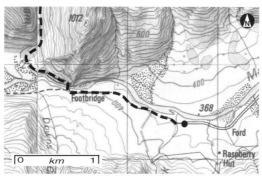

Detail: start of Rob Roy track

TRACK
A good walking track across the bridge and round to Rob Roy Stream, then it gradually gets rougher as it goes upvalley, degenerating into a tramping trail. A steady climb. There are several notable slips, which will probably not improve, and will freak out some people.

WALK TIME AND DISTANCE
3–4 hours (10 km) return.

ONE-HOUR WALK
Seat lookout by Rob Roy Stream return.

ACCESS AND FACILITIES
The Matukituki Valley road is an adventure in itself; good up to the Treble Cone skifield turn-off, it gradually becomes more basic. After a while the road seems to lose most of its gravel, and some parts can get heavily rutted or slick after rain. The major ford is at Niger Stream, by Mount Aspiring station, and if you do not like the look of this then it might be wise to turn back. Beyond here there are four or five more fords before the road ends at the Raspberry Creek carpark. Heavy rain can make any of these fords tricky. It is 55 km from Wanaka, and as they say, half the fun is getting there.

The compensations for coming up the Matukituki River road are obvious.

Sharks Tooth, Matukituki Valley, on the Rob Roy Glacier walk.

This is one of the finest mountain valleys in New Zealand, and you have not even got out of the car. Sharp slabs of mountains bracket either side of the valley, with snowfields suspended in the hanging basins. Waterfalls cut down the valley walls, and the sheer scale of the mountain scenery makes your neck ache. The Rob Roy track leads to a glacier and rock cirque, accessible and awesome.

From the carpark the track crosses a footbridge and skirts the riverbank to a swing bridge across the Matukituki River. There is a short section sidling through bush to a seat and lookout over the valley. The track now climbs steadily up beside the Rob Roy gorge, and there are several slips where the track has disappeared and people have improvised trails across the wet mud and gravel slopes.

A seat marks the halfway point, then the track climbs less steeply, sliding past ribbonwood groves on old slips, and eventually up an old streambed of the creek into the alpine zone. It is not much further to a lookout with information panels — but really the view is language enough.

QUEENSTOWN CITY WALK – QUEENSTOWN HILL
Steady hill to a sculpture

TRACK
Gravelled path, then tussock trails higher up.

WALK TIME AND DISTANCE
2 hours (4 km) return.

ACCESS AND FACILITIES
Access is easiest (that is, highest) off Edinburgh Drive to Belfast Terrace, an area traumatised by a massive subdivision in 2001, but no doubt the mud and debris will have been turned into something nicer by the time you get there.

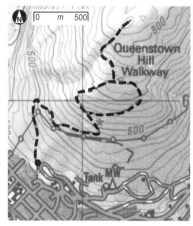

Queenstown Hill is a large, flattish, dome-like peak on the eastern side of the town. Most visitors would not notice it, for it can hardly compete with the likes of Walter Peak and the Remarkables. But there is an excellent walk up it, plus a 'time walk', which is a glorified name for a sequence of information panels. The views anywhere above the treeline are tremendous, and this track is much less busy than Ben Lomond.

The walk is well signposted, and follows a four-wheel-drive track through pine forest up to a stylish wrought-iron gate. The information panels start here, and tell the history of Queenstown from early Maori to the present day.

At the first track junction turn right if you want to keep to the sequence of panels. There is a belt of dark pine forest of Douglas fir, then a rock lookout, then the track breaks out of the pine trees and into the broad tussock country up to a dainty tarn and track junction. On the left is a big metal sculpture, like a Maori kete (or basket), and a soothing view.

For the high point, continue past the tarn for about 20 minutes to the rock cairn. There is an alternative track back from the tarn.

The cairn atop Queenstown Hill.

245

QUEENSTOWN CITY WALK – BEN LOMOND
A classic jaunt to the dominant peak behind Queenstown

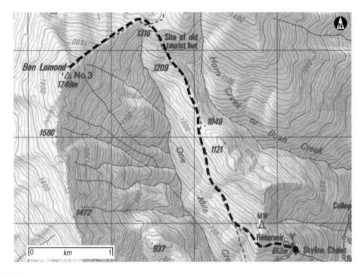

TRACK
Graded gravel path up to the saddle, then a solid foot trail through the tussocks and up to the peak. If you come back via the alternative Ridge Track this has some steep drop-offs.

WALK TIME AND DISTANCE
From the gondola complex to Ben Lomond 4–5 hours (8 km) return; from town to Ben Lomond 5–6 hours return.

ONE-HOUR WALK
Ridge Track junction and saddle return (from the gondola).

ACCESS AND FACILITIES
Most people will go up the gondola and start from there, where the track is well signposted. If you want to save the cost of the gondola you can follow the access road from Lomond Crescent up some zigzags, where at a junction a foot track links with the main Ben Lomond track. Another alternative (particularly as a return route) is to go up the attractive One Mile Creek track, which links up with the main Ben Lomond track.

There are also casual foot trails zigzagging under the gondola pylons themselves, but these are not recommended as they are quite steep. Lastly, from the gondola complex there is the Ridge Track, which climbs up past the paragliding launch area and onto a sharp crested ridge with rock outcrops, meeting the main Ben Lomond track 1.5 km at a saddle. This can be used as an alternative on the return, but it is suited to more experienced walkers.

INFORMATION
Wandering in the Wakatipu, by Becky Reid, booklet.

This is a classic hill walk to a 1748-metre peak behind Queenstown. There are a range of alternative routes and shorter options at the start, but they all coalesce near the saddle and there is no escaping the final heart-pumper to the rocky summit. It should be treated as a full day walk. Take plenty of water.

Once you can tear yourself away from the cappuccinos and souvenirs of the gondola complex there is a good track that (somewhat surprisingly) sidles across the hill and even a little bit down. Once through the pines it meets the historic pack-track, which went across to Moke Creek and the Moonlight goldfields in the 1860s.

Already there are good views of Ben Lomond, and the route becomes obvious as the track climbs steadily past the Ridge Track junction and onwards to the main saddle at 1316 metres. The saddle is a good lunch stop and turnaround place for those who do not fancy the last climb; allow 2–3 hours from the gondola complex.

The foot trail to Ben Lomond is well worn, and negotiates around rock outcrops and tussock faces some 500 metres to the summit. There are no particularly steep parts, and it is easier and quicker than it looks from the saddle. An all-round vista of course.

Nearing the top of Ben Lomond.

SAWPIT GULLY & BIG HILL PACK-TRACK
Wandering water races and rollicking pack-tracks

TRACK
A gravel track on the Sawpit Gully circuit, and tussock paths on old water races and the pack-track up to Big Hill saddle. 300 metres climb on the Sawpit Gully circuit; 600 metres up to Big Hill saddle.

WALK TIME AND DISTANCE
4–5 hours (10 km) return from Big Hill saddle; 2–3 hours (6 km) return for the Sawpit Gully circuit.

ACCESS AND FACILITIES
Arrowtown is 20 km from Queenstown via the Arthurs Point road, or via Lake Hayes. The track to Sawpit Gully starts by the Chinese settlement carpark and information sign. Toilets, and good cafes in Arrowtown.

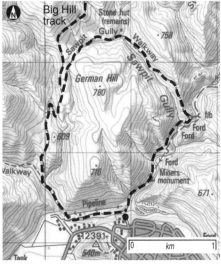

Detail: Sawpit Gully track and start of Big Hill track

INFORMATION
Macetown and the Arrow Gorge, Department of Lands and Survey booklet. This excellent booklet might be hard to get; try the Arrowtown Museum.

This is a walk steeped in gold history, as complex as the numerous water races that were constructed by the diggers of the 1860s. These gold-diggers made the track you walk on, supped grog in the ruined stone hut you rest by, and broke their bodies

Water races over the hillsides on the Big Hill pack-track.

looking for the gold that you will more effectively capture in your photograph of the glorious evening light.

From the carpark, cross the small Bush Creek and follow the pipeline upriver past a multitude of four-wheel-drive tracks. There are steps over the pipeline, and the track wanders through maple and pine forest to a junction, then climbs steadily out of the scrub and winds through a gully onto German Hill or Eichardts Flat. Wide-ranging views here, at the signposted junction of the Big Hill track.

If you are taking the shorter Sawpit Gully option, follow the good track past a ruined stone hut, then sidle down the creek to the Arrow River gorge. The track cuts around schist bluffs, passes the monument to William Fox (the loudest discoverer of the goldfield) and returns to the Arrowtown carpark.

For Big Hill saddle, climb up the worn trail to the elegant water race. This is easy walking as it turns around the corner into the beech forest at the head of Sawpit Gully. Somewhere, the water race disappears and becomes the historic 1864 pack-track (built to access remote Macetown) and wanders around into another bushy gully before striking out into the tussocks.

Fabulous views, and you should not mind the steeper grades now, as the bridle path cuts around into the head of Swipers Gully and reaches the blowy saddle at 1100 metres. It would not take too long to climb 100 metres up onto the small peak to the east, and see on to Macetown and Advance Peak.

GLENORCHY WETLAND
A simple stroll

TRACK

A flat, easy walk on crisp boardwalks, stopbanks and grass paths, though sometimes boggy after rain.

WALK TIME AND DISTANCE

1 hour (2 km) return.

ACCESS AND FACILITIES

The track starts from the wharf in Glenorchy township, or off the short side-road beside the golf course. Toilets, cafes, petrol, store and DoC information centre at Glenorchy.

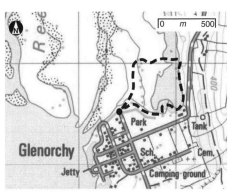

The 1950s American urban mystic and writer Alan Watts called walking a form of wakeful meditation. As the body is exercised, so the mind is soothed, and surely this little track exemplifies the perfect balmful qualities of just strolling along.

There is almost a Zen-like simplicity between the water and the willows on this walk. This small segment of the Rees–Dart delta is a cunning mixture of old river channels, shallow ponds and broad grasslands, and the colours are the soft yellows of the grasses, orange willows and the sharp blue of the ponds.

Across the valley plain are massive mountains, but you tend to get absorbed by the intimate local details. Black scaup dabble on the edges, and grey warblers make sound patterns. There are the customary lookouts, seats and bridges, and really there is not much else to be said. It is magic.

Boardwalk through willows in the Glenorchy Wetland.

INVINCIBLE MINE
Golden views

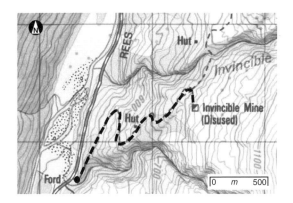

TRACK
An old vehicle and pack-track climbs steeply through beech forest and scrublands. Not marked but obvious.

WALK TIME AND DISTANCE
3–4 hours (4 km) return (allows for some exploring); total climb 500 metres.

ONE-HOUR WALK
Log cabin return.

ACCESS AND FACILITIES
From Glenorchy take the Rees Valley Road some 15 km to the sign. One biggish ford to cross, wretched parking space. Access to the circular buddle is about 1 km further. This is an extraordinary shallow metal cone, some 8 metres in diameter, that separated the various ore materials. It looks quite unreal in the beech forest.

INFORMATION
The Invincible Mine, Department of Conservation pamphlet.

Heavy metal bands of the nineteenth century were rather different from those of today. They were groups of miners following the gold, or the antimony, or the serpentine, or whatever made a dollar, and if it led them into spectacular locations, so be it. The Invincible Mine has one of the best views anywhere. It looks down on the clean crystal waters of the Rees River, and across to the ramparts of snow underneath Mount Earnslaw, although one wonders if the miners had the luxury to enjoy the view.

From the roadside follow the track past the ruined tin hut and into the beech forest. The track was built in the 1880s so that heavy machinery could be hauled up to the mine, so it is a good easy surface. About halfway up there is an old log cabin, then quite a few zigzags to the mine site.

On the left there are seven berdans, revolving metal drums with heavy weights in them that ground the ore down. There is not much left of the battery, and the mine shaft is along a short track to the right. A grill blocks the entrance. The most notable things about this site (apart from the raw silence) are the mullock heaps, or tailings.

The Invincible was a going concern by 1882, with ten stamps in the battery driven by an overshot waterwheel. Yields were good, and in 1884 another company processed the tailings, building a 679-metre chute (think about that for a minute – that is over 2000 feet!) to the valley floor. The material was sent down to a circular buddle for refining. By 1887, however, the quartz reef was 'lost'. The brochure strikes this little epitaph:

> Several other syndicates have tried to work the mine – notably in 1902, 1912 and 1922 – but all efforts to strike the reef came to nothing. In the long run it may be said that it was the reef which remained invincible.

And the view.

Ruined berdans, remnants of the Invincible Mine.

GERTRUDE SADDLE
An awesome alpine tramp

TRACK

A worn trail through tussock and rock, cairned but unclear in places. Near Black Lake there is a wire. You need calm, clear weather to get to Gertrude Saddle itself, although the valley walk is straightforward in most conditions. Suited to experienced walkers and trampers.

WALK TIME AND DISTANCE

5–6 hours (8 km) return, total climb 700 metres.

TWO–HOUR WALK

To top forks return.

ACCESS AND FACILITIES

From Highway 94, turn off down the short gravel road to Homer Hut.

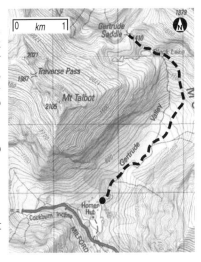

Fiordland is the most rugged part of New Zealand, the valleys so deeply incised it reminded the Maori of their facial moko, and they called it Te Rua-o-te-moko — 'the pit of the tattooing'. In Gertrude Valley the glaciers carved painfully deep, with severe granite on every side, except for the goat path that climbs up to the saddle. This is a tramp rather than a walk.

From Homer Hut, take the worn path through the grasses and follow it up beside the stream. The track is not very clear here, fossicking among boulders, and the easiest route may cross the stream several times, but after a while it becomes better defined and trots alongside the west bank of the stream.

The sheer walls of the Gertrude Valley are awesome, and the track stumbles upvalley, crossing the stream occasionally on its way to the top forks. From here a worn and cairned path climbs more steeply up a slight spur, then sidles around towards the head of the valley. Just before Black Lake there is a steepish section on rock and a wire, which sounds worse than it actually is.

The lake has a magical mirror effect on a good day, and 10 minutes further on there is another large lake. Gertrude Saddle itself is the obvious low and flat point, with stupendous (this is the only time in the book I use that word) views into the Gulliver River. Such travels indeed, to this remarkable place.

Black Lake, on the Gertrude Saddle walk.

LAKE MARIAN
Alpine lake in a Fiordland cirque

TRACK
Good at first, with boardwalks alongside the cascades, then getting rougher towards the lake.

WALK TIME AND DISTANCE
3–4 hours (6 km) return.

ONE-HOUR WALK
Marian Creek cascades return.

ACCESS AND FACILITIES
From Highway 94 to Milford Sound, turn off 4 km down the Hollyford Road.

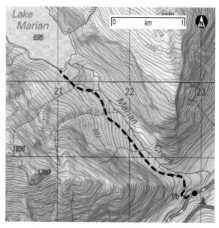

This track leads to a dead-end, an alpine lake in a deep trench, hemmed in by granite walls. Seagulls sometimes penetrate here, but there is not much other sound to diminish the serious silence.

From the carpark, cross the swing bridge over the Hollyford River and follow the well-gravelled track as it wanders through the thick rainforest. Moss literally drips from the trees. After 15 minutes the track gets up on cantilevered boardwalks and verandahs bolted into the rock face, and overlooks the mossy boulders choking Marian Creek, with the water seething underneath. A fine and popular lookout.

It is much less popular to carry on to Lake Marian, and the track gets rougher as it climbs away from the creek. It crosses fern gullies, where there may be a bit of scrambling, and climbs almost 400 metres from the Hollyford road to the lake outlet. There is a sheltered grass clearing on top of the rockfall that shuts the lake in, and a short track down to the lakeside itself.

After heavy rainfall you cannot get near the foreshore, but usually the lake level is low enough to walk around. Rocks provide a back-rest for lunch, and you are almost above sandfly level. It is like another world.

OTHER WALKS IN THE MILFORD AREA
The Chasm, 20 minutes return; Bowen Falls, 10 minutes return; Homer Tunnel nature walk, 15 minutes return.

KEY SUMMIT
One of the best

TRACK
A well-graded track and boardwalks.

WALK TIME AND DISTANCE
3–4 hours (4 km) return.

1.5-HOUR WALK
Track junction.

ACCESS AND FACILITIES
From Te Anau drive 55 km on Highway 94 to the start of the Routeburn Track at the Divide Saddle. Shelter, toilets and carpark.

INFORMATION
Fiordland National Park Visitor Centre, Te Anau.

There is a sprinkling of tarns on this alpine wetland, which overlooks three great valleys – the Hollyford, the Greenstone and the Eglinton. Maori on war parties into the West Coast and carrying greenstone out of it, early settlers looking for cattle country, and goldminers looking for gold all traipsed this way. Now it is walkers and tourists who make the trek up to Key Summit, and admire the rugged panorama.

From The Divide carpark the well-graded track (which is also the start of the Routeburn Track) climbs up through silver beech forest with ribbonwood and fuchsia. The fuchsia has distinctive bell-shaped red flowers in summer. There are several streams to cross, bubbling over pretty waterfalls.

It is about an hour of gradual climb to the turn-off to Key Summit itself, and there are reasonable views here. It is quite a crossroads on a busy summer's day, with walkers and trampers stopping for a breather and a gossip.

The track climbs up through open slopes of flax and tussocks and there is an easy circuit, with plastic information sheets that you can pick up then deposit on the way down. The main track reaches a boardwalk around a beautiful tarn with bog cushions, mosses, and the alpine sundew. A plane table helps you identify the mountains.

The little circuit track goes through pockets of beech forest shaggy with hanging lichen, and continuously enjoys a panorama of mountain scenery that is breathtaking – the Darran mountains, a bite of Lake Marian and the elongated valley of the Hollyford River.

Tarns and walkers on the trek up to Key Summit.

LUXMORE HUT
Garden path up to tussock downlands

TRACK
An extremely well-made graded track on a steady climb up through the bush, then some boardwalk on the tussock tops.

WALK TIME AND DISTANCE
5–6 hours (16 km) return.

ONE-HOUR WALK
Dock Bay return.

ACCESS AND FACILITIES
From Te Anau take the Manapouri Road for 5 km, turning off to the signposted Control Gates. These are a little removed from the carpark and you have to walk down to them.

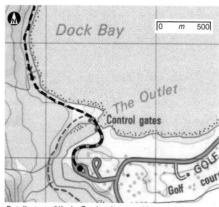

Detail: start of Kepler Track to Luxmore Hut

If walking from the Fiordland National Park Visitor Centre in Te Anau, there is a lakeside path that goes past Te Anau Wildlife Centre and continues around to the Control Gates (about 4 km, 45 minutes' walking one way).

Note: you can get water taxis and pick-ups from Te Anau to Brod Bay, saving an hour's walk each way.

INFORMATION
Fiordland National Park Visitor Centre, Te Anau; *Kepler Trackmap 335/9, Manapouri C43* maps.

This track is a veritable garden path, climbing from the glistening Lake Te Anau to the undulating tussock hills around Luxmore Hut. Despite the 1000-metre climb, and the altitude (1200 metres above sea level), the quality of the track enables many people to visit this alpine region in a day return. The views of the lake and the remote Murchison Mountains are certainly worth the effort.

Cross the Control Gates and follow the gentle lakeside track as it wanders through tall red beech forest. There are occasional footbridges and plenty of birdlife as you pass the Dock Bay picnic and camping area and go on to Brod Bay beach and shelter. This is a sparkling little bay, slightly spoilt by the hungry sandflies.

Now the climbing starts, in gentle, lazy zigzags up the thick-forested hillsides. Not many views, but about two-thirds of the way up you reach a limestone bluff, with some fossils in the rock. It is about 100 vertical metres now to the bush edge, and the track has got squelchier and the forest has changed.

It is a wonderful moment when you burst out onto the rolling downlands, and the slopes are gentle as the track follows boardwalks and tarns another kilometre to the palatial Luxmore Hut. With 60 bunks it is rather a wart on the landscape, but there are fine views from the verandah and lounge. A good place for lunch and a brew-up before the long lollop downhill.

ACKERS POINT
An historic cottage on the way to a lighthouse peninsula

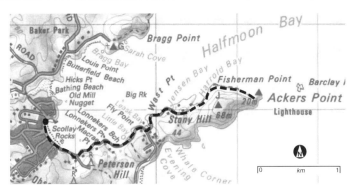

TRACK
Road walk then gravelled path. Some seats.

WALK TIME AND DISTANCE
1–2 hours (6 km) return.

ACCESS AND FACILITIES
Stewart Island, or Rakiura, can be reached by ferry (slow and rough) or plane (fast and not so rough). People with good stomachs or motion-sickness pills will enjoy going over one way and returning the other.

INFORMATION
Rakiura National Park Visitor Centre; *Day Walks*, Department of Conservation pamphlet.

Halfmoon Bay is a beautiful settlement, languid, softly tucked into the bush hillsides, with most of New Zealand's best bush birds perched about the houses as if they own the place, which is probably half-right. Not too many cars, with only 25 km of roads, and electricity has quietened the generators. There is a sense of being at the end of the world here, and the evening sunlight that penetrates the squalls of cloud is quite other-worldly.

Perhaps all this peacefulness will change now that Stewart Island has become New Zealand's newest national park, Rakiura.

From the settlement foreshore, follow the coastal road around the south edge of Halfmoon Bay as it wanders in and out of small bays. In one eucalyptus grove there is a loud colony of kaka, and it is quite likely you will see individual birds up close as they tear at the tree bark for grubs. Tui and kereru (wood pigeons) are equally abundant.

The coastal road climbs up and ends at a stile and signpost, after which an excellent gravel track continues, sidling past Ackers stone cottage. The cottage, built in 1834, is worth the short detour.

The main track cuts around Fishermans Point (good seat here) then out to the lighthouse at Ackers Point, where there are information boards about the little blue penguins and sooty shearwaters, which return to their burrows here at dusk. The views towards Bluff are sometimes sharp, sometimes hazy.

MAORI BEACH
Coastal bridle path to a bonny bay

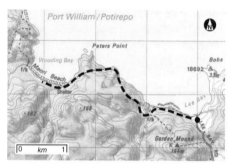

TRACK
Mostly flat walking with some mud.

WALK TIME AND DISTANCE
2–3 hours (6 km) return to Maori Beach.

ONE-HOUR WALK
Little River beach return.

ACCESS AND FACILITIES
From Oban walk/drive over to Horseshoe Bay, then take the road to Lee Bay to the start of the Rakiura Track (5 km).

INFORMATION
Rakiura National Park Visitor Centre; *Day Walks*, Department of Conservation pamphlet.

This far south the sky has a luminosity you do not find anywhere else. The Maori called Stewart Island Rakiura — 'land of the glowing skies' — which is poetic and appropriate, and this walk along an old bridle path takes you out of the scant settlement of Halfmoon Bay into a wilderness of beaches and light.

The Rakiura Track to Maori Beach starts from Lee Bay (through the Anchor sculpture) and the track is well graded, as it was once the main land route to the sawmill settlement at Maori Beach. Birdlife is usually vocal, with bellbirds, wood pigeons, chattering parakeets and kaka. After a kilometre southern rata is particularly evident around the pretty Little River estuary.

There is a footbridge, but at low tide the track skirts the sand. Upstream from the bridge there is a pleasant picnic area and a toilet.

Now the track climbs steeply, and there are glimpses of the bouldery coastline as it wanders across the headland at Peters Point and drops abruptly to Maori Beach. At a lower tide you can cross directly to the beach, but there is a very muddy high-tide alternative track.

Maori Beach, 1 km long, is elegant between its headlands. Behind the beach a massive boiler remains from the days of the sawmill.

OTHER WALKS
It is 2 km on to Port William, with a 150-metre climb on the way. Port William was the site of a failed government-sponsored settlement in the 1870s, but today gum trees are the only reminder. There is a hut, jetty and picnic areas. Add another 2 hours return.

Taking a rest on the way to Maori Beach.

ULVA ISLAND
Birds on paradise

TRACK
Well-maintained bush tracks.
WALK TIME AND DISTANCE
Boulder Beach return 1 hour
(1.5 km); West End Beach return
2 hours (2.5 km).
ONE-HOUR WALK
Nature via Sydney Cove and
lookout.
ACCESS AND FACILITIES
You need a water taxi; check at
the DoC information office for times and prices. Obviously the amount of time you
spend on the island depends on your arrangement with the water taxi, but if the
weather is fine you should take lunch and make it a 3- to 4-hour session. Information
panels, toilets and shelter on the island.
INFORMATION
Rakiura National Park Visitor Centre; *Ulva Island*, Department of Conservation
pamphlet. The latter explains the elimination of predators from the island and some
of its unusual history, including the famous post office that operated from 1872 to
1923.

Not quite at the end of the world, though sometimes it seems like it, is the moody
inland sea of Paterson Inlet. One of the islands, Ulva, has been turned into a sanctuary
for birds and plants, and when the sudden Stewart Island squalls break and illuminate
the forest in gold, you feel that this is a suitable place to find refuge. Dense podocarps
go down to the water's edge and mingle with bright strips of sand. The birds flourish
and sing at this lonely outpost, as they might have sung thousands of years before.

The water taxi drops you at the wharf, and past the information signs you can
wander at will on the tracks. The forest is lush and fertile, with an abundance of
birds that will take absolutely no
notice of you.

I watched baby bellbirds
chasing their mum for food,
brown creepers doing exactly
what their name suggests only
a metre from my nose, and kaka
hacking pleasantly away at the
old tree bark. Tui, parakeets,
fantails, all are here, so for those
few people who make this long
journey down to the near
conclusion of New Zealand, and
to the end of this book, the
rewards are immense.

Sydney Cove, Ulva Island.